Emotional Intelligence Domination

2 Books in 1

Cognitive Behavioral Therapy Made Simple, How to Analyze and Influence People, NLP, Mental Models, Critical Thinking, Empath, Self-Esteem, Psychology 101

BY

Gary Scott

TABLE OF CONTENTS

EMOTIONAL INTELLIGENCE MADE SIMPLE

COGNITIVE BEHAVIORAL THERAPY MADE SIMPLE

EMOTIONAL INTELLIGENCE MADE SIMPLE

8 books in 1:

How to Analyze and Influence People, Cognitive Behavioral Therapy, NLP, Mental Models, Critical Thinking, Empath, Self-Esteem, Psychology 101

BY

Gary Scott

CHAPTER 1
HOW TO ANALYZE AND INFLUENCE PEOPLE

Secrets of Psychologists to Read People As If They Were Open Books

Surely you have wished more than once to be able to read other people's minds. Some are saved with the help of their developed intuition, but if you are not so conscious, you only have one way out: learn to decipher body language.

It is no longer a secret that with the help of nonverbal communication, we get 55 percent of the information. Allan Pease, the famous Australian writer, mentioned it more than once. Expressions of the face, gestures, and body movements can remove the mask from anyone, revealing their real thoughts and feelings.

The wording of Genial. Guru proposes you to pay attention to the signals sent to us by the people around us without even knowing it.

1. Closing the eyes

If a person, speaking with you, closes his eyes, you have to know that he is trying to hide or protect himself from the outside world. This does not mean that I fear you. Rather, the other way around. He wants to take you out of his field of vision. You may have bored it already. Close your eyes and bam! You disappeared.

2. Protecting the mouth by hand

It is a vivid example that we all come from childhood. Remember, how you covered your mouth with the palm of your hand when you didn't want to say something. An adult is the same. Some fingers, palm, or fist help us contain the words. Sometimes we mask it with a simulated cough.

3. Biting the ring of your glasses

Is a friend of yours thoughtfully biting the rings of his glasses? Try to support and encourage him. Surely you will be worried about something and at your subconscious level try to feel safe, as in childhood with the mother's breast. By the way, a pencil, pen, finger, cigarette, or even chewing gum in the mouth also indicates the same.

4. Showing face

Many women use this gesture to attract the attention of men. Supporting the chin on the folded hands, we expose our face to show it, as if it were the shop window in a store as if we were saying: "Here I am so pretty, admire me." Men should remember this gesture so as not to miss the opportunity to make a compliment on time.

5. Stroking the chin

In this way, the person tries to make a decision. At the same time, your gaze can be directed down, up, to the left, or any other side. He does not realize what he sees at that precise moment since he is completely immersed in his thoughts.

6. Crossed arms

It is one of the most common gestures. It is not surprising that many people feel very comfortable with this pose since this gesture helps to isolate themselves from others. Many times we use it when we are not comfortable with something. The crossed arms are a clear sign of the negative attitude of your interlocutor.

7. Exposing oneself

This pose is more open. When a woman wants to like a man, she starts exposing herself by showing her the best sides. She straightens to highlight her breasts and crosses her legs. The folded arms below are a clear signal of attention towards the interlocutor.

8. Leaning forward

When a person feels sympathy for his interlocutor and wants to have contact with him or her, he usually leans forward. At the same time, the feet may remain in the same place, but the body advances instinctively.

9. Leaning back

If the person leans against the back of his seat, he makes it clear that he is bored with the conversation. You may feel uncomfortable in the presence of your interlocutor.

10. Toe, heel

Yes, adults do too. Not only children. This gesture indicates that the person is anxious.

11. Rubbing his hands

It is said that the hands convey what the head thinks. When we rub our hands, we usually express expectations or hope of some success in something. In other words, we make this gesture when we think about future benefits.

12. Handshake "glove"

If your interlocutor greeting you grabs you with both hands, it shows that you can trust him.

13. Squeeze with palm up

The palm-up, covering the interlocutor's hand, indicates empathy, but only if done at once. If the hands were already held for a specific moment and then someone put the palm up, it may indicate their desire to show who is in charge.

14. Squeeze with palm down

By supporting your caller's hand, it is as if you were talking about your willingness to help him.

15. Squeeze with a touch

With the available hand, the person can touch the forearm, elbow, or the back of the person he is greeting. This invasion of personal space shows the need for communication. And the closer the body is, the higher the need.

16. Straightening the tie

Here everything depends on the situation. If it is a man who does it in the presence of a woman, it is highly possible that he likes it. But this gesture can also mean that the person does not feel comfortable. You might have lied or want to leave.

17. Collecting non-existent hairs

It is thus called the gesture of repression. Most of the time, people use it to express their tacit disagreement. In other words, they do not openly express their opinion, but they certainly do not agree with what is happening around them.

18. Feet on the table

This gesture can mean many things: bad manners, disrespect, desire to show off as a great boss, or concern for your health. However, psychologists tend to believe that even if you feel very comfortable in this position. it would be better if you use it at home or in the presence of your family.

19. Riding the chair

A chair is not a horse and its back, although in some ways it seems, is not a shield. Also, it was made for other purposes. So many people are bothered by this way of sitting around because, at the intuitive level, we feel a lot of aggression from the "mounted" person. Typically, dominant people use this position.

20. Playing with the shoe

Cross-legged is one of the most attractive female poses. And if we add to him playing with the shoe half removed, we accentuate it even more. This gesture speaks of a relaxed and calm mood and serves as a kind of green traffic light for man.

21. Eye contact

The eyes are the mirror of the soul and a perfect instrument of communication. There we can read all the feelings and emotions of the interlocutor. Lovers stare into each other's eyes, unconsciously waiting to see how they get bigger. And this shows a lot because the pupils can increase in size up to 4 times, compared to their normal state. And, by the way, if the person gets angry, their eyes become like accounts due to the maximum reduction of the pupils.

How to Analyze A Person
By Their Photos

Have you just met someone, added you to their Facebook, Twitter, or Instagram, and are you wondering what kind of personality you have? Do you want to know what message you give the world with your photographs on the networks?

Since the arrival of the Internet in our lives, the way we have to relate to others has changed radically. Now we have space where others can see what we want them to see. The images we decided to upload to our social networks show much more than we imagine. An Internet profile is a projection of what we want to show the world, our desires, and even our insecurities. That is why, by making a correct analysis of the published photos, we can develop an accurate personality profile.

Tell me what profile picture you have, and I will tell you how you are.

What the profile photos indicate

When we choose a profile picture (whether for WhatsApp, Facebook, Instagram ...), we are choosing our cover letter to the world. After that election, there is a series of mental processes that arise to avoid giving an image that we don't want to give. For example, someone more introvert will have more difficulties in this process, and they may not change their photographs very often. In extreme cases, these people hide behind anonymous profiles.

Some elements that we can analyze from the profile photos are the following:

- **Pose:** People who are not afraid to expose themselves usually go out with open arms, calm and with full-length (or half-body) photographs. However, a more reserved person probably has a more serious photograph, with arms crossed and in a more closed plane.

GARY SCOTT

- **Facial expression:** A wide smile, without touch-ups and head-on, they are usually self-confident, open, and outgoing people. A grimace may be a sign that we want to show "naturalness" but, deep down, we feel insecure and force ourselves to be funny in a photograph. The most serious people (or who use their networks for professional purposes) usually leave with a half-smile or, with an expression without grimaces and sober.

- **If we go out with more people:** Going out with many people in the photo can indicate a tendency to be sociable, they enjoy life more in the company, and a photo alone does not represent them.

- **If it is a photo with our partner:** Although the image we give on the networks about our partner is not reality, uploading many photos or having a profile picture with your partner does not imply anything bad, on the contrary. A photo with our partner means that we have taken the step of showing the world who we are united with and who is part of our life.

- **If it is an old or childhood photo:** These types of images indicate a strong anchor to the past, we may be going through a bad time and do not want to connect with it or, we are simply afraid to move on in our lives.

- **Photo color:** Color is also a crucial element; a black and white photo can be a sign of a melancholic, poetic, or introverted personality. On the other hand, bright colors usually express vitality and joy.

- **If the photo is not of us:** Some people hide behind anonymous profiles, avatars of soccer players, celebrities, or cartoons. These individuals travel through the networks without interest to show their personality, either because of fear, insecurities, or because they do not like to show their lives to a vast audience.

The psychology of colors in profile photos

The study of how colors affect our lives has also reached the analysis of personality, the ones we choose for our virtual presentation letter also show very characteristic features of us.

Black and white photos

As we have commented previously, a black and white photo can be a sign of melancholy and artistic tendencies. Retouching a photograph to remove the shades can also indicate bad self-esteem and, as a consequence, certain insecurity when showing us the world.

Photos with lots of colors

The strident photos, with many shades and full of color, are characteristics of equally strident and striking people. Not only is it a sign of extraversion, but the striking colors also indicate the desire to attract attention and to have a certain presence in the lives of others, whether in the real world or on the Internet.

Photos with blue tones

Using cold tones such as blue can indicate two things: either a corporate personality, sober and elegant, or a tendency to be a cold and calculating person. These tones do not invite you to delve into the personal depths of each one.

Photos with red color

If this striking tone predominates in the photo, we may want to show the energy and passion we have in our day to day. The use of warm colors denotes an intense, competitive, and sometimes aggressive personality.

Half-face photos: Meaning

Not showing our face partially can indicate two very different things:

- **Mysterious personality:** Half-face invites you to enter the profile to discover more, see what that person hides and reveal his personality.

- **Disinterest in social networks:** A person who does not mind being exposed to social networks but does not want to waste time on them. For this type of individual, a half-face photo implies that they have given the message that they don't want to show their whole life on it.

Back photo: Meaning

It is possible that in the profile picture, we do not even want to face, the back photos reflect a certain level of resistance when having social networks and being active in them. In this type of photos, the face is not visible and, therefore, we hide our facial expressions from the world of the Internet.

On the other hand, a photo from behind can also mean that we have gone through a painful time. Right now, we do not have enough courage to show ourselves in the face of a world as extensive as social networks.

Finally, it is worth mentioning that, although it is interesting to know how to analyze a person by their photos. Each individual is a world, a very intricate set of experiences and paths, and that it is better to talk to a person if we want to know them thoroughly.

Five Major Factors Analyzing Personality, According To Goldberg

Lewis Goldberg's personality theory is also known as the "Big Five Model." It stems from a variety of studies in which the excellence of a particular personality trait is repeated as a factor determining people's way of life. I have been talking about this model since 1933, but it was 1993 that was structured as a theory.

The five main personality traits are identified by capital letters and are also known as "main factors." The first is the element of "O" — openness to new experiences. The second is the responsibility of "C." The third is "E" or extrovert. The room is "A" or kind. And finally, the fifth is "N" or emotional instability. The letters from the acronym "OCEAN."

"Each one is like a god, but you can leave it to God."

-Miguel Servet-

Similarly, each of these characteristics is made up of more specific features. From this model, a variety of personality tests have been developed that can evaluate and measure how people have evaluated. Let's take a closer look at the features and characteristics of the model.

Openness to experience, one of the personality traits

Openness to experience ("O") refers to the ability to find new skills, space them in life and creatively visualize the future. Those who have this level at a high level are imaginative people who appreciate art and collaborate with others. They are also curious and prefer variations over every day.

The opposite is people who have closed to an experience they have never experienced before. The opposition characterizes them. This means that they prefer a guaranteed traditional one. They prefer strict routines because they take time to adapt to new things. They tend to be technical and tend to show little interest in abstraction.

Responsibility or factor "C"

This dimension relates to self-control ability and the ability to develop effective ways of acting. It refers to the ability to plan, organize, and execute tasks. You must also be able to achieve your goals, keep on time, and maintain your goals and goals.

People with high scores in this dimension are often seen as organized, reliable, and demanding people. Taking this personality trait to extremes can lead to perfectionism and even work addiction. They feel a great need to succeed.

Extraversion, another personality trait

It has to do with having fun with other people's companies. People who have this most prominent feature feel comfortable when they are with others and act in harmony when they are in a group. They are good people working in teams, optimistic and enthusiastic. Along with others, they are like sea fish.

There is an introverted person on the other side, and it is best to work alone. Often, you feel certain distrust and attention to others. They prefer a small circle of friends and are very uncomfortable with a large group.

"A" factor: kindness

Mainly related to empathy. Those who show excellence in this personality factor understand, forgive, and calm with others. Demonstrate your ability to understand other people's needs and feelings.

The people on the other side are in conflict. These are people who like discussion and debate and want to give their perspective. Hostility is your brand. They can work well in activities that require demonstrations of competition and energetic attitudes towards others.

Emotional instability or neurosis

It specifically talks about the ability or lack of ability that one has to overcome in the face of difficult life situations. People who show a high level of this factor are characterized by unpredictable behavior. They do not maintain a series of actions, but the reasons are not very clear, and their reactions are different.

On the opposite end, some stable people remain attentive and modest in critical situations. They are quiet people who are relieved with the ability to handle difficulties and mistakes. Your emotional state is positive, even in the face of problems.

Read People and See-Through

Honestly, wouldn't it be nice to be able to assess people with lightning speed and to know immediately how to deal with the best? Which buttons do you have to press to reach what you want?

You know instantly which kind of person you are dealing with and which behavior is likely to happen to you from a few perceptions. This knowledge gives you a huge informational edge, while the other person is still completely in the dark, not knowing the number of inferences on their personality you have already learned.

Your ability to perceive what others have missed reading between the lines, after a few sentences, will allow you to get a clear picture of a person and place them in a grid that will allow you to predict the person's remaining attributes and preferences. In short, you can read people and see what really drives them.

Would not that be an incredibly helpful skill? Just think about what this knowledge could bring you benefits. In which situations would you have the decisive advantage? In which situations could you have prevented so much, if you had already known in advance, how a person would probably act? And with which people would it be much easier if you knew exactly how you should deal with them?

We, humans, love to look for patterns in our environment and to recognize them.

Scientifically this tendency is called "Randomness Error". It is one of the automatically occurring attention mistakes that cause us to perceive the reality a bit distorted. In a nutshell, he says that we assign meaning to random events that they do not have. They just happened completely arbitrarily.

However, we try to make sense of everything and therefore recognize seemingly recurrent patterns that help us to categorize events in our environment. Even though these categories often do not exist. And of course, we do the same with our fellow human beings and their behaviors. Of course, this has some advantages and disadvantages.

Classifying people makes their behavior more manageable and allows us to rate the unknown. This seems to be an inherent pattern of human behavior. Evolutionary conditionally was necessary to detect dangers early. Today, it helps us to be better at dealing with people and to assess how they will behave. It allows us to be one step ahead of others.

Already in ancient Greece, the personality of the people was classified in the grid of the temperament theory. Similar to the personality types, according to Carl Gustav Jung, the Myers-Briggs type indicator, or the "Big 5" of the OCEAN model, which is often used in psychology today, people of every segment were given certain qualities.

By recognizing some of these typical behaviors or characteristics, people can be assigned to a segment. Once assigned, one knows which other behaviors and characteristics the classified person is now statistically most likely to have and how best to deal with it.

Of course, this knowledge has not only advantages but also significant disadvantages. Katja Vogt once said that in all the drawers that we humans entertain, unfortunately, only a sock is lost.

This quote nicely reminds us that too hasty conclusions can often have consequences, and many things pass us because of our now active expectation filter. We should, therefore, pay very close attention to whether the model used allows me to assign other unerring drawers.

In our opinion, the models mentioned above have some upgradable points that need to be considered when trying to "categorize" people. First, categorizing bothers us.

We in the NLP are convinced that we can always only recognize tendencies. The world is not black and white; it shows in many shades. And so do personality traits of people.

The second point is that we humans can change and evolve. Such an analysis is static. Just as an exam is just a snapshot, a survey or questionnaire can capture our personality at some point in time based on a set of criteria.

But because NLP itself is a dynamic model and we constantly calibrate our conversational waking ears and sharp eye in conversations and situations, we can easily perceive changes and deviant behavior.

NLP's behavioral analysis is always up-to-date, and its users are aware that human behavior is constantly changing, but they have the ability to respond flexibly to these changes.

Also, many analysis models overlook the fact that human behavior is very context-dependent. I can take the helm in a situation and lead a group safely to the desired point.

Likewise, in a different context, I can sit back, wait and see what the others do, and talk and engage only when I have a clear picture of the situation. Just because I got things going in a context and was virtually the "doer" does not mean that I do that in any other context, let alone that it always makes sense.

But how can I analyze and read people and their behavior with NLP?

The model we use is called MBC - Meta Behavioral Coding. It is our creation and combines the best elements of some well tested and working analysis models.

These include, for example, the metaprogramming from the NLP, which is derived from it specifically for the working context of Dr. med. Rodger Bailey derived LAB® Profiles (Language and Behavior Profiles) and some analysis tools used in profiling and the military.

With MBC, we use a framework that allows us to incorporate human behavior into over 20 facets. Based on the different characteristics and metaprogram combinations, we can assess ourselves and our counterpart very precisely and derive action strategies.

You already know one of the metaprograms if the VAKOG model tells you something. This metaprogram tells you from the language of a human in which sensory channels your counterpart perceives his environment and thus also in which sensory channels you should talk to this person in order to create a good basis for conversation and to prevent one another from talking to one another. Here you can find more about the VAKOG model.

Metaprograms themselves are, therefore, unconscious personality patterns and filters of our brain. These determine our behavior, how we are motivated, how we make decisions, how we value things, and how we perceive our environment. Metaprograms thus help us to see how our counterpart is sorting his reality and what his subconscious personality patterns look like.

Of course, these patterns have a powerful impact on how and what we talk about. From the structure of a person's language, MBC allows us to create precisely those unconscious patterns to hear and to get insights into the personality. A small example. Markus and Christina have just a small disagreement at a meeting.

Markus says: "Before we start, we have to rethink our decisions and analyze together whether we have thought everything through. We can not risk external factors bugging us."

Christina says: "Thinking, even more, does not make sense. We finally have to get started; we're running out of time. We will already be able to handle the external factors when the time comes."

Here different metaprogramming meets, which causes conflicts more frequently. We're talking about the meta-program Proactive/ Reactive. We want to introduce you to this today.

Proactive people are action-oriented and take initiative. They want to do something. The activity and the action are in the foreground. Precise analysis of the situation and the most accurate balancing of all available alternatives usually leave it to others. Much can only be considered for them once you have started. They assume that they have a handle on what happens and can influence environmental factors through their behavior.

In everyday life, they are often referred to as "makers," as they initiate many ideas and take the first steps. This is helpful when an action is required. In extreme cases, the quick start and initiate actions can also happen rashly and anger other people. It may seem that they act like "steamrolling" and could have prevented some with a little more thought in advance.

Leave reactive people to take the initiative to other people. Situations have to "mature" for them to make decisions. They like to let things take theirs to see what impact this has on them. Situations want to be understood and analyzed before an action is taken. Reactive people also need to be completely sure that they have considered all alternatives. They see themselves in the area of the tension of external influences and find that environmental factors influence their behavior.

In everyday life, they are often referred to as "analysts" or "thinkers." They provide valuable solutions and a sharp analysis of problems. The honor of putting the first stone, but May like to take another person. In extreme cases, this metaprogram can lead to an "analysis" loop, as there is always new input to analyze and understand.

There is no action at all until it is too late. Sometimes, other people also perceive reactive people as "passive" because they spend a lot of time waiting and contemplating. This can also make them passengers of their own lives.

So you realize that both Metaprograms have their advantages and disadvantages, none is better than the other. Depending on the situation or task, one expression can prove to be more advantageous than the other. Just ask yourself what expressions Mark and Christina have and how you can recognize them.

How do I know which characteristic my counterpart has?

Proactive:

Are very active in body language and movements, linguistically noticeable by short, sometimes incomplete sentences. Has problems staying calm for a long time.

- Typical sets of proactive people:
- What are we waiting for? Here we go!
- Now it's time to get started.
- Let's get started.

Reactive:

Tended to lean back more often or in a classic analysis posture. Speaks slowly and in longer, nested sentences. Longer inactive phrases are no problem.

- Typical sentences of reactive persons:
- Let's look at precisely what we are dealing with here.
- We should think about that again before we do something.
- Let us also listen to other opinions on this topic.

How can I use these patterns?

Proactive people can be very well used as motivators and initiators of actions. They get things going and start where others are still thinking. But when there is a more prolonged standstill, they become impatient and try to get things moving. They can help get an otherwise reactive team going and prevent over-analysis.

Reactive people are excellent analysts; they weigh, want to understand and act thoughtfully. Especially in situations that need to be controlled in the background, or in an advisory capacity, it is recommended to use reactive persons. They can give proactive doer a clear direction and prevent essential things from being overlooked in a hurry. While the other one is starting to work, they can analyze further in the background and gradually work out new input.

How can you best deal with proactive/reactive people?

If you realize in a group process that proactive members are getting impatient and getting started, but the more reactive ones do not feel ready and need more time, then you can intervene very simply in this process. Split tasks and share the group is the magic formula.

Give the proactive something to do. Let them either fulfill smaller sub-goals or tasks that have already been agreed or give them tasks that need to be done either way. With them, you talk best about what has to be done and done. Once you've told them that, you do not have to worry about anything anymore; the tasks are done independently and quickly.

Thus, you give the reactive persons the time and opportunity to continue important analysis processes and give them the security they need. You give them to understand that this process wants to be carefully considered. With them too, it can help to use partial goals or milestones to make the analysis more precise and faster. Here it is important to set clear deadlines and execute them in order to prevent rethinking.

This way, the situation with Markus and Christina can easily be resolved. Both are focused on a common goal, and Christina can get started, while Markus can calmly devise strategies to tackle external factors. Of course, you explain their tasks to the two ineffective speech patterns that satisfy their metaprogramming.

Speech patterns that you can use to link to them include:

- **Christina:** Do, do, get started, act, now!
- **Markus:** Think, weigh, think, analyze, wait, act, when the time is right!

What brings you now, MBC?

In a nutshell: you can read carefully from the language of your conversation partners and recognize what they need and how they tick. So you know how to explain something "brain-friendly" in their language so that it makes sense to them intuitively and sounds good.

You do not have to rely on a static personality analysis; you have the ability to calibrate your opponent's tendencies with a proven and simple grid at any time and in any context, and so have clear action strategies for you.

Imagine you are in a discussion and know what arguments will convince. In a negotiation, you realize how your demands are being accepted. What if you have to sell something and know exactly how to raise the need for it? Whether you want to motivate, lead, understand, or respond to someone, you will notice a noticeable difference and be able to prevent much in advance.

How to Influence People

When we need to convince someone, we can use many techniques. Obviously, if we make a good proposal, we have valid arguments, and what we want to do is a win-win; it will be easy to convince our interlocutor of our interests.

But apart from the content, there are some small tricks that we can use to influence the people we talk to and achieve our goals.

The way we talk, our attitude, and know how to handle the conversation can be the key to getting a favorable response to our interest.

1. Smile

A smile on your face is the first thing we have to do if we want to influence people. When someone smiles, conveys happiness, and well, and we all like to feel good.

When a proposal is made with a smile on our face, we are more predisposed to accept what they are asking.

2. Take advantage of fatigue

When we are tired, we don't feel like arguing, and we are more willing to say yes (even if they leave us alone).

Cults know this perfectly. Therefore, the sessions where you "brainwash" are always long and exhausting. They know that a tired person has low defenses and is more willing to obey and accept how true what you are saying.

3. Make the ball

The ego is one of the weak points of all people. We all like to be told how good we are, and we are more willing to serve a person who makes us feel good.

It is not easy to flatter without it noticing. So, if you're beating someone to convince him, do it subtly and credibly.

4. Tell him many times YES

If you want to influence someone, let them say yes. When in a conversation, we say many times, yes, our brain understands that we are in tune with the person with whom we speak and the inertia of responding that if it can be an excellent tool to get us to respond affirmatively to what we want.

Cold-door commercials are one of the strategies they use very often:

- Do you want the best for your family? Yes
- Do you like to save on the fixed expenses of your home? Yes
- Do you live in this address? Yes
- Do you like things to work correctly? Yes
- Do you want me to make a special offer for you? Yes

Make the ball and let us say many times IF they are two of the basic techniques of commercials.

5. Do not take the reason from your interlocutor

Showing someone who is not right in what he says and that if you have, it is an excellent strategy to feel good and have the feeling of "having won the argument."

But it is not an excellent strategy to influence another person.

When we argue, most of the time, we end up curling ourselves even more in the position we defend.

If you want to influence another person, you better not discuss and ignore the contrary arguments of the other person (this strategy is one used by all politicians in our country).

6. Extra trick: Use your voice well

The voice is a key element when it comes to influencing others.

There are four aspects of the voice to consider; these four elements, which make us perceive a certain voice differently, are; intensity, tone, timbre, and duration.

On the union of all parties, it will depend on a voice being more or less persuasive. The ideal formula to be persuasive with our voice would be like that; medium-strong intensity, serious tone, opens bell, and medium-fast duration.

CHAPTER 2
COGNITIVE BEHAVIORAL THERAPY

What Is Cognitive-Behavioral Therapy?

For most of the twentieth century, psychoanalysis was the most common type of psychotherapy. Clients had to see a therapist several times a week, often for several years. In the 1970s, a large number of new forms of psychotherapy appeared; many lasted only a few weeks or months.

In 1979, Time magazine announced that there were nearly 200 types of psychotherapy. In 2010, this number would be between 400 and 500. However, a direct comparison reveals that only a few therapeutic methods are instrumental in resolving the problems for which people generally ask for help such as depression, anxiety, phobias, and stress. Increasingly, Cognitive Behavioral Therapy (CBT) is being recognized as the "standard of excellence," which is the best type of therapy for these kinds of problems, as confirmed by over 375 clinical studies since 1977 and current international treatment guidelines, based on the knowledge of experts in the field. For example, the United States National Institute of Mental Health (NIMH) and the UK National Institute for Health and Clinical Excellence (NICH) have concluded that among the various psychological treatments for anxiety and depression, CBT is the recommended first-line psychological treatment.

CBT is effective for all age groups, from infancy to senior years, regardless of educational background, income, and ethnicity. It has also proven effective in individual and group sessions.

Introduction to CBT

CBT is based on an intensive short-term approach (six to twenty sessions) focused on problem-solving. It is a fast, practical, and goal-oriented therapy that allows clients to develop long-term skills to stay healthy.

CBT focuses on the present moment and the problems that occur daily. It helps clients examine how they interpret and evaluate what is happening around them and the effects of this perception on their emotional experience.

CBT does not focus on childhood experiences and events. Still, these can be examined to help clients understand and deal with the emotional disorders that occurred early in life and understand the possible effects of these experiences on how they react to events.

According to CBT principles, what we feel is related to our perception of a situation and not just the nature of that situation. This idea has its origin in ancient Eastern and Western philosophies. It was incorporated into the general psychotherapeutic approach in the early 1960s. In his first work, Aaron T. Beck, the father of CBT, described the negative thought patterns associated with depression (e.g., being critical of oneself, the world, and the future). He also described ways to target and mitigate negative thoughts to improve mood. Later, Beck and his colleagues focused on the content of ideas and thought processes associated with anxiety, as well as ways to deal with anxiety problems. Since its inception, CBT has become one of the most widely used therapeutic methods.

How is CBT happening?

During a CBT, you learn to recognize, question, and change the thoughts, attitudes, beliefs, and superstitions related to your problematic emotional and behavioral responses in certain situations.

By taking note of your thoughts in situations that cause emotional upheaval, you learn that your thinking can aggravate emotional problems such as depression and anxiety. CBT shows you how to mitigate these problems by:

- Recognizing the distortions of your thoughts.
- Considering your thoughts as ideas of what is happening and not as facts.
- Taking a step back from your thoughts to see the situation from another angle.
- For CBT to be effective, you need to be ready to discuss your thoughts, beliefs, and behaviors and participate.

Exercises during sessions. To get the best results, you should also do the activities planned at home.

COGNITIVE BEHAVIORAL THERAPY

What disorders can be treated by CBT?

CBT is effective in treating a wide range of psychological disorders, including:

- Mood disorders such as depression and bipolar disorder.
- Anxiety disorders, including specific phobias (e.g., fear of animals, heights, enclosed spaces), panic disorder, social phobia (social anxiety disorder), generalized anxiety, obsessive-compulsive disorder, and post-traumatic stress disorder.
- Bulimia and binge eating.
- Dysmorphophobia (body image).
- Substance use disorders (e.g., tobacco, alcohol, and other drugs).

CBT can also help people:

- Who has a psychosis.
- Tear off hair or scratch always or have tics.
- Who have sexual problems or relationship difficulties.
- Insomniacs.
- With chronic fatigue syndrome.
- Suffering from chronic pain (persistent).
- Having longstanding interpersonal issues.

In CBT, a similar method is used to treat different emotional problems. However, the method and strategies used vary and are adapted to the problem.

Why is CBT effective?

CBT is an effective therapeutic method because of it:

- Is structured.
- Is problem-oriented and goal-oriented.
- Teaches strategies and develops skills that have proven themselves.

- Emphasizes the importance of establishing a healthy, collaborative relationship between the therapist and the client.

To describe how CBT works, this guide will focus on using this therapy to treat people with an emotional disorder.

Basics Of Cognitive Behavioral Therapy

Most people believe that an event or situation causes their distress: "I quarreled with my con-join this morning, and I am still angry." "My boss said he was dissatisfied with my job; I am discouraged "or" I read in the newspaper this morning that my actions had gone down. It frightens me ". In each example, the person indicates how the situation caused his emotional upheaval.

However, what you feel in a given situation depends not only on this situation but also on how you perceive it or the meaning you give it. This way of seeing your emotional reaction as being determined by what you think of a situation is one of the underlying assumptions of cognitive-behavioral therapy.

For example, a smashing noise near the window of your room wakes you up at 3 am. Your reaction to this situation will depend on what you believe to be the cause of this noise. If you think an intruder caused it, you will probably be scared and will leave the room running to make you safe. If you believe that the noise was created by the person with whom you share your apartment (if any), who came through the window because she (again!) Forgot her key, you will probably experience frustration and irritation and will react by arguing with her. Finally, if you believe that the noise was caused by your partner, who comes to see you for dating, you will probably be excited.

Nature of automatic thoughts

In each of the previous examples, the situation is the same: a smashing noise near the window at 3 a.m. However, you might have a different quick thought to assess the situation, so-called automatic thinking in CBT. It is thought that suddenly comes to mind and determines the emotion you will feel (e.g., fear, annoyance, excitement) and the behavior that will result (p. e.g., flight, confrontation, cordial reception).

These sudden automatic thoughts influence your emotional and behavioral response more than the situation.

Evaluation of automatic thoughts

In general, automatic thoughts are so brief and so quickly replaced by your awareness of the emotions that follow that you might not notice them.

The ability to take note of your automatic thoughts and evaluate them during a troubling situation is one of the essential skills you will develop and practice in CBT. You will also learn to ask yourself the following question: "What came to mind when I realized that I was upset?".

Do the following exercise. Think about an event that has upset you today or in the past few days and has caused you anxiety, sadness, or anger. Try to remember what you were thinking at the time. By recognizing the thoughts you had in this situation, you might discover the automatic ideas that came to your mind that you were not aware of at the time.

By identifying the automatic thoughts you have had, it will be easier for you to determine the nature of the emotion that has resulted and to understand why the situation has so upset you.

Automatic thought patterns

In many cases, when people start to watch their automatic thoughts and take note of them, they discern a pattern. In the early CBT books he wrote in the 1960s, Aaron T. Beck found that a large number of patients who were depressed had automatic thoughts characterized by a negative perception of themselves ("I am good for nothing"). The world around them ("Nobody loves me") and the future ("I'm bad, and I will not change"). This thought pattern has been dubbed the "cognitive triad" of depression.

In the 1980s, Mr. Beck described a pattern of thoughts in tomatoes that seemed peculiar to anxiety. Clients said they had more ideas about threats and danger ("What if something terrible happened?") And the inability to adapt to a situation ("It's unbearable. Cannot continue like this").

The way a situation or event is perceived varies from person to person. However, the nature of the automatic thoughts of depressed or anxious people becomes predictable and conforms to individual characteristics.

The CBT aims, in particular, to help you become aware of your automatic thoughts. It shows you how to step back and question, evaluate, and rectify incorrect negative automatic thoughts. However, CBT does not present positive thinking as a solution to the problems of life. This therapy is intended to teach you how to evaluate your experiences and issues in different ways (positive, negative, and neutral) so that you can draw accurate conclusions and find creative solutions to your difficulties.

Recognition of distortions of automatic thoughts

On the other hand, the negative automatic thoughts of people with an emotional disorder are usually distorted or wrong. For example, the person who says, "I will never find a soul mate" because she had a bad experience at an appointment dramatizes the outcome of the meeting. And is more likely to experience disruption, excessive emotional that the person who says to himself, "This appointment did not go well, but I hope that the next will be better." Here is another example. A student who considers himself "stupid" and "shabby" because he had a bad grade on an exam gets a label and sees things in an all-or-nothing perspective. He is, therefore, more likely to be upset than a student who says, "I did not get the grade I wanted. I will ask for help and study more thoroughly next time."

Distortions of thought amplify the emotional importance of everyday events. CBT aims to make you more aware of your distorted perception of everyday experiences, especially when you are upset.

We all have negative automatic thoughts and cognitive distortions from time to time. However, some people are more likely to have intuitive ideas related to depression and anxiety and to have more cognitive distortions. CBT assumes that automatic thoughts are influenced by two "deeper" levels of thinking that make some people more likely to have negative and distorted views. These deeper levels are called rules and assumptions and fundamental beliefs.

Rules and assumptions

From the beginning of childhood, you learn rules and make assumptions when interacting with family members and the world around you. For example, you may learn rules about:

- How to interact with other people (e.g., "if you have nothing good to say, do not say anything").
- Situations in which it is acceptable to express emotions (e.g., "never show your nervousness").
- Your performance (e.g., "if you cannot do something perfectly well, it's not worth trying" or "I should excel in everything I do").

You may not be aware of these rules and assumptions. However, when you begin to monitor your automatic thoughts in unexpected situations, you will be able to see the patterns of your intuitive ideas that relate to the rules you have learned and the assumptions you make.

For example, if you assume that you have to excel in everything you do, you will be more likely to be confused if you do not get an optimal result (e.g., you fail an exam, you do not receive a promotion, you are not retained for a job) than a person who does not make such an assumption.

The rules and underlying assumptions can cause automatic thoughts.

CBT aims to help you become aware of your rules and assumptions and their influence on the negative automatic thoughts you have in emotionally disturbing situations.

Basic beliefs

Your fundamental beliefs are at the deepest level of cognition, a level even more profound than where your rules and assumptions lie. In general, fundamental beliefs are learned early in life. They are based on rigid and absolute notions of oneself, others, and the world. Examples of positive fundamental beliefs: "I am attractive," "I am intelligent," and "People love me." Examples of negative fundamental beliefs are: "I am good for nothing," "I am weak," "People are dangerous," "I cannot trust anyone," "The world is a scary and overwhelming place."

Aaron T. Beck suggested that people with negative fundamental beliefs are more vulnerable to depression and anxiety than people with positive fundamental beliefs. Negative basic beliefs may be inactive and affect a person only when a stressful life event occurs, such as the death of a family member, a break-up, or the loss of a job. For example, a woman who believes mentally that she does not deserve to be loved can also think that if she does all she can to please her spouse, he may love her anyway. However, if her spouse leaves her, this woman may begin to believe that she does not deserve to be loved, which may make her more vulnerable to depression or anxiety.

One of the underlying assumptions of CBT is that one can learn to recognize, evaluate, and modify underlying assumptions and beliefs just as one can understand and change negative automatic thoughts. As soon as you begin to mitigate your negative assumptions and expectations, negative and distorted automatic thoughts start to diminish. The lessening of underlying negative assumptions and underlying beliefs that give rise to emotional problems alleviates emotional upheaval and partially protects against the re-emergence of depression and anxiety.

In summary, CBT differs from many other therapeutic methods in that it focuses on ways to help you determine the connection between your thoughts, feelings, and behavior. Although the latter are interdependent (they influence each other), CBT emphasizes the role of cognition (automatic ideas, rules and assumptions, and fundamental beliefs) in the appearance and maintaining emotional difficulties such as depression and anxiety.

The purpose of CBT is to help you recognize, evaluate, and modify your usual patterns of thinking for each of these levels of cognition. With the help of the therapist, you will learn that by giving a less extreme, pragmatic, and accurate sense to adverse events, your emotional and behavioral reactions will be less intense and less disturbing. Once you have developed these skills during therapy, you become your therapist and will be able to cope with painful experiences and emotional upheavals.

Cbt And Cognitive Changes

We all have automatic thoughts that spring into our minds. They can be positive, neutral, or negative. CBT is particularly interested in negative automatic thoughts related to intense moods. In the beginning, CBT aims to teach you to recognize negative automatic thoughts and cognitive distortions that occur in problematic situations. Some people develop this skill quickly while others need more time.

Determining the links between thoughts, mood, and behavior

To recognize the automatic thoughts and cognitive distortions that occur in problem situations, you should first talk to your CBT therapist about situations that have upset you recently. This discussion will help you discover the connection between your thoughts, mood, and behavior. Here is an example:

Therapist: Can you describe a situation that has troubled you in the past week?

Pierre: I was in the subway, and I noticed everyone who was in a relationship.

Therapist: What did you feel at that moment?

Pierre: I was sad and angry.

Therapist: What did you think when you were sad and angry?

Pierre: I told myself that everyone seems to have someone in their life except me, and that is unfair.

Therapist: And if it's true that everyone seems to have someone in your life except you, do you think it reveals anything about you?

Peter: Yeah, that I'm a shabby and that I'll always be alone.

Therapist: What did you do while you thought about it and had these feelings?

Pierre: After a while, I could not take it anymore. I got off the metro even though I had not arrived at my destination. I went home, I sat on my bed, and I thought about it all.

Here are the elements of this example:

1. **Situation:** In the subway, Pierre notices the presence of couples.

2. **Mood:** Sad and angry.

3. **Thoughts:** Everyone has someone in their life except me, it's unfair; I am a shabby and I will always be alone. Behavior: Pierre comes down from the subway, then goes back to the house to mull over all that.

In this example, to determine why Peter was sad and angry, we must understand what he was thinking:

- He does not have a romantic relationship, and he wants one.

- It is unfair that everyone seems to have what he wants to have.

- Because he does not have a romantic relationship now, he will never find a soul mate, and he will always be alone.

Challenging and evaluating negative automatic thoughts

As you learn to recognize your negative automatic thoughts, you will also learn to question and evaluate them. One of the main goals of CBT is to help you think of your dreams as ideas that do not necessarily correspond to reality. In other words, your thoughts are not necessarily truths.

To help you achieve this goal, the therapist will perform "cognitive restructuring" exercises that will teach you how to step back, question your negative self-thoughts, and evaluate the evidence that supports your thoughts and the ones that contradict them. You can then determine if your ideas are right or wrong.

In the previous example, a CBT therapist could ask Peter the following questions:

- Among the people you love and respect, is there anyone who is not in a relationship?

- Have you ever had romantic relationships?

- If one of your friends thought of you, what would you say to him?
- Can you ignore experiences you've had that suggest you will not be alone?
- Do you hold yourself responsible for something that is partly out of your control?

This approach is not intended to question Peter's thoughts, but rather to bring him to challenge the accuracy of his automatic opinions in the light of his real situation.

Recognition and correction of cognitive distortions

To recognize and modify the negative automatic thoughts associated with strong emotions, you must also learn to recognize the distortions or "errors" of thinking that occur when you find yourself in a troubling situation or remember such a situation.

Distortions of thinking are more likely to occur when you are troubled because emotional turmoil can undermine your strengths so that you could rely more on shortcuts or more straightforward ways of thinking. We all have distortions of thought from time to time. Here are some examples (Burns, 1999):

- **All or nothing (black or white):** Perceive things in black or white, without greyish zones (e.g., Amina got three A +, two A, and one B + during her session and believes that because she did not get only A, she failed).

- **Rejection of the positive:** Ignore positive experiences and see only the negative side (e.g., John is a dedicated father who helps his son with homework every night and spends as much time with him as possible). As he had to be absent more than usual recently because of his work, Jean thinks he is a "bad father").

- **Over-generalization:** Considering a unique experience as a continual event (e.g., Ingrid was anxious during the meeting, she concluded she would never be comfortable with her co-workers).

- **Mental filter:** Give great importance to a negative detail (e.g., Denis speaks to a group of ten young people in the church, only sees one who does not seem interested in the place of the nine others who listen carefully).

- **Dramatization:** Consider the worst, that is, assume that a situation will be more terrible or horrible than it probably will be (e.g., one morning, as Susan gets up, she notices a redness). On the back of her leg, instead of thinking of all that could have caused this redness, she immediately concludes that she has skin cancer and rushes to her doctor.

- **Reading the thought:** Quickly conclude that a person has a negative perception of you before knowing all the facts (e.g., at the movies, Guy stumbles and topples his popcorn and his drink. world must think he is a shabby man).

- **Personalization:** Believe that things are wrong and that they are the cause (e.g., Charlotte is organizing a party, she notices that two of her guests are alone and do not speak.) She begins to believe that this is his fault if they do not have fun.

Taking note of your thoughts

At the beginning of treatment, the CBT therapist will ask you questions to help you recognize and question your negative self-thoughts and cognitive distortions. As you make progress, the therapist will ask you to complete the thoughts book at home, in anticipation of the next session. Over time, you will become accustomed to completing this register, which will allow you to question and evaluate your automatic thoughts, as well as alleviate the emotional troubles you experience in your daily life.

It is recommended that you complete the thoughts register shortly after the end of the distressing situation or event because that is when you are most aware of the ideas generated by the experience you come from, To live. However, it is sometimes difficult to do this, for example, if you risk exposing your personal life or if the problem arises at work or at another time when it is inconvenient to complete the registration. In such a case, try to fill in the register later in the day before you forget the details. Thus, you will recover more quickly from the trouble you have experienced.

Target assumptions and beliefs

As the therapy progresses, the CBT therapist will introduce other cognitive strategies and home-based exercises that serve to target your assumptions and fundamental ideas.

To identify your assumptions and fundamental beliefs, you can use the register of thoughts, for it identifies situations that cause an emotional disorder and to identify the thread. The CBT therapist can help you challenge and evaluate your assumptions and beliefs and generate insights that will make it easier for you to compose when you find yourself in troubling situations.

Another way in which CBT is used to target the assumptions and beliefs that need to be changed is to write a negative fundamental understanding of yourself on a sheet of paper (e.g., "Unfriendly") and, on the backside, a less disturbing belief that you would like to have (e.g., "friendly"). You will then have to keep a record of your experiences during the week by indicating situations that seemed to confirm your positive or negative belief. In cases where you have gathered evidence to support your negative mindset, you will need to re-examine the situation carefully to identify facts that support and contradict your belief to arrive at a more balanced perspective.

Behavioral experiences

One of the best ways to challenge and evaluate underlying assumptions and beliefs is to test their validity with behavioral experiments. For example, if you think someone will make fun of you if you make a mistake, you might be asked to go through an analysis to determine what happens when you make a mistake. Of course, you will be asked to submit only to the experiences that you think you can do and only when you have learned ways to deal with the full range of potential outcomes that such experiences may have.

When you're ready, you might be asked to make a mistake like purse money while you line up at a store checkout or spill a drink in a cafeteria. You will be able to determine: a) how much people notice your mistake; b) their reaction (e.g., they laugh and ridicule you, as you fear, or they do not seem to notice or criticize you); and c) how you deal with the situation.

In summary, the initial goal of CBT is to help you recognize and modify negative automatic thoughts that cause emotional distress in problem situations. You will learn to identify and rectify negative automatic thoughts and cognitive distortions that arouse intense moods. The thought register is the primary tool used to make cognitive changes. Other cognitive strategies, including the following, are used to reinforce the progress you make when you modify negative automatic thoughts and the assumptions and beliefs they are based on:

- Determine the advantages and disadvantages of these beliefs.
- Study the evidence that supports the assumptions and expectations and those that contradict them.
- Have a less extreme and balanced perception of oneself, others and the world.
- Submit to behavioral experiments.

Use of Cbt for Behavioral Changes

Until now, we have focused on the cognitive aspect of CBT, that is, the modification of cognitive elements, or thoughts, which can cause an emotional disorder. We will now look at behaviors that can aggravate or prolong negative moods.

Changing thinking and behavior changes go hand in hand. If you change your perception of a situation or problem, you could also improve your behavior and vice versa. If you change the way you approach a situation or problem, you may perceive it differently. For example, if you smoke and find new information that makes you think that smoking is more dangerous than you thought, you might decide to quit smoking (a cognitive change leads to a change in behavior). Or, if you stop for a week because you are sick or unable to smoke, you might say, "If I can quit smoking for a week, maybe I can do it for a month." This way of thinking may cause you to change your behavior and try to quit smoking for a month (a change in behavior leads to cognitive change).

CBT uses a variety of behavioral methods and strategies to alleviate your distress. You will find more details on this in the next pages.

Self-monitoring

We talked about the register of thoughts, which recognizes and evaluates negative thoughts and cognitive distortions. The registry is one of the self-monitoring techniques that you will be asked to use during CBT. You could also be asked to do the following exercises:

- Monitor your moods or feelings every day that gives you pleasure or give you the impression of being in control of a situation, for example by giving them a score ranging from zero to 10 or from zero to 100.

- Monitor the symptoms of your problem in specific circumstances.

- Plan activities or monitor the progress you have made to achieve a goal related to your behavior; for example, schedule fitness sessions for the week or record the number of times you have been training during the week.

DAILY Self-Monitoring

By taking note of problems every day, we become more aware of situations that may "trigger" distress. The monitoring forms used during CBT help clients recognize the type of reactions they have in stressful situations. For example, they can determine whether certain events trigger feelings such as sadness, anguish, anger, hurt, or disappointment.

The monitoring forms also allow people who fill them to be more aware of the intensity of their moods. Thus, they can determine if a situation often causes low anxiety, while another condition always causes very intense anxiety.

Finally, the monitoring forms are not just for taking note of problems. They also help people who use them to become aware of the progress they have made. For example, these forms can be used to determine the extent to which a person has achieved a behavioral goal, as well as the events and tasks performed that give him or her the feeling that she or he is in control of a situation. (sense of accomplishment and acquired skill).

In general, people who experience depression or have other emotional problems that disrupt motivation-their activities and engage in an event tend to report a lower level of pleasure than they felt while they were doing it. One way for a person to become more aware of what they are doing with their time, the comfort they have gained from their activities, and their mastery of each activity is to take note of all they have done and felt. If you have a problem with motivation, taking note of your actions can help you recognize that you are having more fun and feel more like being in control of a situation rather than doing activities than when you are doing something. In simple terms, an action, however trivial, can make you feel better.

Self-monitoring Of Symptoms

For almost all clinical problems treated with CBT, there are specialized forms that allow you to monitor your symptoms and take note of them during treatment. Keeping track of your experiences and taking note of them alone can improve your mood and well-being. As a result, clients are generally encouraged to do this after the first CBT session.

If you are following therapy for anxiety, you may be asked to fill out a form where you will describe your particular symptoms, depending on the anxiety problem you are experiencing. For example, if you are undergoing therapy for social anxiety, you will be asked to fill out a form where you will record distressing social situations and those where you have experienced performance anxiety in the past. If you are following therapy for an obsessive-compulsive disorder, you.

Indicate on the form the nature of the obsessive thoughts and distress they caused during the week, as well as the duration and frequency of the compulsive rituals.

Calendar of Activities

You can write down your schedule Which will be used to monitor your activities and give them a score based on the fun and impression of control of the situation they gave you, can also be used to program activities that you may have. Tried to avoid. This calendar can help you decide whether to go to an event or not. For example, if you choose in advance to exercise on Tuesday from 5 pm to 6 pm, you are more likely to do so than if you wait to see how you will feel that day before making a decision.

The therapist may ask you to include pleasant activities in your calendar (e.g., going out to dinner with a friend) and tasks that make you feel like you are in control (e.g., paying bills) for the next week. He will probably ask you to keep a record of the automatic thoughts that you will have as you go about your activities to help you recognize the distortions and other assessments you make that reduce the enjoyment of the activity and the activity. The impression that you are in control of the situation.

Also, the calendar of activities helps you recognize the factors that prevent you from doing specific tasks and divide these tasks into more uncomplicated actions to alleviate the distress they cause and increase the chances of you accomplished. You can define "staggered tasks" so that you will make the parts easier before performing the more difficult and complicated elements. By merely changing the structure of the tasks to be completed and the process you are following, you can significantly increase the chances of accomplishing these tasks.

Exhibition therapy

Exposure therapy is an integral part of CBT in the treatment of anxiety. It aims to reduce the fear of certain things (e.g., insects, snakes) or specific situations (e.g., confined spaces, heights) by gradually increasing exposure to these things or in these situations. To start, you may be asked to think about the idea or situation that scares you or to look at an image that illustrates it (indirect exposure) and expose yourself to it more and more until you can touch this thing or put you in this situation (direct exposure).

By gradually exposing yourself to your fears, your anguish will diminish, and you will learn that your concerns are excessive and irrational. This process is called habituation (or exhaustion of effect).

In general, exposure therapy begins with exposure to situations that elicit mild to moderate fear. The client is then gradually exposed to conditions that create more intense fear. Before starting this therapy, you should rank your concerns in ascending order and indicate all the situations that are causing you anxiety as well as the levels of anxiety associated with each trigger.

At first, the therapist will help you expose yourself to your fears, and as you progress, you will have to expose yourself to it after the sessions. Your progress will depend on the intensity of your fear and your ability to withstand the discomfort associated with your anxiety. You must expose yourself to your fear several times and long enough (usually at least 30 minutes) to get the best results possible. You will learn that your anxiety naturally decreases when you are long enough in the situation that causes fear.

Behavioral experiences

The behavioral experiences described previously allowed you to analyze your assumptions and beliefs. Through these experiences, you will be exposed to a scary situation to determine if your fears will come true. If the result that scares you occurs, the experiments will also allow you to learn how well you have coped with the situation.

Experiences are behavioral because they force you to "try" new ways of thinking by changing your habits, usually by putting yourself in specific situations and choosing a different behavioral strategy.

CHAPTER 3

NEURO-LINGUISTIC PROGRAMMING?

What Is It And How Does It Work?

Neuro-linguistic programming helps us to change behavior patterns and thoughts even very traumatic or rooted in ourselves. In this chapter, we reveal some of the NLP techniques that will help you achieve it.

Richard Bandler and John Grinder created the neurolinguistic programming (NLP) in California (United States) in the seventies. Its creators affirm that there is a connection between neurological procedures, language, and behavioral patterns learned.

The creators of the NLP took three teachers, Fritz Perls, Virginia Satir, and Milton Erickson, and through various studies, they verified that these three people possessed special communication skills that allowed them to obtain excellent results with their patients. That way, they were creating a set of tools that they later called neurolinguistic programming.

"NLP is like the nuclear physics of the mind. Physics studies the structure of reality, the nature of the world. NLP does the same with its brain. It allows decomposing the phenomena in the constituent parts that determine their operation."

(Tony Robbins)

The elements of neurolinguistic programming

It has happened to all of us that we react to a situation, and then our inner voice tells us that we should have said something else or reacted in another way. Actually, our way of responding and thinking is conditioned by a neurological map that encodes and stores our way of responding to a situation.

That map is made up of our past, our present, and our future. And from it, we build our beliefs, lessons, and behaviors learned.

The structures of our mind are so strongly rooted in us that we cannot influence them, at least in a conscious way. The mind works on two levels: conscious (logical thinking) and unconscious (automatic functioning).

The neurolinguistic programming and conscious and unconscious mind

The conscious mind is the always alert one, which allows us to remember dates and names of people, for example. And the unconscious mind is one that activates all behaviors, beliefs, values, etc. that we have learned and that shape our way of acting. It is not always consciously accessible. And, for example, it is what allows us to drive, write an email, or open a window.

For our unconscious mind to "draw" a new map, it has to act with a clear objective that answers the question, what do we want? And the complicated thing is precisely that, that on many occasions we do not know what we want. Therefore, we do not know how to define our objective.

For this, we have to think of something that changes our habitual behavior in a situation, something that is apparently impossible.

The objectives in NLP

The purposes that we propose in the neurolinguistic programming sessions must answer a series of questions. The result is to achieve a significant change in our behavior.

· Is it a positive goal?

For our programming to work, we must define a positive objective. Our goal cannot begin with, "I don't want that ...". It's about highlighting what you want to achieve, not what you want to avoid.

· Does it benefit you?

Your goal should be something you do for yourself, and that depends on yourself, not on others. For example, it is very common that the goal of young people is to finish a university career, but that is not a goal of them but of their parents. You must also control what you do to reach your goal so that it depends on you. We cannot wish as a goal to make good weather on the weekend, because it is not up to us.

How will you know that you are reaching them?

Think about what you will be doing at that moment and how you will feel. Visualize each action, each feeling that this moment provokes, how it smells, what flavor you feel, what you hear, how you move, what you do. In addition to knowing if we are achieving our objective, we will have to set ourselves goals in the short term and measure their fulfillment. For example, if my goal is to find work, a goal will have to be to look for job offers and offers each week.

Is your goal specific?

You must make clear what you want and what you don't. The more defined and detailed your objective is, the easier it will be to establish the steps to achieve it. For example, if we define the objective, "I want to find a job," it is a very generic objective.

But, if we redefine the objective by giving details, we will have much clearer goals to achieve our objective. For example: "From February 1, 2020, I will work in a company dedicated to computer science that will pay me 2000 euros a month."

What resources do you need to make it happen?

Think about the resources you already have and those you need broadly: knowledge, objects, financial resources, help from third parties.

Once our goal is set, we must review our beliefs and values. What we have deeply rooted in ourselves and that prevents us from reaching our dreams. We must change the negative belief structures that make us impede to go towards our goal.

What prevents me from achieving my goal?

One of the biggest obstacles we will encounter on the road to our dreams is the opinions of others. Remember that each person has different perspectives, and we must put ourselves in their place to try to understand their reasoning.

All the way to go towards your goal, visualize your dream, feel how it smells, what is heard, what you touch, and especially the feeling and feeling of happiness that causes you to achieve your goal. And reach your dream! Turn your aspiration into reality!

Finally, for our subconscious mind to learn a new program that allows us to realize our dream, it must perceive the reason, the reason.

In NLP, the learning process is established in four phases:

- **Phase 1:** Unconscious Incompetence. I don't know I don't know.

- **Phase 2:** Conscious Incompetence. I know I don't know.

- **Phase 3:** Conscious competition. I know I know.

- **Phase 4:** Unconscious competition. I don't know what I know.

To unlearn, we go from step 4 to 2 and to relearn from step 2 to 4. Once we have learned the new program, we can apply it at the moment it is necessary. Therefore, NLP helps us create new mental programs that facilitate many aspects of our lives and help us work on goals to achieve what we dream and desire.

The most significant development of NLP has occurred in interpersonal relationships and the workplace. In both areas, you can use NLP to train your skills, overcome obstacles, resolve conflicts, and influence other people.

In conclusion, NLP gives you the necessary tools to control how to respond to your environment, how to perceive it, and thus take steps to make your dreams come true.

The principles of NLP

1. The inner card is unique

One of the principles of NLP relates to the orientation of the people in the world around them. The direction of the person has to do with the inner card. In the early stages of life, the inner card is simple. As we grow, however, the map becomes more complex, and new paths open.

2. The best map offers more than one road

As mentioned in the previous point, the complete map is also more accurate and offers more options to reach a goal or solve the problem. This is related to flexibility and the ability to respond to a vital event in a number of ways. The map is not the area that represents it, but if it is correct, it has a similar structure to the area and is more useful.

3. Every behavior has a positive intention

This can be one of the most discussed principles of NLP. This point refers to the fact that every person and every action has an intrinsic property positive intent. For example, someone may doubt that a smoker has a positive intention to smoke. However, according to this principle, the smoker may smoke to relax or be socially accepted. NLP tries to redirect this positive intention towards a more adaptable behavioral pattern and suitable for the person.

4. The structure of the experience

This principle shows how each experience is composed of a particular structure. Every thought, every feeling, every memory, or experience It consists of a series of elements. This means that if every experience has a structure, its effect can be changed thanks to a change in composition.

5. All problems have a solution

This principle refers to the fact that all problems have a solution. It may seem perfect because sometimes certain solutions can not be carried out. At other times, there will be problems that do not have a clear solution. This has to do with the card the person has The fewer roads or alternatives you have, the fewer solutions you can give to the specific situation. Also, the interpretation of the problem has to do with the content of the map. A richer map that offers more resources will find certain situations less of a problem.

6. Everyone has the strength he needs

This is one of the principles of NLP, which has to do with the personal development of the person, as they are referred to. Everyone has the necessary strength to achieve what is suggested. The problem arises when a person's limiting beliefs influence self-esteem.

7. Body and mind are part of the same system

This principle refers to Man is body and mind. In other words, every emotion and emotion affects the body. This also applies vice versa. For example, a disease that affects the body has psychological effects. Therefore, for NLP, the thought changes that alter physical issues are important. By the way, did you already hear of that? Embodied knowledge?

8. The importance of communication depends on the result

It is necessary to establish clear communication guidelines that do not lead to misunderstandings nor an option for biased personal interpretations by the recipient of the message.

9. There are no failures, but opportunities

When a person moves continuously, they have different ways to reach the goal. The failures must be seen as opportunities, that is, as measures that you can overcome and move in the desired direction.

10. If something does not work, try something else

Sometimes people insist on doing something that does not work, nor do they change the way they act. At this point, the famous phrase "do not expect different results if you always do the same thing" makes sense. NLP Practitioners Want to Help Recognize and modify these behaviors that are not effective and keep repeating with the same stone.

Three keys to NLP to change your life

The keys to NLP (neuro-linguistic programming) can be incredibly useful in changing the way we perceive and interpret reality. We cannot forget that our thoughts and feelings shape everything that surrounds us. Hence the techniques that accompany this approach are useful for us to become aware of it and apply appropriate changes.

In one way or another, we have all heard about neurolinguistic programming. More than psychological theory, we should see it instead as a set of personal development strategies. With them, what their creators, Richard Bandler and John Grinder, were looking for back in the 70s, was to model the abilities of the human being to allow him to achieve his vital purposes by himself.

On the other hand, it should be noted that there is no lack of critical voices regarding this model, who distrusts NLP, seeing it instead as a type of pseudoscience. Now, it should be said that their strategies turn out to be quite useful in many cases, as well as impressive from the psychological point of view. Thus, one of its main objectives is to establish a connection between neurological processes, our language, and behavioral patterns learned through experience.

Thus, by correcting our cognitive representations and removing power from those rigid mental maps that sometimes characterize us, we gradually shape much more adaptive behavior patterns. The keys to NLP are an exciting and useful way to change our reality, to model our mind, our way of feeling what surrounds us to perceive life in a freer, more positive, happy way.

These would be three strategies to achieve it.

1. Dissociation technique

NLP or neurolinguistic programming explains that our lack of confidence, as well as anxiety or stress, are activities, processes, not permanent conditions. The key is, therefore, to control these processes, change them so that they flow in a more appropriate direction and of course, in our favor.

One way to achieve this is through dissociation. The steps would be as follows:

- Identify that emotion that you want to stop, that you want to calm and dissolve from your mind, such as anger, anger, fear, disappointment...

- What we must do is focus on that particular emotion and on a situation that provokes it regularly. For example, I feel anger every time my co-worker speaks behind my back.

- We will visualize that scene as if it were a movie, and what we will do with it is the following: we will provide it with a fun soundtrack to remove drama. Then, we will reproduce it more times in our mind to reduce negative emotions, to perceive that everything is under our control and that this situation, far from affecting us, is already unimportant; It can even prove ironic. The rage has disappeared.

2. Re-frame content

Another of the keys to NLP may be evident to any of us, but it is no less accurate that we tend to forget it or not know how to combine it properly. If we become obsessed with anticipating fatalities, in facing our day to day with fear and always thinking the worst, it is possible that in the end, we will generate our death.

For example, some keep thinking about what would happen to him or her if their partner left him if he betrayed him. Their anguish is such that they end up developing obsessive behaviors, jealousy, distrust, and a whole range of harmful processes that end up crystallizing in their worst fear: the couple ends up leaving them for not supporting that situation anymore.

Thus, one way to control these fears is to make use of content re-framing. It is based on a cognitive technique were to shift attention focused on fear to frame it in other more constructive aspects.

For example, I must stop focusing on the fear of losing my partner to focus on building good times by his side.

I shift my fear of being alone to focus on an essential process: taking responsibility for myself. I must learn to love myself enough, learn to be active instead of letting myself be trapped by fear.

3. NLP keys: the anchoring technique

The anchoring technique is undoubtedly one of the keys of the NLP most representative of this psychotherapeutic strategy of personal growth. It is based on something very concrete: an anchor is a connection between a stimulus and an emotional state. Our purpose is to achieve an adequate mood as well as dominant with which to perform a specific task or face a given situation successfully.

«Every time you are doing the same as most, it is time to Stop and Reflect.»

-Mark Twain-

For example, let's think about those situations that are characterized by generating anxiety or insecurity: exams, speaking in public, approaching that person that attracts us so much. If we can evoke, to put into operation a particular mental state, we will find enough momentum and security to get out (and successfully) of these very ordinary moments. These would be a few simple steps to achieve an anchor based on the NLP keys:

- We will first identify what we want to feel: trust, happiness, tranquillity...

- Now we will try to remember a moment in our life when we feel those positive emotions with high intensity.

- Focus on that memory and "trim" that image, make it yours, keep it alive.

- Now we must choose a phrase that serves as an anchor, "I am at peace" or "serenity," or "everything will be fine"...

- The strategy is to repeat this sequence (desired emotion, memory, visualization, anchor word) daily until it is integrated into our mind. In this way, the anchor will be automated little by little every time we need it.

We are sure that these keys to NLP will have aroused the curiosity of more than one in that broad and always suggestive universe that is neurolinguistic programming. If so, it is possible to say that it is an approach that is within our reach, it is part of the movement that emphasizes our enormous potential as human beings, initiated in the 70s, and that has been consolidating over the years.

The 8 Transformative Strategies of NLP

You may have heard on occasion about NLP or Neurolinguistic Programming as a practice of personal development or excellence, and so it is. A more exact definition would be, a set of techniques aimed at analyzing, coding and modifying beliefs and behaviors through the study of language, both verbal and gestural and corporal. Today we are going to discover the transformative strategies of NLP and why it is so successful.

It is called "programming" because it is an action plan or set of operations that seek a specific objective," neuro " because it studies the processes that occur in the same nervous system and "linguistic" because we use the language (verbal and not verbal).

Do you want to know more about Neurolinguistic Programming? In this section, we explain what it is and the eight transformative strategies of NLP that are used to seek success, quality of life, or overcoming traumas and phobias.

"The brain is not a vessel to fill, but a lamp to light."

-Plutarch-

The NLP method

NLP has occupied a prominent place among the disciplines that assist in the achievement of objectives so that many psychologists, doctors, and coaches apply it in the field of personal development individually or in groups.

One of the foundations of NLP is the evidence that each of us builds different representations of reality to which we add our emotions and language processes.

By modifying our beliefs and emotions, our way of expressing ourselves, we can also change the perception of reality and the self-image we have of ourselves.

On the other hand, Neurolinguistic Programming ensures that memory and imagination use the same neurological circuits and thus have the same impact on the human being. Then, eight transformative strategies of NLP collected by psychologist Jazmín Zambrano in his book NLP for all.

1. Submodalities or learning styles

Submodalities are variants of representation systems, that is, in the way in which our brain encodes and classifies an experience. There are three types:

- Visual (color, distance, depth, clarity, contrast, and luminosity).
- Auditory (volume, tone, rhythm, and pauses).
- Kinesthetic (temperature, vibration, texture, pressure, movement, and weight).

All these nuances would help us, through imagination, to be able to change the characteristics of the memories we have edited as a film of our life and thus modify, for example, the memory of an unhappy childhood.

Another way to apply them would be through "dissociation." We move to the moment in which we live an unpleasant experience; we feel the touch that an object had or see what was happening, and then dissociate ourselves, leave the situation and look at it as if we were outside it, observing ourselves.

For NLP, the objective of dissociating is to remove the emotional power from the experience we have experienced. Thus, the experience loses strength, detaches itself from suffering, and can even be associated with a pleasant moment.

2. Anchoring technique

In the process of the anchoring technique, an external stimulus or "anchor" is associated with a positive behavior that one wishes to acquire. Anchors can be words, gestures, smells, or colors that transport us to a positive state of mind.

An example of this anchorage would be to associate the gesture of touching the ear with feeling good so that, in moments of crisis or difficulties, with that small gesture, we could recover well-being and feel better.

3. Reframe

The reframing, in NLP, consists of modifying the frame of reference in which a person lives the situation to change its meaning. Therefore, the emotional state and the behavior that accompanied it in principle. It is to see the glass half full instead of half empty, find an unexpected edge in the situation that manages to reverse its impact and positivize it.

4. Calibration

This strategy is to recognize the mental state of the individual through his verbal behavior and nonverbal, that is, if you are sad, angry, or even lying. Looking at their behavior, we can get to know each other better and help them in their process of change.

5. Modeling

With the modeling, it is possible to determine how other people acted to achieve success in some area of their life and to imitate them. With the modeling technique, what is attempted is the creation of representation as faithful as possible of another person, especially their behaviors to achieve something.

6. Induction

With the technique of induction, people are guided to certain emotional states to modify painful situations. Either induce feelings of discomfort that match the experience they had or pleasant feelings to address their fears and concerns about these situations.

7. Synchronization

The synchronization would be like a deep empathy, through which the feelings of others are understood until creating a strong link between the conscious and unconscious level of the interlocutor. This technique serves to optimize interpersonal communications.

8. Relaxation

Finally, NLP considers relaxation an effective tool to relieve tensions, expand awareness, and free the spirit. Relaxing is always good to face our day today.

The effectiveness of NLP transformative strategies

The positive thing about the transformative strategy of NLP is that they enjoy great efficiency. Therefore, this type of therapy is so used today. It is important to mention that the strategies mentioned above will not be applied as a whole in all cases. What does this mean? That the incidence will depend on the professional in some more than in others.

With these strategies, NLP pursues a personal transformation that raises self-esteem, increases creative capacity, and helps us express ourselves more satisfactorily by improving relationships with others. Have you ever tried Neurolinguistic Programming?

How to Manage Your Emotions through NLP

Act as if you were already the person you would like to be, and allow your emotions to be the force that drives your engine of change. You are the architect of your reality.

It is possible that you have already heard about NLP (neurolinguistic programming), and that you even have your own coach, or that for now, it is only a trend that attracts your interest but in which you have not yet deepened enough.

As curiosity is often said to be the first step towards knowledge, and if there is a powerful dimension in which we should always be up to date, it is in emotional management.

Neuro-linguistic programming (NLP) is a method that is at the service of Emotional Intelligence through a set of systems to understand and program our behavior. It teaches us to act, to deploy strategies and, above all, to manage.

Because managing is being able to face the problems in our social relationships, learn to make more effective and successful personal decisions.

NLP and our internal programs

We will begin by defining briefly what are the basic postulates of the NLP to have a basic guidance guide:

- Neuro-linguistic programming is a communication, personal development, and psychotherapy strategy created in the 70s.

- All our behavior is a set of habits and actions acquired by all our experiences: they are programming. An example?

In our childhood, they never recognized everything we did well; we only received sanctions, criticisms, and rejections. All this developed in us a sense of helplessness and little confidence in ourselves.

As the years have passed, our "internal programming" has been feeding even more with this feeling.

69

- We have thus established a connection between neurological processes ("neuro"), our language ("linguistic"), and behavioral patterns learned through experience.

People think, feel, and act according to internal programs. NLP offers us a series of appropriate tools to allow us to change, and at the same time, improve all these processes. It is a model of human experience and communication.

NLP bases for emotional management

We will start by telling you that NLP is very useful to complement it with our Emotional Intelligence.

Sometimes, despite knowing, we do not know how to put it into practice, so, for example, it is possible that despite knowing what are the basic pillars of EI, in your day to day, you do not know how to reproduce them:

NLP seeks to model and reproduce competent skills based on emotional intelligence so that we find success and happiness in everyday life.

Emotional Intelligence will be the speaker that will help us communicate, and NLP, for its part, will provide us with practical strategies, through continuous interaction, or "programming," between our nervous system (our "hardware"), and our language, (our "software").

1. When our programming is based on negative emotions

Depressions, states of depression or helplessness, are very common in our day to day. First of all, we have to refocus our ideas on them:

Negative emotions such as sadness, grief, or grief, are not eternal diseases, nor should we resign ourselves to them. It is necessary to manage them to promote CHANGE.

- Do not be afraid of them; do not fear sadness. NLP invites us to know how to administer and accept them so that they are an effective tool. For what reason? Because they are part of ourselves and of a knowledge from which we must understand their origin.

- NLP does not seek to eliminate anything in you. Pain cannot be erased, but we can understand it to offer us teaching, and teaching is a weapon of power.

Why do I feel so downcast? I don't feel well in my work situation. My work generates frustration. What does this frustration tell me? What should I make any changes, maybe? What strategies should I deploy to promote it and find myself better?

- Managing emotions mean making the most of them, making them go from being "negative" to "harmless."

2. Action keys to generate change

- Be aware of your emotions by listening to your body: welcome the emotions and accept them.

- Describe each emotion with words, define them aloud. Name the feeling.

- How is that feeling? Is it healthy or immobilizes you?

- Connect with your own inner strength to transform the unhealthy emotion, or those destructive thoughts into useful dimensions: make your voice act as healing.

NLP requires practice and above all, well and full awareness of our emotions. It is a daily adventure that is worth exercising to get to know each other better and bring about changes.

The Power Of The Mind

We have heard of them, but what are NLP techniques? Indeed, we cannot talk about Neuro-linguistic Programming as a science; hence, it has received some criticism. But it is considered a "model," that is, a set of techniques and theories focused on understanding behaviors and orienting the human being towards self-knowledge and the achievement of objectives.

But we better analyze its acronyms first:

On the one hand, we have the word "programming," which refers to the intention to reprogram behaviors, beliefs, and psychological processes. The "neuro" concept leads us to the idea that all behavior is based on a series of neurological processes. And finally, "linguistic" responds to the concept that all these neurological processes are expressed through a specific verbal and body language.

«NLP is a set of models, skills, and techniques to think and act effectively in the world. The purpose of NLP is to be useful, increase options, and improve the quality of life.»

-John Grinder-

Principles and techniques NLP

That dimensional triad that we mentioned has as an initial objective to understand our internal processes to reprogram the way of communicating and expressing ourselves, in order to change beliefs and make us feel safe to achieve our personal success. A challenge, right? But let us know, in a brief way, some more of its aspects and NLP techniques.

1. The communication

NLP tells us that the way we communicate and the words we use define our reality and the way we understand the world, a personal perspective that sometimes does not match that of our interlocutors.

In addition to this, people have two types of communication: internal (what we think and feel in our internal jurisdiction) and external (where in addition to the words we speak out loud, gestures, postures, and gestures come together).

2. How to process information

People differ in our way by "capturing" the information. Some people are guided more by the visual, others by the auditory route, others by the sensations. Stop for a moment in this idea: How do you remember things more, with words or with images?

Try to remember a moment of your past; how does that memory come to mind? See how you analyze and capture the information around you, if you are, for example, more visual or auditory.

3. The anchor

One way in which to achieve objectives or overcome certain problems would be based on this concept, already used by behavioral psychology and one of the basic NLP techniques.

Imagine a situation that causes us a lot of anguish and anxiety, public speaking, for example. One way to face this reality would be to "anchor" a pleasant, relaxed, and positive moment of our memory, and associate it with visualization and breathing techniques to the "stressful situation."

A walk on the beach when we were children, a sunset with our partner, relaxing music... all this should help us "weaken that fear" and reprogram new realities where harmony prevails. In this way, gradually, we "anchor" in a quiet and pleasant situation to face an event that is stressful for us.

4. The weather

Time has a certain importance for each person, but you must know how to manage it properly. In the past, our memories and emotions come together, a trunk from which good things can sometimes be taken to redirect the "now."

Because it is in the present where sensory experiences prevail, in which the significant events occur and where we must invest all our efforts in view of a good future. Thus, working in the present is essential in NLP to sow the future we would like to have.

The future does not exist yet; hence, it must be established as that point where to place our desires to push our present. Ours now.

5. Systems ecology

People have a system of beliefs and determined values built throughout our lives, which are those engines that guide our neurological axes. "We are what we believe," and beliefs are the conceptions of our world, which promote action and behavior.

Sometimes, these beliefs are so ingrained in our being that we do not even realize if they are beneficial to us or not, we may be hurting ourselves without knowing it... Hence, NLP delves into our systems ecology to make us aware and reorganize these structures more beneficially and optimally.

"The greatest wisdom that exists is to know oneself."

-Galileo-

These are, then, with great strokes, the basic pillars on which this approach of the human mind is based, the Neurolinguistic Programming, where how we interpret our reality and organize the information:

The senses, the language, the time, words, memories, beliefs... are those leaves that make up the tree of our life.

NLP techniques help to vary or focus differently on any of these parts to direct our lives towards certain goals.

Why is NLP so successful?

NLP are methods

NLP is not a universal, universally applicable method. NLP transforms into something that everyone needs right now. The main focus of the NLP is on the uniqueness of the people. Therefore, every method is tuned to the individual. The application of NLP is always based on the analysis of the individual. Only when you know how you or your counterpart is ticking can you use NLP successfully. Knowing to solve a problem, it is important to understand how the problem works. And this is where NLP comes in. The NLP not only looks at what people think and do. The main focus is on how they think. The thought process, the subjective mental process, is considered. NLP helps us to understand this structure of subjectivity. Through this analysis of the individual, you can find out what makes a person successful or how a problem works. When you understand that, suddenly, it's easy to solve a problem or help translate success into another area of life or another person.

Albert Einstein is said to have said the phrase, "The definition of insanity is always the same to do and expect different results." In the spirit of Einstein, an important principle in the NLP is: "If what you do does not work, try something else ..." Hence the claim to work on one thing for as long as the desired outcome established. NLP is flexible and flexible; it adapts to the individual and is, therefore, surprisingly successful.

NLP is a model

NLP is a model of mental processes. A model is, by definition, not the reality but a simplified representation of reality. A model is right to the extent that it allows predictions of real events. One such example is the atomic model. This model of the atom does not pretend to explain reality altogether one hundred percent but offers a critical approach that allows statements about the behavior of atoms and molecules. It even will enable schoolchildren to make accurate statements about the behavior of particles, although the underlying reality is much more complicated. In this sense, NLP does not explain how the brain works but provides a clear idea of the processes of our psyche. As such, NLP provides a critical approach to seemingly inexplicable processes. NLP's model allows us to make changes in our mental processes, which are reflected in changes in real trade. It makes it possible, for example, to change out-of-the-way behaviors and finally implement what we set out to do.

Is NLP dangerous?

We all agree: a sharp knife in the hands of children can be very dangerous. If you use it for cutting bread, it is a useful everyday item. In a surgeon's side, a scalpel can even be a lifesaver. So it is with the model of NLP. Learn NLP to see who is using it and how to protect yourself from negative influences if necessary.

Ways to control anger using neuro-linguistic programming

The method of controlling the anger that I will tell you this time is highly effective. When you're on fire with an angry fire, people don't have good judgment.

In particular, thinking becomes a source of anger, will the words that were full of endlessly anger continued tour came in from the inside of your head.

In such a case, it is necessary to urgently wake up the fire of anger and instantly awaken a philosophical thought. An image is indispensable for that.

If thoughts dominate you, your head will be contaminated with negative words, and you can see the current situation only from a subjective perspective.

On the other hand, if you use the image, you will be able to view the current situation objectively.

If you can only judge the current situation from your point of view, everything else will be distorted. By making full use of the image, the current situation can be objectively recognized, so it becomes possible to separate emotions and think calmly.

1. Rehearsal with image

It is recommended that you first rehearse with an image to control anger. It is a method called dissociation of a technique called neuro-linguistic programming.

Imagine a movie theatre in your head. Then, imagine how you will deal with anger and your ideals.

For example, consider the case where you feel angry with your boss about your poor treatment. In a movie theatre in the headquarters, a dissociate is to imagine the situation where the boss will improve the treatment by telling the boss about the current situation.

By looking at the image in the movie theatre in your head, you will be able to image your actions objectively. By looking at the image repeatedly, it is possible to act in the actual production with the same emotion as the image.

At the same time, like a movie soundtrack If you hear the voice, "If it is, then it will be more effective."

In this example, "If you can analyze your situation accurately without telling your boss about the situation, you will be able to improve your situation."

In neuro-linguistic programming, we associate the experience of the image world with associates, and the creation of a movie theatre in the image world to see the screenings is separated from associates.

Dissociates have the effect of thinking separately from emotions, so they are often used when it is difficult to remain calm, such as anger.

2. Relax with an image

There is a visualization that uses an image as an anger control method that lets you let go of anger without spending time. Imagine a sight where you can relax and enjoy the sight, and your body and mind will be healed in a short time.

I introduced the method of dissociating neuro-language programming. Disassociate was a way of looking at the cinema screening film in the image. It was a way to separate and think about your anger and the situation by having an objective experience like watching a movie instead of subjective experience in the image.

In contrast, immersion in the world of images is called an associate in terms of neuro-linguistic programming. This method allows you to feel the image world more subjectively by immersing yourself in the image world.

It is not recommended to image big emotions such as anger as an associate because the energy of anger is amplified. Still, it is recommended because you can enter the world of images more if you are in a relaxing sight.

Imagine a place or sight where you can relax the most. Thinking for about 2 minutes will calm your emotions to some extent. The first priority for anger control is to control emotions. For this reason, the relaxation method using images is inseparable as a method of controlling anger.

CHAPTER 4

MENTAL MODELS

What is the mental model?

Mental models are thinking devices through which a human being tries to explain to himself and others how the real world works.

It is a kind of internal symbol of hypothetical external reality representation that plays an important role in cognition — that is, in the way we grasp the world. It is the mental models of each of us that define how we perceive what happens around us, how each event will affect us, how we will think, and how we will act. Each person has their own mental model, which is the result of all their experiences, life history, and situations.

In short: the mental model can be described as a broad view of the world gained through past experiences. They are assumptions, generalizations, or even ingrained images that influence the way we see the world and act.

What are the sources of mental models?

Each one's mental models are created primarily from four main sources: the nervous system, language, culture, and personal history.

Check below how the construction of each of them happens.

Nervous system

Also known as a biological filter, it concerns certain limitations as well as the physiological and cognitive abilities that each human being has.

For example, a colorblind person will not have the same interpretation of painting as one who can recognize all the colors of the landscape.

Similarly, comparing human characteristics with that of some animals would also be uneven for us and offer different experiences on both sides.

While man's ear has a limit of vibrations to be heard per minute, something close to 20,000, dogs can hear much louder sounds than we do.

Human night vision also cannot compare with that of a bat or even a cat. Our visual range is infinitely less than that of an eagle.

This impacts the way these living things act.

A shrill whistle may be hurting your dog's hearing aid while you may be hearing almost nothing.

Personal story

We all have a past and carry information over the years.

This baggage of ours in one way or another interferes with our mental models more or less directly, depending on the case.

Elements such as race, sexual orientation, family history, economic status, educational background, parent-teacher relationship, and other variables affect our decisions.

Some behaviors that you may be perceived as obvious, logical, and natural to others may be viewed as unreasonable and purposeless.

This is because creation and past and assimilated values are different from person to person.

Even at the beginning of our childhood, when we do not even have the critical capacity for reflection, information is incorporated into our way of being.

The examples of this mental model filter are numerous.

Imagine a sporting event that has as commentator a former athlete of the sport and a specialized journalist who studied all the theoretical part of the game.

The opinions will be different, as the former athlete tends to go to the practical side, based on his personal experience, having worked in the role. He will bring cases of the profession, situations experienced by him.

On the other hand, the journalist will weigh in on the technical side and the information he has studied and analyzed as one who critically evaluates the sport.

And this happens not only in the professional field but also in the personal.

How many people do not deprive themselves of certain experiences because they have had a bad history in some specific situation?

The important thing is to understand that this filter is about personal history. That is, the present and the future will be impacted by these experiments of yore.

It's up to everyone to deal with their trauma and memories as best they can so as not to fall into an endless looping loop that keeps them from moving on.

Culture

In a way, it is very similar to the previous source of mental models.

The difference is that this kind of thinking pattern, let's call it that, is influenced by the collective imagination and not by the individual.

That is, your view of the reality around you is impacted by the culture you have been subjected to or submitted to throughout your life.

And don't fall into that mistake of believing that your culture is superior to the other. That does not exist.

Western civilizations have different customs from the eastern people, for example, but that does not mean that one is better than the other.

For example, some Arab Muslim countries argue that a man can marry more than one wife.

Can you disagree with the way other peoples view this marriage issue? Of course, you can.

Your customs and personal experience will make you question these values.

It is wrong to be prejudiced with a tradition that is not yours and which you certainly do not fully understand.

As the only filter of mental models of a collective nature, culture can be viewed in two very different ways.

If, on the one hand, it is positive, as it helps maintain order and structure a way of thinking that extends to large numbers of people, on the other, it tends to be limiting and conservative.

Even so, cultural, mental models are the most difficult to transform and adapt to new realities.

The origin of mental models

As we have seen, our mental models emerge long before we were born.

Culturally speaking, its origin points to hundreds or even thousands of years before us.

But over time, our biological limitations, our personal history, and our appropriation for different types of language guide the way we think and act.

It is from this combination of factors that we assemble and firm our opinions.

More important than knowing the origin of these mental models is trying to take the reins on them.

Not getting carried away by the automatism of preconceived concepts is the main challenge of the routine.

After all, it's not because you've always understood a subject in a certain way that you need to go on like this.

Mental models that block creativity

"I can't do it." "I can't do it." "I won't even try because it won't work."

These are typical phrases that we repeat in difficult situations that require going beyond the ordinary.

But maybe it's time for you to rethink using each one.

The human unconscious sometimes imposes barriers to our actions.

It is the so-called limiting thoughts that make us fear new and different experiences.

It is that thinking that only leads to commonplace and prevents something creative from being externalized.

You know those traditional phrases, cliches like "every politician is a thief" or "blonde is dumb"?

The tip here is to put such expressions aside, and allow yourself to go further, understand the meaning behind each story and not just repeat what most propagate as truth.

Cognitive Psychological Foundations of (Misery) Understanding

What does it take for the subjective feeling to come to understand someone or a situation? What must be the case that something is understood well enough to serve as a basis for decision-making, planning, and solving problems? And what, conversely, is the basis for potential misunderstandings and wrongdoing?

In the following section, two theoretical positions in cognitive psychology are first presented - Understanding Propositions and Understanding about Mental Models -, in which the relevance of mental models for the understanding of linguistic utterances is discussed in more detail.

A special case of mental models that is important for the processes of understanding are metaphors, which, in contrast to other linguistic forms of knowledge representation, are also closely linked to pictorial thinking. Based on investigations in the company environment, it is explained, which functions metaphors for processes of the understanding and misunderstanding in the context of knowledge cooperation and knowledge exchange in enterprises and organizations can have.

The propositional model of (mis) understanding

Cognitive psychology knows different models with which it tries to explain the processes of understanding and misunderstanding. On the one hand, the understanding of texts and statements can be understood as the understanding of individual semantic units. In this so-called propositional representation of knowledge structures, statements based on predicate logic are presented as relations between arguments and objects.

Thus, the sentence The Greeks loved beautiful works of art as a relation with the predicate 'loved', the argument 'Greeks', and the object 'works of art' represent. This proposition represents a unity of meaning and represents the fact that Greeks loved works of art. Conjunctions can also be established between different propositional representations of this kind if different propositions have common arguments or if propositions act as arguments of other propositions. With this suggestive form of presentation, entire texts can be structurally broken down and described as a sequence of partly nested propositions. An elaborate model of propositional text processing was developed by Kintsch and van Dijk (1978), who assume that a text is processed in several cycles due to the limited cognitive processing time. By understanding and processing individual propositions separately, until finally, the understanding of the own propositions leads to an understanding of the entire text.

In the propositional model, understanding is understood as a juxtaposition of semantic entities. Understanding is possible if, as in the case of a puzzle, a given set of particles (semantic units) can be put together in such a way that a complete structure is created. Missing particles must be supplemented by the formation of so-called inferences. This understanding of understanding can be described as additive-elementary.

However, that understanding can not only proceed in this additive way was shown by various experiments. If understanding were to be based exclusively on the original propositional model of Kintsch and van Dijk (1978), who sees text comprehension only as linking propositions, the following two textual examples would have to be drawn from an experiment by Sanford and Garrod (Sanford & Garrod, 1981; Garrod, 1982) can be processed with exactly the same speed, since the propositional structure is the same in both cases:

- Anna was on her way to school. She was worried about the mathematics lesson. She was afraid she would not be able to control the class.

- The teacher was on her way to school. She was worried about the mathematics lesson. She was afraid she would not be able to control the class.

Subjects need significantly more time to read the last sentence in Example 1 than in Example 2. In Example 1, the last sentence presents difficulties because the readers imagine Anna in the role of the student based on the first two statements. However, it does not belong to the role of a student to control a school class. Therefore, the last sentence can not merely be processed unhindered, because, based on the last information, a reinterpretation of what has been read so far must be made. In Example 2, on the other hand, this difficulty is not present since the last statement is congruent with the educated model of the teacher role, and no reinterpretation has to be made. Further research has shown that information that is inconsistent in time, space, and also emotionally inconsistent leads to longer processing times. They thus refuted a purely sequential-proportional model of language understanding.

However, the appropriateness of an exclusively additive model of textual understanding is doubtful for other reasons. Thus, in the propositional model of Kintsch and van Dijk (1978), it is assumed that statements read so far are always mentally present to the same extent.

However, it has been shown (Lesgold, Roth, & Curtis, 1979) that in a thematically continuous presentation, relatively much information from previous sentences remains present, while this mental presence in a change of subject or a change in the context no longer given us. Depending on the content and context of a statement, propositional structures are processed differently and remain present in the working memory for different periods.

Overall, it can, therefore, be said that understanding has to involve more than simply linking propositions. Even though propositional representations have an empirically demonstrable significance for the understanding of linguistic manifestations, understanding goes beyond this:

Humans start from the very first information they receive, ideas about what might be meant; they go far beyond what is explicitly said or written. Implicitly, assumptions about the consistency and congruence of situations and contents are also automatically made, which lead to a delay of mental processing during topic changes, changes of context, and so on, and that not all verbal statements are equally present in working memory, All of these processes hinder a purely additive processing and understanding of individual propositions, as postulated by the additive model.

Because of these problems, various approaches have been developed to understand better and explain these phenomena. Common to these further approaches is that they all assume that the complexity and integrity of mental representations do not add up as in the propositional model, but are there from the beginning. As the preceding examples have shown, people from the very beginning make complex notions of a situation that may already apply to information that has already been obtained, and not put it together afterward.

Understanding about mental models

Sanford and Garrod (1981) talk in this context of so-called 'scenarios', which are activated in the understanding. These are understood to mean holistic representations of complex issues, similar to 'frames' and 'scripts' (Minsky, 1975; Schank & Abelson, 1977).

If a suitable scenario is found for any information, the recipient of the information also tries to draw any further information to this scenario and thereby expand and specify the understanding. By activating such scenarios in the process of understanding, the mental representation of a situation goes beyond what is explicitly stated, as evidenced by numerous experimental findings (Garrod & Sanford, 1983).

Van Dijk and Kintsch (1983) have also extended their earlier propositional model, suggesting that propositional representation is complemented by so-called 'situational models' that represent holistic mental models of the situation. Understanding something similar to Collins et al. (Collins, Brown, & Larkin, 1980) under the term 'internal text model.' They point out that the internal model construction has a momentum of its own: As long as the information processing has not been completed, the internal text model under construction still contains spaces. Because of these gaps in knowledge, a person now has very specific expectations of further information, which is not simply passively awaited, but actively sought.

As understanding increases, more and more precise hypotheses about what is missing and expected to be information are being developed. Understanding is, therefore, not simply a receptive but essentially an act of the process, in which the receiver is just as involved as the sender of the information.

The conceptual differences between the different terms 'scenario', 'situation model,' and 'internal text model' are so small that I will follow SCHNOTZ (1988). And will only use the term 'menta-les model' by Johnson-Laird (1983) and which seems to be most appropriate for the characterization of this type of representation.

The statements made so far have not stated anything about how a linguistic utterance is represented in a mental model (En-gelkamp & Pechmannn, 1993). Johnson-Laird (1983) assumes that a mental model is fundamentally different in structure and function from propositional representation.

A propositional representation consists of discrete units of meaning, the propositions, which in turn are built up of linguistic symbols. The syntax determines how the individual units of meaning are put together, thus describing the intended facts of a verbal utterance. For this reason, the propositional representation has relatively proximity to the linguistic structure of the text defined by it.

A mental model, on the other hand, is an 'inner object' that, utilizing the analogy with the original (a behavioral, functional, or structural analogy), can solve tasks and problems vicariously and mentally in this inner object. The exact structure of the mental model is not important as long as there is an analogy between the model and the original.

The difference between the proposition and the mental model is well illustrated by the well-known analogy of feeling 'anger' or 'anger' with the concept 'heat,' which was underpinned by Kövecses and Lakoff (Lakoff, 1987).

Numerous linguistic expressions in English, as well as in German, indicate that feelings such as anger are cognitively structured as if they were hot liquids or heatable objects that must be handled with appropriate caution.

This shows u.a. on the following expressions: 'boiling with rage', 'heated debates','boil the blood','bursting with rage', etc .. Accordingly, you attack angry people, with glove,' and let them first you 'cool your little one' before continuing to talk. In the propositional model, it is now central, how exactly the linguisticsyntactic structure of the individual utterances looks like and how the linguistic symbols are related to each other.

The mental model, on the other hand, does not care about these structural aspects of representation as such the - in this case, functional - analogy of the original, that is, the emotion 'anger' or 'anger' and the model, that is, the properties of heat Objects, is preserved.

The two forms of representation thus differ, above all, in their quality. Whereas a mental model concretizes and contextualizes a linguistic utterance via the formation of analogy and thus always has certain imaginative content. A propositional representation is rather abstract in comparison, but much more precise in the depiction of the linguistic text structure.

Another important difference is that mental models, in contrast to propositional representations, allow not only the mapping of structures but also of processes. Thanks to the mental re-presentation, a process can be simulated before the 'mental eye.'

At the same time, the simulation of processes and actions can already make learning possible and may already lead to new mental models, a series of experimental investigations have been carried out (Brooks, 1968, Kosslyn, Ball, & Reiser, 1978, Metzler, 1973, Shephard & Cooper, 1982). It could be proved that in mental simulations of movements (for example, the execution of the movements in the high jump), the time required for a shift in mind is actually proportional to the corresponding physical movement.

In other words, mental stimulation, so to speak, takes place in 'real-time', although it 'only' runs off in the mind's eye, and is a testament to the fact that mental models are not only formed and psychologically real, but apparently also have close proximity to the original. From the various findings, it can be concluded that in mental simulation cognitive processes take place that is analogous in terms of requirements and course to actual movements.

Mental models and problem solving

Due to the above, it should not come as a surprise that mental models can also have an effect on problem-solving behaviour and on the regulation of action. This aspect, which is central to the operational environment, is to be further elaborated here. Researches by Gentner and Gentner (1983), which asked test subjects how to explain the operation of a switch to switch an electric lamp on and off, show this connection between mental models and problem-solving.

It has been shown that many people imagine the circuit in the metaphor of the watercourse. In this analogy of circuit and watercourse, the cables are equated with tubes in which the water flows in a certain direction.

An electrical load then corresponds to a type of watermill that is put into operation because the water (the stream) is in motion. In this model, the power voltage corresponds to the water pressure that arises from a (power) source, such as a battery, which itself can be thought of as a kind of water tank.

Finally, in this metaphorical model, the switch is a type of valve that interrupts the flow of water as soon as the valve is closed. It would be conceivable and explainable why a consumer no longer functions when the circuit is interrupted with the switch: the (electric) flow stops and the consumer is no longer powered on.

An alternative to the metaphor of the watercourse model is the idea that electric current consists of a multitude of small 'males' that crowd through corridors (cables). The voltage would correspond here to the pressure to which the mass of males is exposed. Closed or open doors would act as switches, and constrictions in the corridors would function as electrical resistors.

Both analogies - watercourse and masculine imagery - are physically incorrect mappings of an electrical switch. Nevertheless, they are suitable as analogies to solve practical problems. Thus, in the event of lamp failure, despite the new light bulb, the heuristic would be suggested in both cases to check that the switch is closing the circuit. The fact that the physical processes are not correctly accounted for or understood is irrelevant for the elimination of the error and for the ability to act.

With these experiments, the importance of mental models becomes clear for human beings. Gentner (1983) have taken their research a step further. The test subjects should not only state what ideas of electricity they have but should also judge how the current changes concerning a comparison circuit in four different circuits.

The problem here was the differentiation of parallel and serial combinations: While the serial combinations of both mental models can be derived equally well (more batteries lead to more power, more resistors to less amperage), this does not apply to the parallel combinations.

Two parallel batteries produce the same amount of current as one, but two parallel resistors provide a higher current than a resistor. The effect of parallel batteries should, therefore, be easier to derive from the watercourse model, the effect of simple resistances, however, easier from the male model. The results of the experiment actually met the expectations: people with a watercourse model solved the battery tasks better, but persons with a male model solved the resistance tasks.

This experiment shows a central feature of mental models: The mental models not only allow finding suitable heuristics for problem-solving, but they also weight the different aspects of the same subject matter differently depending on the chosen mental model. This directs the user to specific solutions while others are out of focus. Moreover, as the examples above have shown, not every mental model is equally well suited to any problem-solving.

These investigations also shed light on how Misunstand s can be explained on the level of mental models: Different mental models of the same subject inevitably lead to mismatches and are thus a potential source of misunderstandings. Besides, mental models not only produce a different situational view and a different evaluation of the context.

They also lead, as the above examples have shown, to a different orientation of attention. So if there is a misunderstanding between two people due to different mental models, then these people will most likely try with very different strategies to resolve the misunderstanding, as they suspect the problem in different places due to their mental models.

Mental models are thus capable of elucidating those processes of misunderstanding that are not caused by missing information or different terms, but by conceptual failures that lead to false implicit assumptions and inferring inferences.

Metaphors: the linguistic representation of mental models

An important question remains unanswered: the question of how mental models are represented in terms of language and how correspondingly the processes of understanding or misunderstanding on the basis of different mental models can be grasped and analyzed based on linguistic utterances. The following explains why metaphors are suitable for the analysis of mental models. Using so-called knowledge management projects in companies illustrates how an analysis of metaphors can be used to show a different understanding of the same subject and to clarify any misunderstandings associated with it.

As the above examples of mental models of the electric circuit (Gentner & Gentner, 1983) have already made clear, metaphors are quite central linguistic instruments of analogy formation. Metaphors allow us to communicate and reflect on maternal models. They are thus one of the most important linguistic instruments of knowledge representation and central to every form of learning and every process of knowledge exchange.

In cognitive linguistics and cognitive psychology, metaphors are understood as analogies in which a so-called region of origin (for example, the water cycle) is mapped onto a target area (for example, the circuit). In this transfer process, the cognitive typology of the structural film of the region of origin is projected with its 'slots' onto a target area. This process of metaphor formation via analogies can be explained again using the example of the metaphor model 'money is water.' In this metaphor model, 'water' is the area of origin and 'money' the target area.

The three slots of the area of origin are thus transferred to the target area, and the abstract good 'money' is cognitively structured and understood in analogy to the watercourse. As the above example shows, not every slot of the originating area must necessarily be occupied in the target area. So there is no metaphor 'money sea' in

German. Due to the underlying metaphorical model of money = water, the term 'money sea' would nevertheless be understood. Conversely, however, in the metaphorical transmission process in the target area, no new slots can be formed that are not already given by the area of origin, because otherwise the underlying analogy of origin and destination would be omitted. The metaphorical expressions thus formed would be incomprehensible. The metaphorical model 'money is water' has led to the formation of a whole series of metaphorical expressions in German, as the following examples show:

The source of money, the flow of money, the flow of capital, the rain of money, money can bubble, dry up, percolate, flow, be made liquid, someone can be liquid or liquid. With someone is low tide in the cash register, someone can swim in money; money can dry out or frozen, someone can turn the tap on, turn it off, and so on.

As the above examples show, these are the so-called lexicalized metaphors, that is to say, those metaphorical expressions that are fixed turns to the German language and are also learned as such in language acquisition. It does not include the metaphors that have been deliberately formed, as found in literary texts, or as they are often used in advertising and politics.

The understanding of metaphors presented here goes back to the metaphor theory of cognitive linguistics, as it was first formulated by Lakoff and Johnson in their 1980 publication Metaphors we live by. Their theoretical assumptions have led to a new understanding of metaphors and have inspired a wealth of publications and empirical research in cognitive linguistics and cognitive science, especially in Anglo-Saxon countries. The original theses of Lakoff and Johnson have been revised several times by the authors themselves and further specified (see Lakoff 1987, 1993; Johnson 1987, Ortony 1993). The approach of Lakoff and Johnson is based on the following central assumptions:

- In the formation of metaphors, originally sensual experiences (for example, the experience of drinking water in which one can swim) are transferred to abstract content according to the principle of analogy (for example, money, electricity circulation). Through this, the metaphorical transmission conveys a quality of experience as well as a help for cognitive structuring, which makes abstract circumstances tangible and understandable. Metaphors thus enable both complexity reductions and the creation of a meaningful reference to already existing experiences.

- The model concepts underlying the metaphor are not an expression of language but an expression of thought. They, therefore, refer to the cognitive structuring of experience, which in turn, determines action and thinking.

- Metaphorical expressions can not be arbitrarily generated and combined. What is considered to be an understandable metaphor and socially acceptable in a particular linguistic space is determined by cultural and social conventions, which are reflected in the lexicalized metaphor of the language and are themselves subject to historical developments. For example, the development of the car or the computer as everyday utensils new metaphors arose as gas, optimize interfaces in the team, and so on.

Further explanations of the concept of metaphors and the theoretical foundations of metaphors can be found in Moser.

Lexicalized metaphors have several properties that are of interest for the study of understanding and misunderstanding:

- The use of lexicalized metaphors is compulsory in both everyday and specialist jargon. It is difficult to form a whole sentence without lexicalized metaphorical expressions. Thus, access to mental models through a metaphor analysis is possible on the basis of almost any linguistic material, irrespective of whether this is in oral, written, or electronic form.

- Metaphors and their correct use are learned implicitly through imitation in language acquisition and later further differentiated and expanded based on experience, for example, in the context of professional socialization and the acquisition of a specific subject-specific language. In this way, specific cultural and subculture-specific peculiarities emerge in the specific metaphor used of a person, which has emerged from a specific context of experience and action.

- The use of lexicalized metaphors is usually unconscious and automated, as is the application of grammar and syntax rules. The mental models underlying the metaphor and their significance for the understanding of complex and abstract facts usually become conscious only when learning a foreign language or due to special pieces of training (such as the metaphors workshop presented below). Thus, the use of metaphors should hardly or only to a limited extent, be subject to self-presentation strategies. Should, therefore, allow a relatively 'unadulterated' access to the implicit knowledge represented in the mental models.

Despite these important properties of metaphors, and although there are too many theoretical approaches to countless approaches, especially in cognitive psychology, cognitive metaphor theory has so far been perceived only marginally in psychology. Theoretical references are in psychology, as already shown, in particular to the theory of mental models, to work on analog closure and problem-solving and the schema term in cognitive psychology (Anderson, 1996). An overview of psychological work on the meaning and effect of metaphors can be found in Moser (Moser, 2001b).

The function of metaphors for knowledge representation

Under the current buzzword 'knowledge management' projects in many companies and organizations are about making the knowledge of people involved in the work process more visible; thus better sharing knowledge, documenting existing knowledge and generating new knowledge in the work process (Moser, 2002, Moser, Clases, & Wehner, 2000). The knowledge of the employees and especially the implicit knowledge and experience are among the most important resources of a company and are central to long-term success (Moser, 2001a, 2003, in press). Ultimately, knowledge management companies hope for economic gain when, through improved knowledge sharing and better exploration of existing knowledge, knowledge loss can be minimized, and fateful and costly misunderstandings prevented. Since many companies are increasingly working in interdisciplinary teams and the individual team members often have to work in different locations and primarily have to communicate electronically, the communication skills of the individual employees are subject to ever-greater demands. One of the biggest challenges for successful knowledge management is the so-called implicit knowledge of the employees, as reflected in mental models, for example, because this knowledge is difficult to grasp (Moser, in preparation). Experts are characterized by the ability to efficiently and quickly arrive at the right problem solutions based on their mental models, which they have built up over many years of experience.

If this implicit knowledge contained in mental models is to be made explicit, the language is of crucial importance. On the one hand, language is the medium in which different implicit perspectives on the same object and implicit knowledge about this object are depicted. In knowledge management projects, implicit knowledge must, therefore, be captured to a significant extent via an analysis of the respective audio-specific language. Communication and language-analytical procedures are, therefore, central methods in knowledge management. On the other hand, language is also largely the medium of the representation of implicit knowledge as well as the medium of reflection and discussion of the meaning of this implicit knowledge.

It is outlined below how metaphors can be used to analyze mental models and to explain implicit knowledge. The metaphor analysis has an advantage over other language-analytical methods that it can be supplemented and supported very well with pictorial representations. Specific to knowledge representation, there are several other points to mention in connection with metaphors:

- The formation of metaphors is one of the most important cognitive strategies for the representation of complex and abstract issues in both subjects and everyday language. This is especially true for such abstract terms as experience and knowledge, which try to capture knowledge management projects. Precisely because these facts are so abstract, metaphors are a central means of making them tangible, as they reduce their complexity.

- The formation of analogies in general and of metaphors in the specific is central to the acquisition of new knowledge. The analogy allows us to structure and understand the new and the unknown along with the experience of the known. It is, therefore, indispensable to constantly build analogies in order to remain able to act and to decide even in uncertain and new situations. Familiar metaphorical thinking models are applied to new knowledge, and the metaphors generated in this way are used to structure the new knowledge base.

- Each metaphor model highlights certain possibilities and excludes others. So the metaphorical model 'money is water' defines what can be done with money (flowing, freezing and so on), where it comes from (it feeds on sources), and so on. In addition to this representation of declarative as well as process-dural knowledge about money, the metaphor model 'money is water' on a more general level also implies that money and cash flows are as natural as rain and snow and subject to corresponding natural laws. It can be assumed that metaphor models also have an effect on the direction of attention and can, therefore, potentially be effective in guiding the action.

In the context of knowledge management projects and the processes of knowledge exchange and cooperation; It is important that the use of metaphors can significantly increase the vividness of a problem or fact, and thus its communicability and transferability.

Finally, the emotional content of metaphors should not be neglected. As the following examples of metaphor models of knowledge management show, the respective emotional content that is conveyed is very different and has a central motivational as well as demotivation function.

CHAPTER 5
CRITICAL THINKING

What Is Critical Thinking?

We can read that the man arrived at the Moon or that he never succeeded, observe the report of the results of a scientific experiment, or we can watch on television what we believe can be a mass demonstration.

We can believe in it or not do it, taking into account that what comes to us from the media, what we read, what they tell us... all this can be the product of an error or due to biased interests or opinions.

Today we have to be able to doubt everything, reflecting and evaluating what we perceive or what communicates to us. That is why we can ask ourselves about the ability to perform this screening. What is critical thinking and how to develop it?

Critical Thinking: Defining the Concept

Critical thinking is the capacity manifested by the human being to analyze and evaluate the existing information regarding a subject or given, trying to clarify the veracity of said information and reach a justified idea about it, ignoring possible external biases.

We apply critical thinking to try to discern the reality of what they tell us and perceive from the analysis of the reasoning used to explain it. In a manner analogous to what Descartes proposed, it is about doubting the information, dogmas, and absolute axioms that surround us until we ourselves can give them truthfulness or otherwise ignore them. With this, we seek to have a justified idea of reality and not blindly accept what others tell us.

This type of thinking, linked to skepticism, helps the human being to create his own identity, appearing throughout development and being especially visible in adolescence and from it. It is not about bringing the opposite to the world, but about being able to elaborate on our point of view based on the verification and contrast of data. What is intended with critical thinking is to eliminate fallacies and biases that compromise the objectivity of the investigated data?

Critical thinking is closely related to other capabilities such as creativity, logic, or intuition, allowing us to develop new strategies and ways of seeing and perceiving things. Having a good capacity for critical thinking helps us avoid conformism and move forward as human beings, avoiding that there is only one way of seeing the world.

Critical and non-desiderative thinking

Before, we have indicated that critical thinking helps us not to get carried away by the opinions of others and consider this something totally true and correct. However, we must not confuse critical thinking with acting on our impulses.

While being critical of what is taken for granted is a great help to improve ourselves and create new ways of seeing the world, that does not mean that we have to depend on what we create without further ado. This could lead us to think that what we want or think about something is the truth, which in turn can lead us to commit cognitive biases.

For example, a person with major depression may believe that his condition will never change and that everything he tries does not matter. This does not mean that this is the case, finding (either alone or with professional help) in your life positive things that will help you improve your condition.

Critical thinking in itself implies being able to set aside the different fallacies and biases to focus on seeking a truth that is as justified and reasonable as possible, seeking evidence and evidence that what is said or done is true. It is based on the search for objectivity, bypassing the subjective and manipulative elements that other people or even one can introduce in the analysis of information.

What skills does having critical thinking imply?

We have made a description of what is critical thinking. However, it is worth asking what exactly is necessary to have it? Having a critical thought means that the individual who has it has some degree of the following skills or traits.

1. Capacity for reflection

To be able to have a critical mindset, it is necessary to be able to reflect on things in abstract terms. That is, being able to associate the information that comes to us with its meaning at both a superficial and deep level. As well as the implications that such information has with respect to the rest of reality.

2. Flexibility

Critical thinking implies the ability to doubt that what we perceive or believe we perceive is true, accepting the possibility that there are alternatives other than the one or proposals. Thus, some mental flexibility is necessary that allows us to visualize that other perspectives than usual can be objective and produce the desired results.

3. Logic and bias detection

The ability to visualize the logic or lack of it in the things we analyze, as well as the possible failures and biases the affirmations and thoughts may have regarding them, is fundamental in this aspect. If we are not able to detect specific aspects of the argument that do not just correspond to reality or to those that lack explanation, it is not possible to make a founded criticism.

4. Theory of the mind

It is necessary to bear in mind that all the affirmations and opinions are elaborated by human beings, who present their opinions based on what they consider correct. Thus, knowledge may be biased even on purpose, if an objective is sought with its transmission.

5. Ability to doubt things

In order not to accept any explanation, it is necessary to be able to question the truth of it. However, the doubts must be limited to the reasonable. Otherwise, the existing principle could be doubted. And while it would be a critical type of thinking, excessive skepticism would not lead to any resolution.

6. Motivation and curiosity

To doubt something, it is very useful that what we doubt is significant. We can be critical of something that does not matter to us, but the presence of high motivation and curiosity regarding the subject or the arguments given implies that we will try to find a truthful and justifiable solution.

Methods to Enhance Critical Thinking

Critical thinking is a very useful capacity and nowadays very sought after by society, both at work level and in other aspects of life. Therefore it is of great interest to be able to enhance it. For this purpose, we have various activities and habits that can be useful to us.

1. Try to keep an open mind

We all have our opinions about our surroundings. However, to think critically, it is necessary to keep in mind that ours or the explanation that society offers may not be the only one of the most accurate. It is more complicated than it seems, but we must allow in our mind the acceptance of other positions, however different they may be from our own.

2. Try to train empathy

Being able to put oneself in the place of others makes it easy to understand how they have reached the conclusions they have reached. Some activity that can facilitate empathy is the realization of role-playings, theatre, or the expression and communication of emotions and thoughts to others.

3. Actively participate in debates

The best way to increase competition incapacity is to exercise it. Therefore, participation in forums and debates is very useful, when confronted in them the opinions, beliefs and data found by different people.

4. Analyze texts and videos

The analysis of different materials can help improve critical thinking ability. It is especially important to observe the possible objectives or the reasons that a person may have to create such material. You can start with simple material and clearly based on subjective elements, such as opinion columns or advertising elements. Later we can move forward incorporating more technical and apparently objective material.

5. Avoid bandwagon and underdog effects

Many people join an opinion because it is either supported by the majority or ignored by it. It is necessary that our thinking is not influenced by the fact that others pay more or less attention to the fact or information in question.

6. Question stereotypes

Society constantly generates stereotypes regarding a large number of issues. Try to choose one of them and look for information that puts it in question to see how well it serves to explain reality.

7. Search and compare contradictory elements

It is easy to find publications on controversial topics on which there is no clear or certain general opinion. Looking for two conflicting opinions and analyzing each one of them allows us to observe what weaknesses these arguments have, helping to be able to analyze other future information.

8. Research and train

In order to discuss something, it is necessary to know what we are talking about. Being informed about what is happening in the world will allow us to put into perspective the information we receive from abroad, including the medium through which we have been informed.

9. Learn to separate information from what it causes you

Emotions help us give an internal meaning to what happens to us, and we live. However, in many cases, they cause us to behave or think in a certain way solely based on these feelings. This can lead us to consider what something makes us feel like the only truth.

10. Try to listen to your intuition

Despite what has been said in the inner point, sometimes our mind acts in a concrete way that we cannot explain rationally. Intuition is sometimes conceptualized as the result of the unconscious processing of information, that is, as the realization of an internal analysis of information that we have not processed on a conscious level. However, keep in mind that this intuition may also be biased.

Ancient Mental Modes

Making a decision is as much art as science. The goal is not to make the perfect decision, but to learn to make better than average choices. For that, we need either luck or better mental models. And since having more luck is not on the agenda, we'd better look for ways to get better models.

It is better to be about right than completely wrong. (John Maynard Keynes)

The idea, in the words of Charlie Munger (billionaire, Warren Buffet's principal associate, and one of the most important contemporary thinkers), is to construct a canvas of mental models. His system is a sort of decathlon for the mind: not just a few areas introduced in school, but a broad range of fundamental knowledge about the world that will serve us in every aspect of our lives.

Why mental models?

Mental models are a way of analyzing the world. A set of tools to help us think. These models are not there to tell us what to think, but how to think.

All models are fake. Some are useful. **(George Box)**

The idea is to focus on models that can be applied daily rather than endlessly debating their accuracy. As historian Yuval Noah Harari explains, "Scientists usually assume that no theory is 100% correct. Therefore, the truth is a poor test of knowledge. The real test is its usefulness."

Even Einstein's theories were not perfect: general relativity explains how the universe works in most cases but is no longer applicable inside black holes in particular. But it remains incredibly useful, not just to improve our understanding of the world. Our GPS, for example, must take into account the effects of relativity to give us the right direction.

These models must above all be useful to us. Then you have to have several available. The nature of human psychology is such that if you only use one or two models, you will distort the reality so that it conforms to your model. At least that's what you'll think.

If the only tool you have is a hammer, you will tend to see any problem as a nail. **(Abraham Maslow)**

If your model directory is limited, you limit your chances of finding a solution. Paradoxically, the more you are expert in a field, the more this problem will be pronounced. Indeed, the more you master a model, the more likely you will use it to solve the problems you will face. Competent people in a specific area can quickly develop a confirmation bias that will penalize them when making decisions.

You can only choose the best tool if your toolbox is complete. Hence the importance of having several models at your disposal.

How to Choose Mental Models?

Here again, we can draw inspiration from Charlie Munger, who argues that the basis of your intellectual pyramid should be composed of great ideas from major academic disciplines. Roger Kaufman suggests the same thing, namely, to learn the fundamentals of the three oldest and unchanging bodies of knowledge:

1: Inorganic systems (13.5 billion years) We will deduce the mathematical and physical laws that govern the universe.

2: Organic methods (3.5 billion years of biology on Earth).

3: The history of humanity (20-30,000 years if we consider the cognitive revolution).

These are the great basic ideas of each fundamental discipline, things that should have been learned in the first lesson of each subject. These are the general principles that govern the world. The fundamental laws in physics. The most useful mathematical tools. Important concepts in psychology and biology. The basic principles of the economy and markets.

Starting from these ideas, we can begin to build our canvas of mental models. The problem is the lack of good ideas; we all have them. But we tend to love our good ideas too much and use them excessively, which makes them as dangerous as bad ideas. Do not try to screw a screw with a hammer. Your problems will become much easier to solve if you use the right tools.

The famous investor and professor Benjamin Graham explain it this way, "You can have many more problems with a good idea than with a bad one because you forget that the good idea has limits."

The solution to this problem is to increase our repertoire of ideas and models and to put them in competition with each other. When you are in a situation where Model A will tell you one thing, and Model B will tell you another, you will be on the right track.

It is on these basic principles that we must focus your efforts. Behind every new idea presented as the revolution of the moment, there is certainly a more important, more fundamental idea that already exists. The "new idea" is just an application of one of the basic principles, packaged in a new sexier format. And yet we spend most of our time running behind the latest fashion ideas. This is true in all areas, whether in finance, health, or marketing.

It's not about suppressing our intuition or preventing our brain from operating the autopilot (we need it to function properly on a daily basis), but to use these models for important decisions. This approach of mental models puts things in the right order. Learn the basics first, then use this database for everyday decisions.

Here is a list of the most useful mental models.

General concepts (7)

- Inversion
- Second-order effects
- Circle of competence
- Ockham's shaver
- Hanlon shaver
- The map is not the territory
- Mr. Market

Mathematics (8)

- Compounding interests
- Law of Big Numbers (error of the casino player)
- Bayesian Inference
- Back to the average
- Game theory
- Normal distribution
- Thick-tailed distribution (Extremistan)
- Multiplication by 0

Systems (8)

- Scale effect
- Law of diminishing returns
- Pareto Principle
- Feedback loop & homeostasis
- Gresham's Law
- Black Swan & Antifragility
- Via negativa
- Lindy effect

Biology (3)

4. The hypothesis of the Red Queen
5. Number of Dunbar
6. The founder effect

Psychology & Judgment (17)

- The Zeigarnik effect
- Fundamental attribution error
- The do something syndrome or naive interventionism
- Confirmation bias
- Group Thinking
- Endowment effect and loss aversion
- Pavlovian packaging
- The tendency to envy/jealousy
- Halo effect
- Availability heuristic (anchor bias and sunk costs)
- Forgetting the basic frequency
- Social proof (security in number)
- Consistency bias

- Retrospective bias
- Influence of authority
- Survivor bias
- Bias of excessive trust

Microeconomics & Strategy (3)

- Opportunity cost
- Comparative advantage
- The dilemma of the prisoner

Learning From Critical Thinkers

Until recently, I had never stopped to question myself about the difference between critical thinking, critical thinking, and critical judgment. As stupid as it may seem, I have always made the duty to develop the "mind-thought-judgment" critic (s) of my students, and that of my own daughters ... without, however, know the fundamental differences between the three concepts. So I widened the subject, and I share my thoughts around the place of the school, including.

The critical mind that nurtures critical thinking

At first, the critical mind is a general predisposition that the human has to interpret various realities, tangible or not, is a critical way, that is to say in a way to appreciate something based on criteria. Predetermined by the thinker. In this respect, the mind nourishes thought.

Critical thinking: mobilizing reason in a reflective activity

For its part, critical thinking is the capacity to mobilize reason in a reflexive activity. Indeed, in a world in constant turmoil, where we are constantly bombarded with information, it allows us to take the time to analyze objectively (or rather aiming at objectivity) what the universe sends us. It makes it possible to go beyond the simple theoretical and informative activity at the base of our own knowledge, created from that of others and from what emerges from nature, to question it and to draw, in a way, our own conclusions. According to an investigative activity. The goal of this exercise is to take action: "coherent relativism encourages action as much as the reason" (Barrau, 2016: 82).

The activity is rigorous and coherent: "coherent relativism (...) is an additional requirement. It does not deny the importance of the truth or its effectiveness within a system, but it questions, beyond the legitimacy of this system" (Barrau, 2016: 80). This coherence is confirmed by a rigor that makes the critical thinker go further in his intellectual activity: he verifies the sources, compares them with other sources, he identifies the nuances, he identifies the bases of consensus and objectification.

In the process, he becomes aware of his own biases and challenges them openly. He also crosses the opinions of others, especially at a time when so-called "social" traditional media are increasingly pouring into pre-formatted information in the form of editorials.

Critical thinking is, therefore, a complex intellectual activity since it is self-regulating, self-correcting, and resulting from a metacognitive activity. On the one hand, it allows a specific rectification of one's own thought to flesh out the quality of the conceptions of reality that are, in fact, dynamic. We correct our conceptions on a regular basis, and, beyond the awareness of our own cognitive biases, we use the reason to override them in our quest for certain truth, the most objective possible. On the other hand, this high-level thinking requires the ability to think oneself thinking (do you still follow me?) by adopting a critical stance not only about our beliefs but also about our own (meta) cognitive mechanisms. In short, critical thinking is the antidote to "magical" thinking.

Critical judgment, or the search for objectivity

Critical thinking leads to critical judgment, which is essentially a search for objectivity. This research is, in fact, a criterion-referenced evaluative activity:

What will produce a good judgment will be the use of criteria, i.e., points of reference or "reliable reasons," or in other words, the reasons for which the greater acceptance shared by Public opinion comes from a safe, objective and trusted character by subject matter experts. The criteria can be very varied in their forms, be formal or informal, but their primary function is to "provide a basis for comparison." To guarantee the value of judgment, they fulfill three conditions: adequacy to the problem, strength, and reliability.

- Kerhom, 2016

The search for truth is accomplished in the process of objectification in which there is a certain consensus in knowledge and sets various scales distinguishing what is acceptable or plausible in a given community from what is not. The objectivation criteria are therefore shared and recognized within the said community.

If we recap ...

The critical judgment, thus the culmination of the spirit that initiates critical thinking. When the mind triggers the critical thought and that it is translated into a thoughtful, objective, even perfect action

(Aristotle speaks of entelechy), we go from the act which is essentially virtual to the action (what Aristotle calls "power"). The first act is the acquired skill. It's the potential and the ability to act, but without the action. It's the human potential of power. As for him, the second act is the competence in the action, the competence in exercise. It's human in power. The one is accomplished through his thoughtful actions.

From the mind to the thought, to the judgment that determines the action, the critical approach aims to make the human an improved version of itself, which, in a way, reminds me of the concept of the mentality of the growth of Carol Dweck (2006). Stating, essentially, that the human is a lifelong learner and that, thanks to this, combined with a reflexive thought, he is in continuous improvement throughout his life.

"Exercising critical judgment": a key competence of the QEP to ensure the sustainability of democracy.

The critically-minded-judgment-judgment trio pioneered in our school's thanks to the competence of "exercising critical judgment," the third cross-curricular competency resulting from the Québec Education Program (QEP).

If we rely on the ministerial document (2006), the development of critical thinking is essential because it is important "to go beyond stereotypes, prejudices, preconceived ideas and intuitive evidence to avoid that the mere expression of 'opinion is a place of judgment.' Indeed, we cannot say that our students are not critical. Criticism is easy: young and old have all understood this. However, to sit this criticism on an approach that aims towards the goal and from which one tries, by all means, to extract the emotional and the irrational, is another story. Clearly, it is easy to claim to be "critical" or claim to be critical!

High school students are at a time of development where they are particularly keen to assert themselves, to debate their convictions, and to have their legitimacy recognized. They are increasingly able to grasp the complexity of certain issues, to rely on facts, to focus on their own point of view, and to separate the emotional and the rational.

Ministry Of Education, 2006

It would be illusory to claim that one of the aims of the school is to develop critical thinking (as defined above at least), and it is for this reason that the school environment emphasizes the development of judgment. Critical, a manifestation of the early development of such thought. Studies must sharpen critical thinking.

Cross-curricular competencies, at least in Quebec, are the PSEQ's dislikes. However, at the time of the alternative facts and fake news, "exercising critical judgment" emerges as a key competence to ensure the durability of democracy:

"The true critical spirit, the one that helps us to thwart the alienation sometimes represented by the suggestions of our intuition, can only be acquired through persevering exercises. This work, so necessary for the advent of a democracy of knowledge, can only be done by insisting on it throughout the educational period and in all subjects as soon as possible."

BRONNER, 2013, P. 226

The role of teachers

Developing critical thinking in young adolescents, the same ones who learn to challenge the established order is a dangerous adventure! It is difficult to teach young people to develop this spirit when, in many cases, school strategy is based on coercion and dogma. We expect our young people to be docile and to respect the rules of life without complaining. It is also expected that they will assimilate all the content transmitted to them without questioning them. In short, we teach those dogmas, recipes, procedures without their having the right to question them. "Unfortunately, at present, and for ages, education serves a goal of social conformity primarily so that everyone remains in his place.

At the opposite of the spectrum, some, like Albert Jacquard, says bluntly: "the goal of teachers should be to make trouble." We must cultivate the doubt and teach why and how to question things to tend towards mental autonomy properly: "the doubt has heuristic virtues, it is true, but it can also lead, rather than autonomy cognitive nihilism".

Essentially, what is desired is that young people understand three things that are the foundations of critical thinking and epistemological reasoning:

- How do we know what we know?
- How is this knowledge validated?
- What does this knowledge serve?

Yes, "the critical path is narrow," but it is under the benevolent guidance of the teacher that the student will be able to venture there. The narrowness of the path is not necessarily related to the critical aspect of the trip, but rather to the scope of the inherent responsibility. "The aim of the school is, first of all, to promote the emancipation of a subject, a future citizen whose freedom and responsibility go together." In a society where there is much more emphasis on rights and freedom, the responsibility that flows from these same rights and responsibilities is overshadowed. Hence the importance, in my opinion, of developing not only the critical spirit but also the ethical spirit.

We all aspire, in education, for our young people to become responsible citizens, hardworking and productive workers, and open and empathic parents. These aims are noble:

The formation of the person as an independent subject who has developed the basic skills to be autonomous in today's world. And whose critical spirit has been trained by aiming at the acquisition of the basic knowledge to be able to learn all the life and participate in debates on the scientific and socially vibrant issues that cross it.

It has two important environments where this critical spirit can be developed: at home and at school. The school is the middle par excellence to achieve it since it is a social microcosm and an experimental social environment. The pupil has all the necessary supervision to learn and develop all these deeply human skills that are referred to when one approaches the question of soft-skills or savoir-être.

How to develop critical thinking in class?

Critical thinking is a valued skill that does not develop on its own, of course. The teacher is thus invested with an important mission: to evolve the child's natural intellectual puerility:

But they [the students] will only learn to exercise critical judgment to the extent that the teachers themselves will be role models and given multiple opportunities to express their opinions, to discuss them with others, to confront them with different points of view and analyze their merits.

MINISTRY OF EDUCATION, 2006

In class, students are often mobilized to learn how to solve problems. To do this, the teacher teaches them an approach that they reinvest in the learning activities imposed by teachers. These redundant activities, often called "drill" in jargon, are actually recipes that are taught and then applied. But to work on the development of critical thinking, another approach is needed:

It is better, for the formation of their scientific and critical spirit, to seek less often to put students in a situation of problem-solving, but in return to let them, at least sometimes, really carry out an investigation to solve them.

CARIOU, 2004

Our young people, just like us, are exposed to the worst deception. And, of course, they are naive, gullible and vulnerable. They must therefore be immersed in authentic situations in which they can exercise their critical spirit: "To train the scientific and critical spirit of the students is good; to give them the opportunity to exercise it in society is better. One of the aims of any teacher should contribute to the student's mind so that he can naturally decide between dream, fantasy and reality. For example, teachers might ask them to analyze advertisements, infomercials, political speeches, public statements, debates, and so on. They could embody characters in a role play. They could design a marketing campaign for a multinational, or write an almanack or an astrology report. The possibilities are endless!

It is necessary to "teach young people the critical spirit, protect them against the lies of speech and print, create in them a spiritual ground where credulity cannot take root ... and especially the warn against human testimony.

In short, the critical spirit serves the student to know how to protect himself against others, certainly, but also against himself, who might be tempted to miss his own "critical ethics." It reminds me strangely of the test of three Socrate sinks (assuming that it is indeed he who has developed this test!).

In short, what matters to us is to develop the intellectual rigor of our students, but also that they know how to take care of their word. We want to arm them with what is more powerful: a mind that knows how to doubt at the right moment, without sinking into mistrust. It is this same doubt that has managed to resist the worst dictatorships, and that ensure the preservation of democracy in our societies.

Skills for Critical Thinkers

Thinking is something we all do naturally. The differences of our thoughts probably emanate from our prejudices and/or more or less erroneous conceptions.

Our prejudices and distorted visions could result from assumptions we made or from information given to us and taken for truth.

Questioning, questioning our assumptions, and the information we are exposed to will help us develop our ability to think critically.

Critical thinking is a very complex process used to understand better, acquire knowledge, and solve problems.

The process of critical thinking requires maintaining an open mind when collecting and interpreting data.

This process requires that each likely response be carefully evaluated to identify its 'likelihood of accuracy.'

Critical thinking has been defined in many ways. Some think that having a critical mind is a higher-order skill that makes it possible to evaluate the arguments and judgments that may lead to the formation of certain beliefs.

Others believe that critical thinking involves identifying and analyzing arguments using reasoning skills.

Both definitions imply that arguments must be examined to determine whether the information meets universal intellectual norms. These global intellectual norms test the quality of information:

- Clarity of information
- Accuracy of information
- Relevance of information
- Depth of information
- Logic of information
- Importance of information

- Fairness of information

The concept of universal intellectual norms favors critical thinking.

Several other concepts emerged in an attempt to clarify the skills needed for critical thinking.

All involve an interpretation (categorization, clarification of meaning ...), analysis (examination of ideas, identification of arguments ...), evaluation (assessment of claims, evaluation of arguments), inference (questioning of evidence ...), explanation, self-regulation (self-examination, self-correction) and deduction (reasoning by analogy, formulating hypotheses, modeling, forecasting ...).

Although these concepts may explain the skills needed for critical thinking, the process of critical thinking can be more clearly explained.

Critical thinking starts with finding an answer to a question. One of the most important techniques used in critical thinking is to ask questions. While the critical thinker might accept the first answer given, he will challenge all the answers given to him.

Critical thinkers must be able to maintain control of their mental activities, use their critical thinking to make sense of their world by carefully examining their thinking and the thinking of others in order to improve their understanding.

The critical thinker must be able to follow the inconsistencies in his reasoning.

10 characters you are a critical thinker

Critical thinkers are able to analyze problems from a variety of perspectives, resulting in more success in business and life. Discover your ability to think critically today. With these ten signs, you are a critical thinker.

1. You receive your messages from a variety of sources.

Critical thinkers know that partisan politics come into play in every mainstream media outlet, so they try to learn about the world from a variety of sources that offer different journalistic voices. They're looking for places like The Wall Street Journal for a Conservative Perspective, Salon for a Liberal Approach, First Look Media for a more aggressive approach to investigative journalism, and perhaps even follow the political thread on Reddit for a Smorgasbord that offers every conceivable taste.

2. You can have reasonable discussions with people you disagree with.

Critical thinkers are not afraid of a healthy debate. They believe any conceivable opinion should stand up to scrutiny, so they welcome talks with people on the other side of the spectrum. Although unlikely to change their minds because of these discussions, they are grateful for the opportunity to learn more about their fellow human thought processes.

3. You are ready to change your mind if you find you were wrong.

Critical thinkers know that it is impossible to always be right in everything. They are open to the possibility that no, they did not find out everything, and when that happens, they are ready to admit it.

4. They resent people who resort to personal insults of commentary threads.

Critical thinkers are often frustrated by the total lack of rationality that surrounds them on the Internet. While aiming to focus each conversation on the current issue, others inevitably resort to ad hominem attacks and personal attacks, and insulting tactic that makes a critical thinker slam the laptop and leave.

5. You develop as a person every day.

Critical thinkers wake up every day and are thrilled to have another opportunity to hone their thinking skills. They hide the shackles of their egos and wear an outfit of modesty because they know that they still have much to learn.

6. You are fascinated by how things work.

Critical thinkers have an insatiable thirst for knowledge. Her friends might accuse her of being bookworms, news junkies, or academic addicts; But they agree with that because they would not trade their childish curiosity for anything in the world.

7. You have creative, innovative, original ideas.

Critical thinkers would rather innovate than vomit. They value learning from the successes of others, but they make original ideas that are anything but "predictable" or "conventional."

While a critical thinker is typically a plus, there can always be too much good. These last three signs that you are a critical thinker are some common pitfalls to watch out for.

8. Analyze problems that require only a simple solution.

Critical thinkers are sometimes guilty of turning a small problem into a larger one. Your brain works at a high level, looking for complex solutions to the complex problems of life. However, the best solutions are often the simple ones.

9. They expect too much of themselves.

Critical thinkers are typically confident (and rightly), but sometimes they forget they're the same as everyone else (and just in case you were unaware, being human means we're all flawed by nature), We all have those moments when we lose our senses or make a bad decision; Being a critical thinker does not free you from this reality, but it often amplifies the following stress. Critical thinkers should cultivate an attitude of patience and let go of their need for perfection.

10. You do too much thinking and do not do enough.

Critical thinkers would be wise to develop behavioral habits to offset their tendency to rethink. No matter how powerful your brain is, it will not do you any good if you do not actively pursue your ambitions.

How We Influence Our Thoughts

"He who can change his thoughts can change his destiny."

Stephen Crane

Our belief systems are socially constituted, and in this sense, we will be mediated or influenced by the specific historical moment, which we have had to live. What is posed from this perspective is that human beings are rational beings that can adequately process the information "we receive from the outside world," and which we access when we start our mental processes.

According to this, we can understand that our ideas or thoughts will then be nuanced by the information that we are acquiring from our socio-cultural environment, from what we observe or that we can experience through others, throughout our lives.

On some occasions, human beings start-up erroneous and distorted thinking processes, which lead us to invalid knowledge (in the form of dysfunctional negative automatic thoughts).

Automatic thoughts: they are conclusions, judgments, and interpretations that appear automatically when we face different situations. When these automatic thoughts are distorted, we tend to have adverse reactions, as if it were a continuum that generally affects our emotional state and on many occasions, our interaction with others.

According to Aaron Beck, these distortions of thought are described as follows:

Hasty conclusions

To many of us, it has happened to us, that they introduce us to someone and for some reason, we don't like them, at that moment in our mind a message "sure you believe a lot" appears and when we know you more, we realize that we think wrongly.

Precisely this distortion of thought is present when we draw a contrary conclusion about a person or event without sufficient evidence to support it.

Catastrophism

It has happened to you that you are late for work and the transport does not pass, or the traffic is hefty, and you automatically think "I will not be on time, surely my boss will realize, he will scold me, he will threaten to say goodbye and in the first chance it will."

As we can see, this distortion implies considering the worst possible outcome of an event (making a storm in a glass of water).

The mental filter also called selective abstraction

Imagine you turn in a job at school, and the teacher congratulates you but makes some suggestions to improve your work further, at that moment you think "I don't know why I make so many mistakes if I had already made this observation" (omitting the praise entirely).

When we have this distortion, we focus attention only on SOME, mostly negative aspects.

Magic thinking

There are times when you are invited to a party, and you know that someone who does not as you will go, and you think, "I'm going to have a terrible time." At the end of the party, you get bored or angry with yourself, assuming you already knew what would happen, without analyzing that perhaps it was your behavior that did not help you to have a good time.

When you have this distortion, we believe that just thinking something and this will happen. It leads us to predict a negative result and believe that it is true.

Dichotomous Thinking / All or Nothing

Has it ever happened to you that you are preparing the food, and almost at the end, something does not go as expected (you forget some ingredient or something is spilled), and you think "everything goes wrong."

This distortion of thought implies the belief that everything is wrong or nothing is right, considering only one aspect of the whole situation.

Mind reading

Imagine that you are walking down the street, and when you pass a group of people, you stumble, immediately you think, "They must think that I am a fool."

When you have this distortion, we draw an arbitrary conclusion that someone is thinking something negative about us without evidence about it.

Overgeneralization

You have met someone who, having a bad experience in a relationship thinks "all men (or women) are equal" or "I will always be alone."

It is because this distortion leads us to draw conclusions based on little information and apply them to many situations.

Disqualification of the positive

Imagine that you arrive at work and they are waiting for you with a surprise party, at that moment you think "sure they do it by commitment" (completely disqualifying the excellent intention of others).

This distortion leads us to reject or make less positive aspects or attributes.

Magnification or minimization

It has happened to you that you decide to start a new exercise routine, you arrive at the park, and after running a few laps you feel exhausted, and when observing other people with more energy, you think "I can't believe I get tired so fast, I don't serve for this."

This distortion implies the tendency to magnify our defects or minimize our virtues.

Thoughts "Should"

It is widespread to hear that people always demand aspects of the personal lives of others, some people think "maybe they are right, they should already be married" or "they should have a bigger house."

This distortion refers to having internal expectations or demands about the behaviors or abilities of oneself or of others, considered as an unobjectionable code.

Labeling

It happened to you to see someone lose weight and think, "sure you are sick." Or have you met someone who you suggest going to the psychologist and thinks, "of course not, I'm not crazy."

Precisely this distortion implies establishing negative labels for oneself or others, with which we describe their personality or behavior.

Perfectionism

Have you ever met someone looking to get 10 in all their subjects to consider themselves a good student? Or someone who, when making a mistake, thinks "not to be good enough in what he does."

As we can see, this distortion implies setting goals or expectations that are too high on the performance of oneself or others.

Personalization

Many of us have experienced a situation in which we feel guilty or take responsibility for something that does not concern us. For example, when we see that our partner is distant and we think "sure I said something that bothers him" (without considering that his emotional state may depend on something alien to us.

This distortion implies assuming causality in situations or actions of others without supporting evidence.

In the process of cognitive therapy, therapist and patient actively work to find these mistaken representations of reality so that with therapeutic techniques, the patient can improve their thoughts. Make them more valid or functional; in any case, it is sought that these thoughts are more adjusted to reality, improving their mental processes.

This process occurs as follows:

- The therapist and the patient collaborate to identify distorted cognitions, derived from assumptions or maladaptive beliefs.

- These cognitions and beliefs are subject to logical analysis and empirical testing of hypotheses (through experience), which leads individuals to adjust their thinking with reality.

- The goal is to correct the distorted processing of information, as well as the maladaptive beliefs and assumptions that maintain our behaviors and emotions.

CHAPTER 6

EMPATH

Definition of Empathic

Empathic is an adjective that applies to an individual who manifests as the quality of empathy. This quality basically consists in the ability to put yourself in the place of another person, to try to evaluate the actions based on the situation that that particular person has around them. This type of quality is highly valued by the fact of building trust in the person who owns it; in fact, the empathetic individual takes the causes of others as his own. Empathy is also largely related to compassion, with the idea of sharing the passions of others.

Empathy is a characteristic that is usually present in some areas of art manifestly. Indeed, if we refer to the case of fiction, whether written or represented, we can verify that the best exponents in its generation have been characterized by the fact of being extremely empathic. In this way, empathy presupposes an in-depth knowledge of people. This knowledge, that leads us to examine deeply human nature, the fears, and hopes that move men in a recurring way throughout history. With this knowledge, a good storyteller can make your characters credible, act on mobile phones that are credible, and make readers or an audience feel reflected or represented in some way.

In acting, empathy can also be a useful element. Indeed, an empathic actor is one who can understand the emotions that go through people, emotions that must be represented for a certain audience. It is known that one of the main techniques used to develop a credible performance is to try to put yourself in place of the character in question. In this sense, the behavior before a fictitious personality would be the same that should be adopted before a real one; However, this process can only be effective if there is ample empathic capacity concerning people in general.

Beyond these concrete utilities, the truth is that empathy is a basic condition of any morality. Indeed, every position that can serve the common good is based on the fact that the conditions to which all men are subjected are similar in a profound sense, a circumstance that an empathic individual recognizes profoundly.

Application Of Empathy In Different Areas Of Life

In psychotherapy means empathy strategy mood transferring the patient to the doctor. This allows the therapist to experience the emotions and mood of patients and, therefore, to understand they better. It is an active process of empathic understanding. This is necessary because patients deny that stressful emotions usually refuse to fight or avoid. The therapist must, therefore, adopt a correction, accepting, and appreciative attitude so that he can better understand stressful emotions and more effective appropriate therapeutic measures.

In management and in particular, in the direct management of staff who play motivation, involvement, and motivation of employees play a central role. The motives and motives of the employees on which their behavior is based cannot be directly observed; they can be tapped only through empathy considerably. Also, many designs are affected and may vary depending on the situation. In principle, other people can only attract (or prevent demotivation), if it is understood not only rationally, but also Imitation. For these reasons, empathy is an essential part of leadership.

In marketing, especially in personal sales and marketing knowledge and technology-intensive products and services, the employees in question must empathize very well with the thoughts and feelings of the customer and the offer to possibly adjust to the - often unspoken - to adjust to motives and wishes. Empathy is, therefore, an essential condition for the efficient organization of the sales process and particularly important in the development of sales skills.

As an example from psychology, the concept of "or social intelligence", the premise of the research on "Emotional Intelligence" by David Wechsler, argued that an important role, both in this discipline and in management theory, assumes and today the day under the keywords "self-regulation" and "Volition" have changed.

The Importance
Of Empathy And How
To Develop It

Many define themselves as empathic, but few are willing to understand each other in a couple or family quarrel. Some people understand each other only when one has experienced a similar situation. On the other hand, empathy is practiced and developed. It is not necessary to experience a similar situation to understand what the other feels.

Empathy is important for a healthy relationship, lasting friendship, and harmonious working relationships.

Each is forging a reality of its own. Our genes and our environment define us. We are influenced by the environment more than we think. For example, culture, people we meet, marketing, the economic context, our education have an impact on our way of seeing the world. Moreover, many of the prejudices one may have about others are, in fact, a social construct.

Empathy helps to understand the other person and to see through his eyes his perception of the world. According to the Larousse, empathy is: "[the] intuitive faculty to put oneself in the place of others, to perceive what they feel."

Empathy is not to be confused with sympathy. Being nice is feeling what others are experiencing, but you have to understand that when you feel it is with your perceptions. In other words, even if you live the same emotions of the other, you do not try to understand what the other lives in his shoes. We then tend to rationalize what the other lives, whereas to have empathy is often to listen and say, "I do not really know what to say, I'm grateful that you told me this."

Take another example: you make a road trip in the snow, and you do not have a shovel with you. A car slows down, and the driver tells you, "Oh, you're bogged down" and leaves. It is an act of sympathy.

While another car stops and the driver gets out of his car to lend you a shovel. That's empathy.

Empathy is crucial because it helps us understand what others are feeling and respond appropriately to the situation. Here are 12 tips for developing it:

1. Be an Active Listener

Most people speak twice as much as they do not listen. Carried away by their enthusiasm, they leave little room for each other. And when they listen, it's more to answer than to understand.

While passive listening allows people to hear and respond to demand, active listening means that the person listens to each word, imagines the emotions that underlie what is being said, and retransmits regularly what is heard. Active listening encourages us to connect more deeply.

The more you listen actively, the more you will be able to read a person's emotions through words, tone, and expressions.

Becoming an active listener increases levels of empathy, but also helps to create positive feelings in the person who communicates with you.

Six principles of active listening:

- Forget anything that could distract you, devote yourself fully to the conversation.
- Maintain constant eye contact.
- Offer a real space of expression to your interlocutor by giving him the necessary time to express his thought without interrupting it.
- When finished, summarize what you understood and ask if it is correct.
- Ask relevant questions without judging.
- If the person is emotionally fragile, allow them to express and feel their emotions in a safe environment.

2. Express Your Point of View

After listening to the other person, you can express how you feel in the same situation. Imagine what your interlocutor is going through. Put yourself in his place, live the moment as if it happened to you, and let your emotions guide you. Once you feel these emotions, express them. The other person will feel understood and heard, and a true connection will be created (provided it is authentic).

3. Be Vulnerable

As we tend to equate vulnerability with weakness, it is an area in which we rarely engage in the risk of being rejected. Yet, it helps us connect to others. It presents us as human, with flaws, wounds, and fears. This feeling of similarity allows us to identify ourselves.

After listening to someone, think of a similar situation in which you have already been. Remember your feelings at this time and share them. Do not hesitate to share your interior landscape, your emotions, your insecurity, your fears. It is an ideal ground for a relation of quality.

4. Do Not Make Assumptions

To assume is to express preconceived ideas that are not based on any deep understanding. In this way, you take a shortcut to solve a problem without considering a more global vision.

When you make assumptions, you suggest premature answers. Take the time to listen and understand. Give yourself a moment of reflection to avoid getting into hasty and inappropriate explanations.

5. Use Your Imagination

Creating a connection is essential. But you may not be able to identify with a lived experience. In this case, be creative. Imagine this situation and the emotions you might feel. This projection ability is fundamental to developing empathy.

The commitment required by reading works of fiction promotes empathy. When a person gets lost in a story, his attitude and intentions change to reflect that story. The reader has the feeling of entering a new world because of the empathy he feels for the characters. This approach requires creative work. It is therefore about developing your imagination.

6. Spend Time Helping Others

Studies show that volunteering makes you happy. Putting yourself at the service of others increases empathy, and empathy increases self-satisfaction. Creating social connections with those who are not part of our immediate social circle and working to improve the lives of others contributes to our well-being.

7. Practice Benevolent Meditation

We know that meditation is a good instrument for mental health, but meditating specifically on compassion helps us become more empathic people. Benevolent meditation is a form of meditation that asks you to focus your thoughts on the desire for well-being for others. It's also a great tool for managing depression, stress, and anxiety.

8. Cultivate Your Curiosity

Being curious can help you increase your level of empathy. It turns out that empathetic people are also curious about strangers. The more you encourage your own curiosity, the more you broaden your network of knowledge and gain a broader understanding.

Be curious about the people you meet. The more you learn about how others live and think, the more tools you have to exploit empathy.

9. Try Another Person's Life

Experiential empathy is the most difficult - and potentially the most rewarding - of all. It involves changes in your beliefs, priorities, and relationships, and allows you to make new friends while changing your point of view. It means gaining direct experience of another person's life.

Imagine, for example, having someone else's life for a day. Try to consider all aspects of this new life and the possible consequences of your thinking.

10. Forget The Judgments and Criticisms

Declaring that just going forward does not make you an emphatic person. You must feel pain and distress. For this, it is necessary to set aside one's own analysis grid and refrain from judging or criticizing it.

Try to better understand each other's point of view without saying it's good or bad. In this way, you will be able to reach a deeper level of understanding.

11. Offer Your Help

It shows that you see what the other person is going through and want to make their life easier. Providing help is an excellent act of empathy because it shows that you are ready to take the time to devote yourself to another person.

Keep in mind that we tend to want to fix what is broken when the person in need often only needs to be heard and recognized at first. Problem-solving can come later when a trust relationship is established.

You don't want to kill me, the story about empathy

Look me in the eye and tell me if I really should die. What do you feel knowing that you are going to kill me? I know you don't want to do it. Make this a story about empathy. In your hand, is rewriting this ending.

Look me in the eye and tell me if I really should die. You know you don't want to kill me. You could take advantage of your work as an executioner to write a story about the empathy you feel right now. When you read it in a few years, you will be surprised. I imagine you will know what empathy is, yes, surely you know it. Try to put yourself in my place and try to imagine what someone who is about to die can feel.

Come on, dig into yourself, think that I can be your brother, that you could be me. The answer, what justifies my death? You point me with the barrel of a shotgun that isn't even yours. You have been told to kill me and do not hesitate to do so. Or so it seems. But I do know that you doubt. You don't want to kill me; you don't want to end my life.

We may be different, but you know that this is not enough reason to execute me. My body will end up on the ground emanating a trail of blood, and you will go to dinner with your family. You will know that you have killed an innocent man, and you can still eat. But I know that inside, you will be suffering.

In your story about empathy, you can talk about Robert Vischer, do you know who he is? He was a German philosopher of the nineteenth century who first used the concept of empathy. Although the German word he used was translated as 'feeling inside.' Interesting, right?

I have no choice

I have no choice, but you do. You can let me run away, and nobody will know. I will go far with my family, beyond these borders. Tell me, what do you gain with my death? What do you gain by shooting me in the head? Nothing, you win nothing, you might think that you are a good soldier, but who is going to kill me, after all, it's you.

I want to think that if you were ordered to throw yourself into hell, you would not obey the order. Try to imagine that your criteria can direct your actions. That there is a possibility, more or less remote, that you follow that opinion that you have reached for yourself.

Who is your superior? What did he tell you about me? What do you know about my life? I will give you some information about when you write your story about empathy. Do you know that I have a five-year-old daughter and a three-year-old son? They are beautiful. My daughter, Luisa, always climbs into my bed in the morning and wakes me up by grabbing my hair. He tells me that his dad sleeps a lot. My son, Marco, laughs a lot with his sister. And now, you're going to leave them without a father. I will not see them again.

Tell me, please, do you think they deserve this? A father, you don't know; a father who has been told to get out of the way by having his own ideas, his own political ideology. You are mine, maybe not politically, but in this, in the human. I see it in your eyes. You have been told not to speak so as not to make love, but your eyes cannot help communicating: they have not left you completely blind. Your tense face shows that you only obey to survive.

«Little soul of mine, tender and wandering, guest and companion of my body, you will descend to those pale, rigid, and bare places, where you will have to give up the games of yesteryear.»

-Emperor Adriano-

Behind the tree

Why do we hide? Why do you put me behind a tree? Are you ashamed of what you are about to do? Do not hide my death. Do not hide your murder. You have been told to kill me; that is how the country works now. Do it where you can see us, I want you to see how you end my life. Let them see your face when shooting; let me look at them when my heart no longer beats. Do not hide what you will do. No, do not do it. Do not hide orders.

I know you listen to me. Of course, you listen to me. In your future story about empathy, I know you will leave writing that you were listening to us all. It is unavoidable. You become brave before your superiors, but you are scared to death. The only thing that comforts you is that the idea has not come from you.

You think you only obey one order that your responsibility in this action is minimal. I would like you to answer me and tell me if you are so annulled if you really believe that because it is not your idea, your responsibility disappears. If they ordered you to kill your son, would you do it? You would kill him, not those who ordered it.

When you write your story about empathy, make it clear that the one who pulls the trigger is you. And that you might not do it because nobody else will see it — just you and me. You have options. You are part of a system that has made you believe that people like me must die. But you don't believe it, don't you? I know that it is not. Surely you are a good father. Tonight kiss your children when you get home. Do what I cannot do.

Without rancor

The night is about to fall, and you have me leaning against the tree. The sun goes down, looking for the horizon. I could run away, but I know I would end my chances of survival. In the end, we end up accepting our destiny. The question is whether this was really my destiny. How many have you killed before me? Were they all poets?

Do you know? I don't blame you; I don't hold a grudge against you. Maybe in your place, I would do the same, or maybe not. Don't think I'm mad at you. Now I am not furious with anything. I just want peace. My children, my wife, my parents... I hope you are well. I will miss you. At least you could tell them that I remembered them before, say, leaving. I hope that one day you will write your story about empathy in which you can see what you might feel, but that you are not authorized to express.

I think the time has come. You are loading the shotgun, and you are pointing me. You still have time. I'm still alive. You don't want to kill me, you know it. Can you really sleep tonight knowing that you killed an innocent man? Can you look at your children feeling proud of what you have done? You know you don't want to kill me. You could already have done it; however, you haven't ...

"When the pure forms sank under the cri cri of the daisies, I understood that they had killed me."

-Federico García Lorca-

Instrumental empathy:
the basis of psychological manipulation

Instrumental empathy is very present in narcissistic and psychopathic profiles. They are people who intuit our emotional realities but choose to put them in their favor for an end.

Instrumental empathy is that dimension that often characterizes the psychopath or narcissist. Because beyond what we can think, these profiles do identify and read our emotions. Now, once they do, they use that connection to manipulate us, to take us to their land and reach a goal without experiencing any resentment for it.

In social articulation, empathy is in the quadrant of the positive and the desirable. We forget, perhaps, that less shining and complex reverse that presents this dimension. Thus, it is common to tell ourselves that people capable of harming others, whether physically or psychologically, lack that ability to empathize with each other.

However, studies such as the one published in the journal Brain and carried out by doctors Harma Meffert and Valeria Gazzola, show us something that should be taken into account. The mirror system, that is, the ability to tune into the emotions of others thanks to mirror neurons is present even in psychopaths who have come to commit criminal acts.

However, this connection is brief, punctual and aimed at specific purposes. Therefore, they would not lack empathy; on the other hand, if there seems to be a real concern for those who suffer, since they rarely identify with the emotions of others. What they do seem to experience is the clear desire to instrumentalize the other.

"Whoever fights with monsters takes care of becoming a monster."

-F. Nietzsche-

Instrumental empathy: I feel your pain, but I don't care.

Thanks to cognitive neuroscience, we have made many discoveries in the understanding of human behavior. One of them is to realize, for example, that the empathic process takes place in many areas of our brain. Different skills are required to make contact with the realities of others, to know what the other feels, what he may be thinking, and what we would feel instead.

Thus, experts in the field such as Dr. Frans de Waal, a well-known primatologist, points out that sometimes these processes can appear differently in each individual. That is, there are people (primates included) who understand the emotional reality of their peers and are motivated to do something to benefit that peer.

Instead, others identify those emotions and choose to do nothing about it. They don't feel that need, that motivated behavior. There is also a third way. It is that which erects instrumental empathy and defines an individual who, being aware of the emotions of others, uses them for an end. There is an action, and it is none other than manipulating and causing harm without charge of conscience or remorse.

Characteristics of instrumental empathy

People with instrumental empathy are often as charming as Sibylline. They are because we come to think that whoever we have in front truly cares about us. We convince ourselves that the feeling is authentic and that the behaviors they carry out are noble.

However, these behaviors have an end. These types of traits are, as we say, very common in psychopathic personality and even in narcissists. They can also appear in interested and selfish people. Let's see, however, what are its characteristics:

It characterizes cognitive empathy. That is, they have an idea of what the other person feels by looking at their behavior, expression, tone of voice... They understand but do not deepen, they never show an emotional empathy, where they «feel» in their skin what the other experiences.

Christian Keysers, from the University of Groningen, points out that people with a psychopathic profile feel emotions. However, their empathy seems to have a kind of "switch." That is, it is a process that comes and goes. When it appears, it does so briefly and on time, and when it does, it looks for a goal. They take information from us to know vulnerabilities and to be able to use, manipulate us.

That can we do before someone who does not empathize "emotionally" with us?

Instrumental empathy is not comparable to emotional empathy. There is no deep connection, they are not put on our skin, and there is no express desire to promote our well-being. Moreover, what they will generate in the short and long term is damage, a violation. Therefore the question that remains on our horizon is: what to do before those who do not connect emotionally with us?

A study carried out in 2011 and published in the Journal of Personality, and Social Psychology showed that individuals with a narcissistic profile were aware that others did not have a very positive image of them. They knew they generated distrust.

However, this did not worry about them. Even more, it was no reason to promote any change in them.

Therefore, we are facing personality profiles where we not only identify an absence of authentic emotional connection. But also, they do not mind generating damage or worry about the negative attribution we have of their person. They are highly pathological figures where many other psychological disorders are often constellated. Therefore, they will rarely take the step to seek or accept professional help to generate changes.

Randall Salekin of the University of Alabama, an expert in psychopathic personality, is currently carrying out mental "remodeling" programs to work on these aspects. The purpose is very ambitious: to ensure that authentic emotional empathy is activated in this sector of the population.

For our part, if we intuit someone who applies instrumental empathy, the most appropriate thing will always be to establish an adequate distance — a personal security barrier.

Listening without empathy: emotional disconnection

Listening without empathy hurts. However, it is also worrisome that those in front of us understand what we feel at the same time, but nevertheless, do nothing about it.

Listening without empathy is looking without seeing. That is to say yes, with the face while the mind is absent, disconnected, and emotionally removed from the one in front. Few skills are as essential to building strong and meaningful relationships as communication and empathic listening, were to know how to connect with the eyes, feelings, and will.

Only a few months ago, Yale University psychologist Paul Bloom, a specialist in cognitive sciences, went around the world following controversial comments about empathy. According to him, this dimension has a little positive. However, to understand what he meant by these words, it is necessary to deepen his message.

According to Professor Bloom, at times, behind this dimension hides an act of sibyl in falsehood. One can, for example, empathize with what the couple is explaining to him, but give him exactly the same. That is to say, we all, in some way, are able to fit ourselves in other people's shoes, but then act with total indifference.

Therefore, we could conclude with a total success that empathy does not help much if there is no proactive attitude, an authentic sensitization, and an active attitude towards those in front of us. Moreover, as Professor Bloom points out, sometimes there are people who carry out certain behaviors based on empathy, but do not do them to help others, but to feel good about themselves.

All this perhaps encourages us to refine a little more the idea we have of this characteristic. It is not enough just to be there, to feel, and to show that we understand each other's reality. It is necessary to manifest that feeling, that bonding actively.

«The most precious gift we can give to others is our presence. When our mindfulness embraces those we love, they bloom like flowers».

-Thich Nhat Hanh-

Listening without empathy, a sadly common behavior

Listening without empathy is something more common than we might think at first. Moreover, sometimes we tend to ritualize our daily interactions so much that we do not perceive that lack of emotional connection, which, almost without knowing, we are directing to those in front of us.

A very characteristic example is those parents who respond almost automatically to their children when they explain something to them. Are those phrases as manidas as "yes that drawing is very beautiful" or "really? How interesting", while they are picked up from school or while they are busy with other things and the little ones try to explain what they have done during the day.

These dynamics do not mean that we love our children less at all. It means that sometimes we don't have time to be present and we just listen without empathy because life is busy, because our journeys make our minds everywhere (and nowhere at the same time).

Non-empathic responses that hinder the emotional connection.

We have all had that same feeling. That where we are talking to someone who remains absent, who says yes with his head while his thoughts are light kilometers away. However, it is common that there are other types of situations where they give us a kind of answers, comments, or reflections that, far from helping, act as walls. As fences in the emotional connection.

They are the following:

- **Advisory response:** what you should do...
- **Emphatic personal response:** You are an exaggeration, but if that is nothing!
- **Corrective:** What you say is not so.
- **Interrogative:** And now, why do you say/think/do that?
- **Excuse answer:** I know what worries you, but I can't help you right now because…

As we see, with this type of response, we realize that sometimes it is better that they had not told us anything. Thus, another problem is often added to listening without empathy: issuing answers that break empathic understanding.

Cultivate authentic empathy with an active attitude

We can all (and surely will be) empathic people. Moreover, studies such as that carried out by Dr. Anthony David of the Institute of Psychiatry, of DeCrespigny Park, in London, show us that it is already possible to measure empathy and obtain our empathic coefficient.

If we did, we would undoubtedly realize that we all have this dimension, but something we usually fail in is one of its key dimensions: social ability. That is, we are empathic, but we do not use this competition effectively. This sometimes means that we limit ourselves to listening without empathy, that we understand the other, but respond inappropriately or that the other person does not feel that we understand them authentically. Therefore, we need to keep in mind the following keys.

How to use empathy effectively

Empathy requires time and knowing how to be present without haste and excuses.

The empathic attitude is worth first of all the look. We need to look at the other without judging, with closeness and affection.

Second, we must know how to respond. Criticism, judgments, or "I would have done in your place" do not help in these cases.

In turn, empathy needs, above all, to be proactive. Because who does see that he understands but does nothing, cheats, and fails. Because to make us believe that we are valuable, but neglecting ourselves later, leaves a mark and hurts.

To conclude, let's not assume that we are all experts in this area. We always have something to learn, to polish, to improve in everyday practice empathy. Let us, therefore, begin with ourselves to give the best to others and thus take care of our relationships as what they are: authentic treasures.

People lacking empathy, disinterested by others

Some people are a light in our path and others who become darkness that hinders our walk. Similarly, some people would do for us to the unimaginable, and others who would not move a finger for our well-being. The truth is that each of us relates differently to each context. Consequently, some relationships enrich our path and others that not so much; the latter can occur with people lacking empathy.

Have you ever noticed that there are people who do not understand that you make mistakes? Have you been related to people who don't consider your thoughts and feelings? These are people who do not have empathy, people who are not interested in putting themselves in the place of the other.

Empathy is the ability to understand the vision of the reality of the other to perceive and be aware of their feelings. It happens that there are people who do not have this quality, so we will tell you what these people are, what disorders may be associated with them, and how to relate to them.

The less empathetic you are, the fewer friends you will have, putting yourself in the place of another helps you grow as a person as our relationships flourish.

Things that do not do without empathy

People disinterested in others, could not get to have certain attitudes, because they do not have the ability or interest to understand and perceive the feelings of the other. There are cases of selfless people who lack empathy, so here are some of the things they don't do:

- **Worry about you.** They don't pay attention to you, or because they are focused on themselves, or because they don't care what happens to you.

- **Sensitize** Although you tell them what you think and feel, they show no interest in perceiving and understanding what is happening to you.

156

- **Trust.** By not perceiving what we think and feel, those without empathy do not feel safe to expect anything from us.
- **Believe in the feelings of others**. People disinterested in others doubt our emotions. Therefore, they are cold before them.
- **Have compassion** They do not feel an impulse to relieve the pain or suffering of other beings.

If you have these characteristics in mind, it may be easier to see in your environment who are not empathic. Keep in mind that for all types of relationships, there are nuances, there are people who have little capacity for empathy or too much.

Lacking empathy, selfish

People lacking empathy do not put themselves in each other's shoes. Therefore, disregard the feelings and thoughts of others. One of the most outstanding characteristics of the selfless in others is selfishness.

Thus, those without empathy can be very selfish because they think about their own well-being and leave the needs of others aside. Then, take advantage of the situation to benefit. In this way, they take advantage of us.

Also, they take to limit the fact that relationships have to be reciprocal. Then they only give if they receive something in return. Thus, they do not give details selflessly. They relate in a utilitarian way, making manipulation a way of life.

Thus, those without empathy can be cold people, since we experience the unpleasant situations in which we feel little understood because they are looking only at their well-being. These are unfriendly people who do not connect with others.

Disorders associated with those without empathy

We can all be lacking empathy, sometimes. However, some people usually carry this feature by the flag. Some psychological disorders are closely related to the lack of empathy; we talk about them:

- **Narcissistic personality disorder.** People are self-centered, have extreme concern for them. And leave others aside. The lack of empathy in this personality disorder has to do with not seeing beyond themselves.

- **Psychopathy.** It is that people cannot adapt to social norms and find it difficult to connect with others, so it is understood that they lack empathy.

- **Borderline personality disorder.** The person usually has emotional instability, so it is difficult to maintain stable relationships. They have more difficulty understanding and predicting how others feel.

Now, when you make an effort to explain to these people the reason why their reactions hurt you, they usually do not understand it and even make you feel guilty by turning it around, insisting that it is you who has misbehaved. Be careful; the lack of empathy can cause a lot of pain in those who do.

How to face those without empathy?

Some people lacking empathy not only have a hard time understanding us, but they manipulate us to get what they want, we give you some ideas to deal with these people:

- Set limits You decide how far people can get with you, don't let them pass from there.

- Choose your friends well. If you feel that you do not see beyond your needs, do not choose it. It will cause you discomfort.

- Assertiveness applies. Communicate what you want to say in the best way. Thus, it will be clear what you feel. In this way, you will not confuse a person without empathy with the difficulty of properly transmitting what you want to say.

- Stay away if you don't feel an emotional connection. If you do not perceive that a connection of your thoughts and feelings flows with those of the other, stay away, you may face a lack of empathy.

Now the extremes do not lead us anywhere. Sometimes we can be wrong and see only our interests; it does not mean that we are not empathic. The important thing is to know how to choose which people are nearby. And, in whom do we place our trust because we know who we can count on in difficult times.

People lacking empathy are true disinterested by others. So, they are not able to put themselves in our skin to understand what we feel and think. Besides, they do not see beyond their world, so they remain in their comfort zone.

Run away from people who turn your speech around to make you feel guilty. They just try to take you to their land to get what they want. So, they are controlling people, and cold, who neither truly express what they feel, nor will they understand the situation you are going through.

Great Readers Are More Empathetic

Reading and empathy are related. Admit it, if good readers know something well, it is that few things are as intense as those connections we make with the characters in the books, suffering their tragedies, moving us with their achievements and feats. That ability to empathize with these stories is also a way to grow, to evolve in many ways.

Doris Lessing once said that nothing manages to stimulate our spiritual, social, and emotional development so much as fiction books. The brilliant writer and winner of the Nobel Prize for literature could not be more right with her words. In fact, in a study conducted by psychologists David Comer Kidd and Emmanuelle Castaño, of the New School for Social Research in New York, the same intuitive conclusion is reached.

"He who reads a lot and walks a lot sees a lot and knows a lot."

-Miguel de Cervantes-

Fiction books, above all other genres, force us to immerse ourselves in a wealth of exceptional psychological nuances. The plot of the story, the paths of a narrative capable of awakening emotions, fears, doubts and passions favours an endless number of internal processes, introspective dialogues and dynamics that come to show us something that we undoubtedly already intuited: reading and empathy go from hand.

Literary fiction improves our social empathy

Possibly, no one had so much mastery when creating characters like Charles Dickens. In its extensive bibliography, we find the most varied psychological archetypes, the most varied, dark, wonderful, and perfidious personality profiles that we can find in any society. About 989 characters came out of his pen, and all of them served for several generations of readers to learn much more about human character, boosting almost without realizing their social empathy.

This is what the Kidd and Chestnut psychologists have been able to demonstrate. In their article published in the Science magazine, they point out that reading and empathy are intimately related because they help us to reflect on the conventions, stereotypes, and prejudices. To immerse ourselves much more in the intimate micro-universe of each character, understanding, empathizing with him, and sometimes identifying ourselves with their thoughts, opinions, and experiences.

Much of that psychological awareness, acquired in the pages of all those books that we "devour" regularly, we transfer to the real world almost without realizing it. It is a piece of baggage of wisdom acquired in fiction literature that also helps us deal with the complexities of our environment in many different ways.

So, if there is something we all know is that people in real life are not as easy to understand as in books. In our day today, there is no external narrator or an omniscient voice that reveals what is in the depths of that companion we like, that friend who fails us, that tyrant boss who asks us to reach certain objectives, forgetting the conditions in which we work.

However, great readers have special solvency to know what is behind certain behaviors, empathize much more, understand, discriminate, are alert, and are more skilled when it comes to an understanding of the complexity of human psychology than the one who, by example, rarely open a book.

"The less you read, the more damage does what you read."

-Miguel de Unamuno-

Reading and empathy, a precious socializing influence

The professionals who have been dedicated to psychotherapy for several decades explain that people's problems have changed over the past 30 years, as have the clothes we wear or the technology we have. We are increasingly affected by issues of self-esteem and emotional conflicts that arise from an unpredictable, nonlinear, and yet very interconnected world. The feeling of loneliness, fallibility, and uncertainty is robbing us of the internal balance.

One proposal that many psychologists usually make when they work with their patients is that they read. Beyond the therapy to follow, the person is generally recommended to increase their reading hours. The socializing influence of books helps us not only to reflect and understand much more this world, sometimes so challenging. It allows us to be calm, makes better inferences, develops reflection, and empathize with those who surround us and, above all, with our own needs.

Reading and empathy are healing. Reading and empathy are liberating; they invite us to deepen the dilemmas of life, we learn to be more compassionate, to connect much more with people to understand them, to learn from them, and allow us to grow, evolve spiritually as Doris Lessing said at the time.

To conclude, remember the healing power that books can have. Especially fiction books. Bringing them, for example, to the little ones from an early age will provide them with great psychological and emotional tools so that they also have a much more apt, sensitive, and enriching social conscience.

For our part, let's not forget how valuable the great classics can be for us. There are times when we need to reflect again on various questions about humanity, and for that, nothing better than to visit Dostoevsky, Tolstoy, Dickens, Chekhov, Charlotte Bronte, Jane Austen, or Herman Melville.

CHAPTER 7
SELF ESTEEM

Definition of Self- Esteem

Self- esteem is the generally positive assessment of oneself. For psychology, it is the emotional opinion that individuals have of themselves, and that exceeds rationalization and logic in their causes.

In other words, self-esteem is an evaluative feeling of our set of bodily, mental, and spiritual traits that form the personality. This feeling may change over time: after five or six years of age, a child begins to form the concept of how other people see it.

The maintenance of good self-esteem is essential in any psychotherapy, as it usually constitutes a recurring symptom in different behavioral problems. Therefore, some psychologists define self-esteem as the function of the organism that allows self-protection and personal development since weaknesses in self-esteem affect health, social relationships, and productivity.

The concept of self-esteem is very important in the field of psychopedagogy. This discipline considers self-esteem as the cause of constructive attitudes in individuals, and not its consequence. This means that if a student has good self-esteem, then they can achieve good academic results.

Self-esteem is also usually a value analyzed from self-help, with thousands of books that teach how to protect and encourage it. However, there are sectors of psychology that believe that self-help can be detrimental to the individual since it promotes a narcissistic profile that affects social relationships.

What causes low self-esteem?

The thoughts you have about yourself seem absolute realities, but they are not only opinions. They are based on the experiences you have had in life and the messages that these experiences have provided so that you form an image of who you are. If you have had bad experiences, the assessment of yourself is likely to be negative. The crucial experiences that help forge these negative or positive beliefs about ourselves are possible (though not always) to occur at an early age.

What you have seen, felt, and what you have experienced during childhood and adolescence, in your family, school, or the community, in general, have a determining effect when it comes to valuing yourself in the future.

Examples of these experiences are presented below:

- Systematic punishment or abuse.
- Failure to meet parents expectations.
- Not meeting the expectations of the group of friends and colleagues.
- Be the "scapegoat" of other people in times of tension or distress.
- Belong to families or social groups characterized by lack of affection and disinterest.
- Be treated as the black sheep of the family or school.

How to be realistic to improve our self-esteem?

Improving our self-esteem is one of the pillars of many interventions in therapy; one of the elements that are part of the base on which we build the rest of the intervention. This is because good self-esteem strengthens our immune-emotional system and sustains our resilience, arms, and legs with which we swim. Understood its importance, now the question is, how to improve our self-esteem?

Achieving it, as well as facing other psychological challenges, requires that we implement various tools/strategies. This is because the sinking of our self-esteem can have roots in different factors. One of the most important is the system of powers with which we work and the degree of influence we think we have on what happens to us.

"Low self-esteem is like driving through life with the handbrake on."

-Maxwell Maltz-

What is causal attribution, and how can it harm our self-esteem?

Generally, when there is a deficit of self-esteem, we consider that what happens to us is a consequence of our own internal factors and that we cannot change. That is, we attribute to ourselves the cause of that "misfortune." Let's give an example. What will a person with low self-esteem think when suffering a breakup? Most often, in these circumstances, it is that he or she believes that the relationship has ended his fault.

Thus, negative thoughts of the type "I am not good enough for him/her" will appear, "I do not deserve," "I am to blame for this having come to an end." The reality is that when a relationship partner ends, usually divided responsibility. This does not usually fall only on one of its members, although one or both feel it that way.

In this way, when there is a sentimental break, it is normal for "thoughts of self-criticism" to appear. Frequent to this type of thought can appear precisely the self-esteem, that if it is healthy, it will lighten weight and avoid sinking. That is, we will be more realistic with the causal attributions we make in this regard. And the same happens for the rest of our life. People tend to make stable and internal attributions about what happens to them.

But not only that, but they also tend to make external attributions of that good thing that happens to them. That is to say, they believe that when they are promoted at work, for example, it is because their boss is a good person, but not because of their merits at work level. What happens with this? That way, it is impossible for them to feel good about themselves when they are rewarded or reinforced.

"Until you value yourself, you will not value your time. Until you value your time, you won't do anything with it"

-M. Scott Peck-

Learn to modify the causal attribution to improve our self-esteem

Now, what can we do to change our causal attribution and thus improve our self-esteem? Let's start by moving away a bit to take perspective. So we can make a general assessment and adjusted to reality and not only focused on failures or problems. As happens when we compare our life with that of others in social networks, it will be of no use to us that this causal attribution becomes too optimistic because then the clash with reality will be worse.

Therefore, we must question to what extent we influence what happens to us (for better or worse) and what other factors have intervened to give a certain outcome. Thus, we have to learn to attribute the good that happens to us if it is due to something we have done. In this way, we will learn and improve our self-esteem.

In the same way, we have to see if the bad is attributable to causes related to ourselves or not, to stop blaming ourselves for events in which our influence has been minimal or zero. Also, if in the event we do have a good part of the responsibility, it will not help us to punish ourselves after having analyzed the fact and having learned.

This will make it more complicated for us to repeat mistakes in the future and for our self-esteem to be damaged.

«When you recover or discover something that feeds your soul and brings you joy, take care of loving yourself enough and make it a space in your life.»

-Jean Shinoda Bolen-

Following this line, we can continue to evolve and improve. In this sense, being able to analyze ourselves realistically will help us to have a tighter view of our strengths and weaknesses. This will improve our self-esteem and facilitate our empowerment, as we will be able to choose better the objectives in which we invest our resources.

Strategies to increase self-esteem

Self-esteem, and more specifically, its state and its influence, has become a crossroads for many. Some countless books and articles show us as a panacea. If you have it, everything will flow, they announce. If you don't count on her, everything will go wrong. The problem is that self-esteem is built mainly in the first years of life, and it cannot be passed twice. That is why many wonders: is there any way to increase self-esteem when it is not well-grounded?

The answer to that question is yes, of course. When someone has highly favorable conditions, it is easy for their self-love to take root from the first years of life. This will give you particular strength and more chances of finding well-being and happiness. But if this does not happen, it is also possible to repair roots that are not so strong.

Another question appears on the horizon: why increase self-esteem? Although it seems obvious, sometimes it is not so. Lack of self-love is the seed of many inconvenient states, the factor that increases your risk. It also usually results in a constant nonconformity that finds no relief. Make it realistic to set realistic goals and achieve them. In short, it can make life much more complicated. To avoid this, we will present three effective strategies.

"We all know that self-esteem comes from what you think of yourself, not what others think of you."

-Gloria Gaynor-

1. Develop a reminder, a technique to increase your self-esteem

There is a large part of our behavior that we are not aware of, or at least not always aware of. Most of the time, we can't say precisely why we think how we think or feel how we feel. We simply experience it this way and not otherwise, but we ignore why. All that information is in the unconscious, or at least an important part.

The truth is that when there is no self-love, the mind operates in such a way that it overlooks many positive aspects of who we are. That is when a reminder becomes a valuable instrument to increase self-esteem.

It is simply about taking a written inventory of the best of us. What you like about yourself, what you achieved today, the obstacles you have overcome. Specify what your virtues, abilities, and skills are. Write down your good deeds. And, above all, check this list frequently. You will help your mind to function as an ally and not as an enemy.

2. Identify destructive approaches

When self-esteem is injured, we tend to see the world from a very dark perspective. In one way or another, we project our discomfort to our surroundings. In this way, we end up focusing more on the negative than on the positive of reality.

There are also unconstructive habits such as comparing ourselves with others, getting scared when we are about to achieve some important achievement, or being carried away by inertia because we have a hard time believing in our own dreams.

It is worth keeping an attitude of observation in front of ourselves. The goal is to detect all those lines of thought that lead us to feel bad. Most likely, we will see black things not because they are like that, but because we have created the habit of interpreting them that way. By observing and identifying this, little by little, we are freeing ourselves from these destructive customs.

3. The exercise of the five fingers

This is an exercise proposed by the psychologist José Ignacio Fernández. It can be very effective in increasing self-esteem. It includes a series of very simple actions to improve mood when there is decay.

The actions to be carried out are the following:

- Relaxation. The first is to inspire and expire deeply to achieve a state of greater relaxation.

- First mental image. It is advisable first to extend your hands and then join the index finger with the thumb. In that position, remember some moments in life in which we have felt loved or protected. For example, a moment of helplessness where another was interested in taking care of us.

- Second mental image. Now you have to put your thumb together with the middle finger. Then evoke some situations in which we have had success or achievement.

- Third mental image. Join the thumb with the ring finger. Then bring to mind some noble act that we have performed.

- Fourth and last mental image. Finally, the thumb and little finger come together. Then you must remember someone who is truly loved or loved.

This exercise is useful in those moments when there are many reproaches or a lack of confidence in ourselves. It is very effective both to find a balance at the moment and to increase long-term self-esteem. Remember that, regardless of the circumstances, we can always change and learn to be happier.

Self-esteem and depression, how do they relate?

Self-esteem and depression have a significant bond. Thus, and although the origin of depression is clearly multifactorial, clinical studies reveal that low self-esteem maintained over time makes us much more vulnerable to this type of condition. Not accepting ourselves and lacking positive feelings towards one's own, leaving us without psychological resources.

We understand self-esteem as that set of feelings generated by self-concept. In this way, while self-concept encompasses all that set of ideas and beliefs that define the mental image of which we are self-esteem, outlines above all a basic emotional component for human well-being.

Low self-esteem makes us feel bad about ourselves, generates disconnection, dejection, and great vulnerability when developing various psychological disorders.

Knowing this, it cannot surprise us those psychologists and psychiatrists take this psychological dimension into account when it comes to an understanding of depressive spectrum disorders. However, in the Diagnostic and Statistical Manual of Mental Disorders (DSM-V), low self-esteem is not included as such among the criteria that a person must meet to be diagnosed with depression. However, dimensions such as the "feeling of worthlessness" do appear.

Researchers of personality psychology, meanwhile, have always shown great interest in the relationship between self-esteem and depression. For the latter, the question would be the following: is self-esteem a factor capable of promoting depression? Or is it depression itself that ends up undermining one's self-esteem? Let's see it below.

Self-esteem and depression: two models to explain their relationship

Many times we get up, shower, have breakfast, and go outside without knowing that we are naked. It doesn't matter how warm we go or the brand that our jeans or shirts have if every day we face the world with low self-esteem. Because through its thin slits and weak armor, everything comes in, abuse, fear, insecurity, negativism ...

It is clear, however, that depressions have, on average a rather diffuse and multifactorial origin, without forgetting those endogenous factors that we cannot always control. However, no one can ignore that every mind covered by this low self-esteem results in low effectiveness in dealing with and managing the simplest problems. Moreover, the glass of these glasses by which the person with weak self-esteem observes the world is usually, on average, quite dark.

However, the only way to demonstrate that link between self-esteem and depression is through scientific studies, and especially through longitudinal research. Thus, and only as a more recent example, the University of Basel published in this same year a very illustrative work on the subject that can give us some answers. Let's see them.

The vulnerability model

According to the vulnerability model, there are people with a personality profile characterized by habitually low self-esteem. According to this point of view, this psychological pattern will negatively process life events. It will also lack basic skills, such as resilience.

- They are often promoters of reality to defend against, to distrust, and in which to always position themselves as a victim or secondary actor instead of conceiving themselves as protagonists of their own stories. Deserving of opportunities and promoters of positive changes with which to overcome negative events.

- Moreover, the authors of this work could see that in many cases, people with low self-esteem tried not to refute but to verify their negative self-concept by paying greater attention and relevance to the negative comments of the people in their environment.

- Self-esteem and depression are related to the vulnerability model to designate those people without resilience and low emotional solvency.

The scar model

Let us now to the opposite view. According to the study, as mentioned above, something that could also be seen in the longitudinal study is that depression itself is often the one who shapes low self-esteem. All that legion of desperate, negative, and exhausting feelings that orbit the depressive mind are those that directly undermine self-esteem.

What do we stay with? With the vulnerability model or with the scar model that advocates depression as a cause of low self-esteem? The American Psychological Association (APA) is clear: weak self-esteem is another risk factor when developing various psychological disorders, including depression.

Moreover, in one of the publications of this institution, he warned that self-esteem and depression are so strongly correlated in cross-sectional studies, that it is a priority to develop adequate prevention strategies in the adolescent population. The number of diagnoses does not stop increasing in this sector. And what is worse, also the number of suicides.

The vulnerability model is, therefore, what we should all keep in mind. Somehow, it also fits with Beck's cognitive triad model on people at higher risk for depression. Namely, they are profiles with a negative view of the world, people who do not trust the future, and who also perceive themselves as beings worthless.

These kinds of attributions, of such limited and gloomy approaches, do not lead anywhere. And less to the expression of a meaningful, optimal, and hopeful life. Self-esteem and depression, therefore, maintain a bond of union that we cannot neglect. Let us, therefore, invest in that plot of our personal universe. Keep the garden of our self-esteem strong, bright, beautiful in all its aspects and corners.

Improve your self-esteem with mindfulness

Defining self-esteem is not a simple task. We could say that it is the emotional part that derives from our self-concept, that is, the emotions that are born from how we look. These emotions, in turn, would generate thoughts, behaviors, and emotions that would tend to reinforce this self-concept. That is why improving our self-esteem is such an easy and difficult task at the same time.

On the other hand, mindfulness encompasses a set of proposals with a common objective: to recover full consciousness, mindfulness, or attentive and thoughtful presence, which consists of being present in the here and now, being observers of what happens to us without judging. It's about us experimenting, having openness to the experience with the least possible prejudices and filters.

When you are no longer able to change a situation, you have the challenge of changing your attitude towards it.

The ladder of self-esteem

We will attend to self-esteem as a principal element, especially sensitive to five processes. They would be the following:

- Self-knowledge Knowing ourselves, with our defects and our virtues. The positive or negative is part of our way of understanding life, not to be confused with the socially accepted. We can hear what others think, but it is we who finally introduces each element into its drawer, forming our ethics and thus conditioning our self-concept and our self-esteem.

- Self-Acceptance Accept what we cannot change now or that it is better not to change because really trying would have a cost in resources that we cannot assume. In any case, far from the projection of the future, the present offers us the possibility to reconcile with the person we are now.

- Self-assessment It is the ability that people have to value our virtues and abilities, both physically and intellectually. This step is one of the most important: some of us have a hard time separating those skills in which we are good from those in which we are not so much.

- Self-respect Many people think that they do not deserve what they have or can have. Respecting us means giving way to an internal dialogue that does not destroy us, nurturing emotions of negative valence or initiating behaviors that harm us to punish or rebuke us.

- Self-improvement Getting to know each other is the first step to improve ourselves. If we manage to perform the four previous stages, we can enjoy a good self-concept and healthy self-esteem.

Improve self-esteem with mindfulness on how to do it?

Once we know the five factors that influence, and much, in our self-esteem, we will see how we can work them through the meditative practice of mindfulness. It is about working them one by one, based on a plan and following an order.

To improve self-esteem with mindfulness we will perform a series of exercises and guided meditations focused on each of the components of self-esteem that we have been detailing before.

Guided meditations are a good tool to work on improving self-esteem with mindfulness.

· **Self-knowledge**

The practice could be introduced as follows:

- We will adopt a comfortable, calm, and relaxed posture, having our mind in the here and now, moment by moment. We catch air and are observers of our breathing, becoming aware of how air enters our nose and widens our lungs from the abdomen. Finally, we expel the air.

- In the first place, we will try to focus on three defects, and then on three virtues. Once we are aware of our defects and virtues, we will observe them as part of us. Remember that they are necessary and make us unique and special. Thus, we will observe them without judging them, without judging ourselves.

We gently open our eyes and move slowly.

Duration: 10-15 min.

Understanding who you are is much more important than pursuing what you should be. Because if you understand what you are, a process of spontaneous transformation begins, while if you try to become what you should be, there is no change: only the old will remain with a different appearance.

· **Self-acceptance**

The process of self-acceptance is, without a doubt, the most difficult step of personal improvement. Almost all people want to improve something of themselves by not being happy with any content of their being, either concerning their body, their personality, or about their way of acting.

As with self-knowledge, we are going to do a practice related to meditation, but now focusing on self-acceptance. Accepting the qualities we don't like is not easy, but it is necessary to improve our self-esteem.

We proceed again to adopt a comfortable and relaxed posture. We take a breath and focus on our breathing. We leave our external prejudices and assessments behind and limit ourselves to accepting them. We accept who we are with our positive and negative qualities, our strengths and weaknesses, our lights, and our shadows.

We focus our attention on those defects that we have previously identified and observe and accept them as part of us. Let us repeat the following sentence when we observe the defect, "I accept myself completely and deeply" or what is the same, "I love and respect myself completely and deeply."

As for the virtues, we catch air again and focus on one of them; we watch it, watch and let it go. We proceed to wake up from this state of meditative semi-incoscience and slowly open our eyes, move our hands, legs, and other parts of our body. As we see, improving self-esteem with mindfulness is possible from self-acceptance.

Duration: 10-15 min.

Wanting to be another person is wasting the person you are.

· **Self-assessment**

This phase is not a good time to be modest, but quite the opposite. Take a notebook and write down any aspect you are good at and value it as it deserves.

Now do not worry about trying to rank these aspects. Each one of us has different qualities, and we must be proud of them.

No one can make you feel inferior without your consent.

· **Self-respect**

The needs and desires are inherent to the fact of living and are part of any path to happiness. Let's try to respect ourselves, look for our skills, and try to keep a space for positive Valencia emotions in any circumstance.

Let's try not to blame ourselves for mistakes and not to calculate feelings of happiness as opposed to other people. If we believe that we are doing something right, there is nothing wrong with feeling happy about it.

If the grass looks greener on the other side ... Stop looking, stop, and compare, stop complaining, and start watering the grass you are standing on.

· **Self-improvement**

As the last point to improve self-esteem with mindfulness, after having seen the different grades, we reach self-improvement. If the person knows each other, he can always improve himself in his personal life.

It is important, as we have said, to know, accept, value, and respect us. Only in this way, we can overcome and improve our self-esteem, which will help us make appropriate decisions and solve solvency actions or our daily problems.

As we have seen, it is possible to improve self-esteem with mindfulness. To do this, we must know, accept, value, and respect ourselves too, later, overcome. It is important to follow the points just noted. It is impossible to be happy with ourselves and to overcome ourselves personally if we do not, consequently, follow the different steps.

Personal integrity, a pillar of self-esteem

To have proper self-esteem, we should work certain aspects, such as personal integrity.

For Nathaniel Branden, a renowned psychotherapist, a doctorate in psychology and self-esteem specialist, the development and strengthening of this is based on six pillars. The last, but not least, is personal integrity. We will talk about him in this section.

According to this prestigious specialist, to have healthy self-esteem, at good levels that make us feel happy and satisfied with ourselves, it is essential to work the following points, in the same order they appear:

- Live the present consciously.
- Total acceptance of oneself.
- Accept that one is responsible for oneself that is, self-responsibility.
- Pay attention to yourself or what is the same practice self-affirmation.
- Have purposes in life.
- Respect personal integrity.

To improve self-concept, and indirectly self-esteem, it is necessary to be clear about personal integrity. So the first step we are going to take is to define it from a psychological perspective.

What is personal integrity?

If we use the definition provided by Nathaniel Branden, we will say that it is "the integration of our ideals, convictions, norms, beliefs on the one hand and our conduct on the other side. When our behavior is congruent with our values, when our ideals and practice agree, we have integrity."

So, based on it, we will say that personal integrity appears when we act in accordance with our value system. Thus, if we believe that in life, one must act in one way and act oppositely, the dissonance is likely to appear an unpleasant sensation that generates a conflict with self-concept.

Now, if we proceed according to our desires and values, with the principles, convictions, beliefs, ideas that are paramount for us, we will be protected against this disharmony. Our vision of I will be aligned with the elements listed: a union that will transmit peace to us.

Of course, it is for this union to occur; it is important to be clear about your principles, values, convictions, ideas, beliefs. We talk about yours really, not those who have instilled or try to impose. No matter what family, friends, co-workers, etc. tell you. It is an exercise in honesty with oneself, the product of sincere, internal dialogue.

Why is personal integrity a pillar of self-esteem?

"Developing our self-esteem is to expand our ability to be happy."

-Nathaniel Branden-

Self-esteem marks the decisions we make, impacting our health and well-being. It will condition our life on all levels: work, social, playful, etc. Besides, it will spread in all these dimensions through a backbone: the attitude.

Hence, it is essential that we have a healthy level of self-esteem and, for this, in addition to working other personal facets, the work of personal integrity is essential, since, the more our way of living with our values coincides, more health You will enjoy our self-esteem.

As we conduct ourselves according to our convictions, our conscience will feel good. In this mental scenario, it will be easy for our mental state to become infected, and also to recognize ourselves in what we do, reinforcing our self-esteem.

For example, a person places his trust in you, he orders you to do a job, and you do it well, in the time you can, without continually postponing it and charging him a fair price. This, in addition to making you look good with the other person and feeling the satisfaction of a job well done, will make you feel happy with yourself because you have acted according to what you think needs to be done.

This will cause you to feel good, improve your self-esteem. In this way, you will identify doing things this way with that well-being, creating a habit that will make you live with personal integrity. All while your self-esteem grows, since you accept yourself, you value yourself and love yourself. That is why it is very convenient to work personal integrity, taking care of one of the fundamental pillars of self-esteem.

Relationship between low self-esteem and self-sabotage

The relationship between low self-esteem and self-sabotage forms a lethal alliance. To the insecurity are added those obsessive and persistent thoughts that dare to take away values, opportunities, and potential. It is like living under the perpetual domain of fear.

Low self-esteem and self-sabotage constitute a two-headed creature capable of devouring all human potential, all worth, and personal integrity. The lack of self-confidence and insecurity is often accompanied by a voiceover that, with a malevolent tone, tells us, almost every moment, that we are fallible, that we will achieve nothing, that it is useless to have hope and hope.

If we could put a speaker to the thoughts of at least 50% of the people we meet daily, we would discover something revealing and scary at the same time. In their minds, there would be no lack of limiting thoughts, negative self-assessments, and self-criticism. We all, somehow, act as enemies at some time during the day.

Self-sabotage is common, and as such, we can open the door to this uncomfortable tenant at some point in time. Now, the problem occurs when we grant excessive power and give that weak voice a fixed place in our lives. No one deserves an existence where you stand as your worst enemy, and that this is so is basically due to that low self-esteem neglected and long forgotten.

"A person cannot be comfortable without their own approval."

-Mark Twain-

Low self-esteem and self-sabotage, when we have been undervaluing for years

We know that low self-esteem and self-sabotage are related. However, what is the first? Is the low appreciation towards our person, or is it that negative internal dialogue that weakens self-esteem more and more? We cannot separate one thing from the other, because everything is a continuum, everything responds to a mental approach focused on failure, insecurity, and lack of self-confidence.

In this way, some can say with all the good intentions of the world to that friend, to that coworker that of 'you have to love yourself more, you have to take care of your self-esteem.' However, they may not know how to perceive themselves in any other way. That low self-esteem may be present almost from childhood, shaping a type of approach and mental pattern that is very difficult to tear down — there where a negative attribution and self-sabotage is almost chronic.

Thus, in a study conducted by Jennifer Campbell, from the University of Vancouver, Canada, he points out something relevant. Self-esteem clarifies self-concept. Promoting healthy self-esteem will help us build a resilient personality with better resources.

On the contrary, if fears, insecurity, or fear of not being up to the expectations of others weigh too heavily since our early years, it will not be easy to change our approaches from one day to the next. It requires, without a doubt, deeper craftsmanship.

There is a 'Trojan' in your thinking, get rid of it

When low self-esteem and self-sabotage are those eternal constants in our lives, we must become aware of something. There are certain 'Trojan' or viruses in our mental focus. They are specific codes of thought that are installed in our mind with a very clear purpose: to interfere with projects, destroy dreams, become someone we do not like.

Don't blame your education or what other people have told you or made you believe about yourself. Self-esteem is erected by you and only you, depending on how you speak to yourself and how you interpret each experience, each event that surrounds you.

Eliminate those Trojans by sanitizing your internal dialogue. Eliminate the 'I can not,' the 'I am going to go wrong, I am not worth it, they will think of me that, surely I fail.' Don't invalidate yourself as a human being; if you are here, it is for some reason, so clarify your goals, your purposes, your reason for being.

Doing nothing is also self-sabotage, move

When we talk about self-sabotage, we instantly visualize someone thinking about negative things about himself. Now, we must bear in mind that self-sabotage is a prism with many faces. One of them, perhaps one of the most relevant, is procrastination, not reacting to what hurts, worries, or scares me. Leaving projects, leaving something for fear of failing or not daring, etc., all this also ends up undermining our self-esteem.

If we really want a change and also enhance our positive self-perception, let us intelligently dispose of our forces. Being proactive, finishing what we started, acquiring commitments, and finding ways to enjoy trails, generates high satisfaction.

Against low self-esteem and self-sabotage, responsibility

To overcome low self-esteem and self-sabotage, you need large doses of responsibility with oneself. No one else will do it for us. Moreover, in our day to day, things will always happen that will put us to the test, which will require us to know how to react, adapt, and respond. Doing it in the best way is our obligation.

Therefore, to achieve strong self-esteem, it is not enough to love each other very much, a vital history is also necessary for which the edges are integrated - errors, traumas, disappointments, etc. - and assumed the dissonances and contradictions. At the same time, it is a priority as well, that we learn to be compassionate with ourselves to tolerate mistakes but demanding enough to overcome each day.

Self-sabotage is the echo of a voice that does not love us, and as such, we must free ourselves from it as soon as possible. Life is already complicated enough for us to live inside us with someone who likes to invalidate us. Such work requires time and perseverance, a firm commitment to practice daily without rest and without surrender. Let's always keep it in mind.

CHAPTER 8

PSYCHOLOGY 101

Psychology

Psychology or psychology is a social science and academic discipline focused on the analysis and understanding of human behavior and mental processes experienced by individuals and by social groups during specific times and situations.

Psychology has a vast field of study, since it focuses on the human mind and experience, from various perspectives, currents and methodologies. Some of them are closer to the hard sciences and the use of the scientific method, while others do not consider it appropriate for the object of study, and prefer to build their own methods and approaches.

In this sense, this social science is interested in the processes of perception, motivation, attention, intelligence, learning, thinking, personality, love, awareness and unconsciousness, but also interpersonal relationships and by the biochemical functioning of the brain.

The professional practice of psychology, on the other hand, is usually divided between academic research, education, and educational innovation, or clinical exercise, that is, therapeutic work to understand and solve various emotional, psychological, or affective diseases in their patients. The latter is known as psychotherapy.

Psychology should not be confused with psychiatry. The latter is a branch of medicine that studies the biochemical behavior of the brain, without generally dealing with the emotional or experiential content of patients. Nor should it be done with psychoanalysis, which is an interpretive and therapeutic discipline derived from the studies of the human mind of Sigmund Freud.

Origin of psychology

Psychology is a relatively new science, detached from philosophy since the eighteenth century, following the philosophical doctrines of empiricism, which began to understand human behavior as a series of stimuli and responses determined by our biology.

Thus was born psychophysiology, the precursor of the psychological field. With the entry of formal sciences into the panorama of knowledge, the possibility of psychology no longer merely theoretical, but even experimental begins.

The first experimental psychology laboratory was founded at the University of Leipzig, Germany, in 1879. From then on, various branches of theoretical and practical exploration of the human mind would emerge, inaugurating a very vast and diverse area of knowledge as it is today.

Branches of psychology

Psychology has a huge number of branches and divisions, which can be grouped into two sets according to their common characteristics, in this way:

Basic psychology. Located as a field of knowledge between the biological of man and the social or human, it focuses on understanding and gathering information about the basic processes of human thought. It comprises the following sub-branches:

- Cognitive psychology. Study the mental processes that allow the knowledge, that is, experience. The perception, the memory, the language, and thought are their areas of interest.

- Psychology of learning. It is dedicated to the study of the processes of adaptation and more or less permanent change in the individual, that is, how human beings learn.

- Evolutionary Psychology. He studies the different stages of growth and development of the human psyche throughout his life.

- Psychopathology. The study of "abnormalities" or disorders of the psyche, from an eminently descriptive method.

- Psychology of art. Study the phenomena of creativity, creation, and artistic expression from the human mind.

- Personality psychology. Try to build models of understanding the human personality.

Applied Psychology. Also called professional psychology, it is the basic psychological knowledge put at the service of solving specific problems of society. It comprises the following sub-branches:

- Clinical Psychology. It is the one that deals with patients, attending to their mental and emotional sufferings and allowing them to lead a life as functional as possible according to the case.

- Educational psychology. It is focused on the learning and growth of the individual that collaborates with the construction of school habits and environments that are more conducive to form the coming generations.

- Child psychology. Together with the child-youth, they specialize in emotional or mental problems during the early stages of human life.

- Social psychology. It focuses on human groups and human interactions, emphasizing the importance of the environment in the configuration of the psyche.

- Industrial psychology. Similar to the social one, but applied to the diverse work environments and mental situations involved in the work.

- Forensic psychology. Collaborate with justice in the mental understanding of criminals, homicides, and other borderline situations.

- Sports psychology. He applies his knowledge to the athletic and sports field to understand what happens there mentally and emotionally.

Humanistic Psychology, What Does It Consist Of?

Humanistic psychology has as its main characteristic to consider the human being as a whole, knowing that multiple factors intervene in mental health, personal growth, and self-realization. Among them converge and interrelate aspects such as emotions, body, feelings, behavior, thoughts, etc.

We are not mistaken if we say that this approach, this theoretical and practical perspective stands today as one of the most remarkable psychological currents. It is a legacy that is worth knowing, and that can undoubtedly provide us with valuable tools: self-knowledge and self-discovery, skills for change, social relationships, strengthening self-esteem...

"I realize that if I were stable, prudent, and static, I would live in death. Therefore, I accept confusion, uncertainty, fear, and emotional ups and downs because that is the price I am willing to pay for a fluid, perplexed, and exciting life."

-Carl Rogers-

Few approaches to psychology directly focus on the positive features and behaviors of the human being. It is from these dimensions that we must start to promote healing, growth, and change. Within ourselves, there is a highly valuable capacity that can guarantee our well-being and balance.

How does humanist psychology arise?

Kirk J. Schneider psychologist, psychotherapist and one of the most renowned exponents of humanist psychology explain in a study published in the American Psychologist that today this approach, together with that of positive psychology, configure an advance within the field of behavioral sciences and psychotherapy itself.

We are facing an effective current to treat a lot of psychological disorders. It is also useful as a growth tool and to improve family relationships. Thus, and in spite of how consolidated it is possible to say that this current of psychology is relatively young.

Humanistic psychology appears in the mid-twentieth century as an alternative to the two main forces: behaviorism and psychoanalysis. Its purpose was to give a different response, addressing the problems of the human being and offering a perspective from the field of health, rather than disease.

The freedom of the individual and existentialism

This perspective opted for a more holistic vision and less focused on the pathological, on the influences of the past or the environment to enhance the positive side of human nature. Thus, theories such as Abraham Maslow's about needs and motivations established a basis for shaping another kind of philosophy. She was joined by names as relevant as that of Carl Rogers, who emphasized, for example, the freedom of individuals when taking the course of their lives.

In this way, the humanist therapists of this era firmly believed that people are intrinsically motivated to self-realize, to move towards their own goals, and thus achieve the healing, wisdom, or personal summit to which each one aspires.

The person is also considered as an individual being, who needs to be attended in a multidimensional and personalized way. The roots of humanistic psychology are in turn within the philosophical current of European existentialism, an approach led by names as relevant as:

- **Jean-Paul Sartre:** "Man is born free, responsible, and without excuses."

- **Jean Jacques Rousseau:** "Man is good by nature; it is a society that corrupts him."

- **Erich Fromm:** "If I am what I have and what I have I lose, then who am I?"

- **Viktor Frankl**: "Man is self-realized to the same extent that he commits himself to the fulfillment of the meaning of his life."

These authors have a vision of the human condition based on freedom, the meaning of life, emotions, and responsibility. They consider the individual as being responsible for their life and their actions, capable of finding their path to freedom.

Main precursors of humanistic psychology

We talked about them just now: Abraham Maslow and Carl Rogers can be considered as the main precursors of humanistic psychology. Let's get to know more about them.

· **Abraham Maslow**

Most of us know Abraham Maslow for his famous pyramid of human needs. It establishes a hierarchy with different levels of needs and motivations, starting from the most basic (physiological), until reaching the top where the self-realization would be: concept created by Maslow when considering that when the human being has satisfied all his needs It is when he reaches a stage of development of his vital impulse.

"The basic element of the field of knowledge is an intimate and direct experience. (…) There is no substitute for experience. "

- Abraham Maslow -

Maslow's contribution to psychology is immense, especially as regards the field of personal growth. Today, we continue to review and update concepts such as self-realization. And an example of this is the study conducted by Professor Willard Mittelman of the University of Georgia, where he proposes replacing this term with "experiential openness."

· **Carl Rogers**

Carl Rogers opted for a novel vision of doing therapy, that which facilitates a more direct relationship with the "client" (a term coined within psychology because it is considered more appropriate than "patient"). In his book, Client-centered therapy shows how, in his clinical experience, he rejects directive techniques, showing a closer relationship with his clients, thus favoring a more meaningful encounter with themselves.

His contribution to psychology from this perspective is of great value since he considers the individual capable of finding within him all the resources necessary to maintain a balance in his life.

For Rogers, people who go through a moment are because they are "asleep," and they need to wake up through their inner wisdom. The therapist serves as a guide for them to find their answers since they rely on the self-healing ability of each individual.

Characteristics of humanistic psychology

Contemplate a broad and holistic perspective

It is characterized by seeing the person as a whole, globally. Each of the aspects having the same relevance: thoughts, body, emotions, and the spiritual realm. These aspects interrelate and converge with each other. They are the main way for the individual to find himself.

Human existence occurs in an interpersonal context

Therefore, they consider that the relationship with others is very important and necessary, taking into account the context in which it is produced for the individual development of the human being.

The capacity for decision and personal development

People can make their own decisions, to take responsibility for themselves and to undertake development and deployment of their potential.

Also, personal development is promoted and facilitated. The psychologist serves as a tool for the person, so that she, through her abilities, can come to understand and develop.

The value of inner wisdom

People have an innate tendency to self-realization. The human being can rely on the wisdom that starts from within since all healing is found in his answers. For this, it is necessary to understand that it is not necessary to control the environment or control one's emotions until repressed.

To conclude, humanistic psychology focuses on the individual from a global vision, understanding that all aspects that make up the human being are important. He is considered a unique being, responsible for his own experience, capable of becoming aware of his resources to develop, reach self-realization, and discover his potentialities.

What has applied psychology?

Psychology is often conceived as a large tree with infinite branches were to try to understand human behavior. Thus, and among all this set of derivations and sheets, a particularly useful one is distinguished: we speak of applied psychology, one that tries to give concrete solutions to the problems that occur in our daily lives.

It is possible that more than one reader feels somewhat surprised. Isn't that what psychology has always done? Is not this science has focused since its inception in help and support to respond to the needs of common and complex human beings? Well, it should be said that as surprising as we think the answer is no, it was not always the case.

«Intelligence consists not only in knowledge but also in the skill of applying knowledge in practice.»

-Aristotle-

Psychology in its origins was more focused on the collection of information and the compression of psychological processes as elementary as attention, memory, learning, or language... All this exciting, immense, and always constantly expanding area configures what is known as "basic psychology."

For its part, it was not until the late nineteenth and early twentieth centuries when, thanks to the German-American psychologist Hugo Münsterberg, there was a new leap in the history of psychology. This vast science was finally oriented towards the search for practical and real solutions for the human being, using all that knowledge generated by basic psychology to transform our scenarios, to enhance the learning, well-being, and health of people. As we can see, it is almost impossible to conceive both areas separately. Basic psychology and applied psychology are two fundamental branches of the same tree. A spectacular tree that will never stop growing to improve our environments and our quality of life.

Hugo Münsterberg: an objective man who laid the foundations of applied psychology

They tell the biographers of Hugo Münsterberg that he used to read Kant and that although at first, he had a good relationship with William James after he proposed to work in his Harvard University psychology laboratory, things between them did not end too much well. It is said that William James had some interest in investigating the so-called paranormal phenomena, something that the disciple of Wilhelm Wundt could not conceive and accept as being a staunch lover of the objective, and in essence, of the practical.

Münsterberg cataloged everything that escaped the logical and the tangible as the "psychology of abracadabra." Perhaps because of this, and knowing that his main interest was to increase productivity in companies, he always felt a certain tension with those academic colleagues who understood psychology from the laboratory. From the point of view of observation and experimentation in order to publish an article and perhaps collapse some theory preconceived by other colleagues.

If there was a reason why Hugo Münsterberg laid the foundations of applied psychology, it was for a very specific objective: he wanted to improve the skills of workers in that context where industry and Taylorism already demanded new profiles. People fitter and qualified to A more complex work environment.

Thus, and although Münsterberg passed away early with just over 50 years, his contribution to the field of applied psychology was decisive, while immense. He established the origin of industrial psychology, developed multiple tests on professional capacity, and even laid the foundations of legal psychology by creating a scale to assess the reliability of testimonies.

The different aspects of applied psychology

We said at the beginning that much of the tools and knowledge used by applied psychology start directly from basic psychology. Now, it should be said that as always happens when we carry out any practical work, the application and development of work end up generating new knowledge, new data, and concepts. Therefore, it is not difficult to understand that many times applied psychology can gain some independence from that sister branch that is basic psychology, and that tries to give rise to it.

In this way, we also understand that applied psychology can have infinite fields of action, areas that cover many of our most everyday contexts; and where, thanks to its immersion, we can find solutions, enhance skills, improve processes, innovate, etc. Let's see some examples below.

That theory that finds no practical application in life is acrobatics of thought.

-Swami Vivekananda-

- Health Psychology. Although this area has points in common with clinical psychology, it can be said that they are two different disciplines. Health psychology analyzes the relationship between behavior and physical disorders and seeks to prevent and treat different diseases.

- Clinical Psychology. It focuses its field of work on preventing and treating dysfunctional behavior to improve our quality of life and our mental well-being.

- Sports psychology. It seeks to enhance the performance of athletes, reducing, for example, anxiety and improving teamwork of sports teams.

- The psychology of organizations. This is, together with clinical psychology, the two best-known aspects of applied psychology. In this case, what is sought is to improve the work environment, solve problems, train, train, enhance skills, manage the human resources of any organization...

- Educational psychology. We are facing another important area, where applied psychology uses basic to improve teaching, methodologies to understand how students learn and provide them with better resources and mechanisms in their day to day.

- Environmental Psychology. In this case, we have an area as essential as it is interesting to understand how people relate to their environment and how the environment itself can affect our behavior.

- Forensic psychology. In this case, the professional's work is not limited only to the investigation of crimes or any criminal act. The validity of testimonies, custody conflicts, attention to victims, etc. is also analyzed.

- Advertising psychology. Something we all know is that advertising is an integral part of the consumer economy. Understanding what drives the buyer to choose certain products, knowing which unconscious processes regulate their desires and needs, are critical aspects of this exciting area of psychology.

As we see, each field of action gives rise to a differentiated profile in the exercise of the profession. They are aspects of applied psychology that are part of our society where we certainly lack many more fields to be detailed, such as emergency psychology, road safety, aging, etc. They are only small examples that give us to understand the multiple scenarios where psychology can be valuable, where good professionals will always try to respond to any need, to any problem.

Wisdom from psychology

Wisdom, which is usually understood as an exclusive product of experience, goes further. Thus, this section presents definitions given by different authors, such as Sternberg, while certain ideas are demystified, and the problem of their measurement develops.

Wisdom, beyond popular conception, has been studied by intelligence experts and psychologists. Wisdom can be defined in scientific terms, beyond the attribution of knowledge that we usually give to our elders.

In this section, we are going to talk about what the science of psychology understands by wisdom. It is a difficult concept to study because of the diffusion of its limits and how complicated it is to use scientific methodology with internal elements.

What is wisdom, according to psychology?

Wisdom can be defined as a set of knowledge that is possessed in the pragmatics of life at expert levels. Many have been the authors who have tried to identify the components associated with wisdom.

The components that are usually grouped around wisdom are:

- Interpersonal skills: Level of knowledge, sensitivity, and sociability when interacting with other people. Interpersonal skills lead one to adapt to the needs of the interlocutor and squeeze the interaction with the other in the most effective way.

- Judgment and communication skills: Wisdom, which is usually related to experience, implies knowledge and advice. Therefore, wise people are individuals capable of advising on problems and giving pragmatic solutions that others would not reach.

- Understanding: Wise people, having been able to cultivate emotion and along with their vital experiences, are individuals who understand and can empathize.

- General competence: This would be the most known or attributed to the wisdom component. Wise people are intelligent, educated, have high knowledge in different fields, and know how to communicate it.

Does wisdom necessarily imply knowledge?

Experts allude that the two most relevant factors of wisdom are exceptional understanding and the skills of judgment and communication. Therefore, there may be wise people but, because of vital vicissitudes, do not possess great knowledge about the world.

All the aforementioned components, therefore, appeal to a construct of wisdom that alludes to affective and interpersonal aspects. In other words, a definition that goes beyond the cognitive.

· **Wisdom according to Holliday and Chandler (1986)**

For these two authors, wisdom implies sagacity, involvement with others, consideration, insight, intuition, knowing one's limitations, reason and logic, experience, logical mind, good problem solving and error learning. The wise person is an information seeker who uses the data he has well.

The definition of Holliday and Chandler tends more to relate wisdom to cognitive factors and aptitudes that allow a person the proper and brilliant problem-solving.

· **Wisdom according to Sternberg (1985)**

Sternberg, on the other hand, defines the wise as someone sensitive, sociable, with good judgment and communication skills, who understands life, who has learned from experience and is able to combine different points of view.

In addition to all these interpersonal and emotional faculties, it also defines the wise person as someone intelligent, cultivated, and with great general skills.

How do you analyze wisdom from science?

In some way, we can assess the level of a person in the dimension through standardized tests and qualitative procedures. There would be two large groups:

7. **Planning tasks:** Subjects are presented with a test in which a person has to make a decision. This decision is about life in certain circumstances. It can be a younger person, with aspects to take into account in the decision making... In this test, the person responds aloud with a plan that covers what he could do, what would be the impact of said decision in the coming years, and what other information you need to make the decision that may not be found in the presentation of the task.

8. **Review tasks:** Situations arise in which different people - who adopted different paths at a crossroads - have to review the decisions made. The subjects evaluated reexamine those decisions, responding aloud. They reconstruct and evaluate what the protagonists of the story would say as they grew older.

9. **Task example:** Tadeo wants to get married.

An example of a task to evaluate wisdom could be the following:

"Tadeo is an 18-year-old boy who decides to marry her boyfriend, whom she has known for nine months."

Based on this statement, the person has to think out loud what Tadeo should consider making this decision. Reconstructs, from Tadeo, the history, the moments of it, possible explanations that have led him to make that decision and evaluations about it.

Can you train wisdom?

Many are the authors who have spoken of the components of wisdom, although there are fewer who agree. However, this does not take away so that it is being analyzed how a person can improve in those components on which there is a greater consensus.

For example, what it is about promoting in decision making is contextualism, relativism, and uncertainty. The only decision-making factor that has been trained is relativism, and the calm or restraint it offers. However, the goal of "training" wisdom still seems too risky.

What does science forget?

One part that does not usually measure standardized tests is emotional and affective factors. You are better suited to evaluate different dimensions of intelligence, such as logical-mathematical intelligence or spatial intelligence.

On the other hand, to date, several definitions of wisdom survive without there being a very broad consensus around one of them. It is an open field, and therefore, it is a complicated task to measure it. This disparity in assessing wisdom can mean that we currently have very biased results referring to the different groups that have been studied.

Can knowledge be inherited?

An extraordinary study conducted at the University of Tel Aviv on the heritability of knowledge has just been published. The results of the investigation call into question the famous Weismann barrier, one of the basic principles of biology...

A recent investigation carried out at the University of Tel Aviv has just put in check one of the basic principles of biology: the Weismann barrier. This study is the first step to future research on the heritability of knowledge; that is, the study opens the door to the possibility of inheriting the knowledge of past generations.

The team of Professor Oded Rechavi, from the Department of Neurobiology of the Faculty of Life Sciences Wise, together with the Sagol School of Neuroscience, has discovered an RNA-based mechanism that encourages the response of neurons to the environment to be inheritable. An acquired information that would affect the behavior of the progeny.

The experiment, which was presented on June 6, 2019, was carried out on a species of worms, the nematodes (Caenorhabditis elegans). The team showed how nervous system cells could transmit information to subsequent generations of worms.

The germline and the controversy of inheriting the knowledge

It seems that the mechanism of RNA regulation would allow the nervous system of living beings to communicate with the germline. This line would affect the behavior of the following generations. This is the great novelty that this study brings.

So, if this research is right, it would mean that the nervous system can control the progeny. The discovery collides head-on with Weismann's barrier, one of the most accepted principles of biology, although very controversial and widely discussed in recent decades.

The Weismann Barrier

Weismann's barrier is the theory that ensures that the acquired characteristics are features of soma cells and that in no case are they transmitted to future generations. This barrier is what differentiates, according to Weismann, the body's soma cells and germ cells (ovules and sperm cells).

Freiburg A. Weismann, was a German biologist and geneticist, who presented his conclusions on hereditary information, the inheritance germplasm, in the book published in 1892.

According to their theories, they affirm that the changes in the germinal plasma produced by environmental influences would only affect the inheritance if they occur in the germinal plasma. Still, they would not do so if they occur in the soma (body) of the cell.

Many have since been the voices in the academic world that have argued that the somato-germinal barrier does not work that way. However, this theory has been taken for years as the basis for rejecting the inheritance of acquired characters.

The investigation

The recently presented study has turned the Weismann barrier. The most advanced systems have been used for this study. The latest CRISPR-Cas9 gene-editing tool was used to create a variant form of a mutant gene or allele. A genetically encoded calcium indicator (GECI) and calcium image analysis, GCaMp2, have also been used.

For this purpose, worms were designed to produce RDE-4-dependent endo-siRNA only in neurons. The purpose was to understand the inheritable effects of neuronal RNApn (small nuclear RNA). Genetically encoded calcium analyzes allowed the observation of neuronal activity through optogenetic systems.

Inherit knowledge: how it works

The research concluded that the RNA of the neurons regulates the germline genes and controls the behavior of future generations. This mechanism would control the expression of the germline gene for several generations.

More specifically, it is the neuronal RDE-4 that controls chemotaxis for at least three generations. It would do so through the

ArgonauteHRDE-1 that is restricted to the germline.

An open the door to research

This discovery about the mechanism of RNA that makes communication between the cells of the nervous system and germ cells possible to allow the heritability of the information acquired in the following generations can change the way we understand the process.

New research in the future could confirm the functioning of this mechanism in the rest of the animals and in the human being. Undoubtedly, the implications of this study on the knowledge we have about genetics, evolution, epigenetics, and the heritability of intelligence are enormous.

Similarities And Differences Between Psychology And Sociology

Social psychology and sociology, could you say what differentiates them? Although they may seem the same, they are different. On the other hand, it is no less true that they share some elements in their definition and that the birth of one depended, in part, on the other. At first, there were only sociology and psychology. A part of psychology was interested in social and group processes, thus emerging social psychology. Therefore, the names are related. Social psychology comes from the integration of psychology and sociology.

Sociology, on the other hand, was also interested in the individual processes that psychology studied. The interaction between subjects and their environment became the object of reflection by sociologists, thus moving away from other macro-sociological approaches. Therefore, we can find that there has been a great influence of one over the other - and vice versa - in the evolution of both so that its evolution is largely common.

At present, both fields of knowledge in their evolution have tended towards specialization. Each has invested its efforts in increasingly specific and particular aspects. The result has been that both have ended up isolating themselves. Thus, sociologists have focused on macro variables, such as social structure (Bourdieu, 1998) or migrations (Castles, 2003), while social psychology has focused on micro variables such as group identity (Tajfel and Turner, 2005) or influence (Cialdini, 2001).

A love-hate relationship

It is noteworthy that both sciences share a common object of study, human behavior. However, social psychology would become a branch of psychology that studies how the environment directly or indirectly influences the behavior and behavior of the human being (Allport, 1985). For its part, sociology is a social science that is dedicated to the systematic study of society, social action, and the

207

groups that comprise it (Furfey, 1953). You could say that both study relationships between people, but from different perspectives.

The fact that each one has its watchtower in different places means that one can get rich from the other, while the differences between the two are accentuated. One of the main differences between the two is that psychology studies the effect of the social on the individual, while sociology focuses on the collective phenomena themselves. In other words, social psychology studies human behavior at the level of the individual and sociology at the group level.

· **Social psychology**

Social psychology has as its ultimate goal the analysis of the interaction between the individual and society (Moskovici and Markova, 2006). These interaction processes take place at different levels, which are usually divided into intrapersonal, interpersonal, intragroup, and intergroup processes.

In short, processes between people and between groups. In the field of interpersonal processes, the differences between people, information processing. How this information is used within the groups is studied. As for intergroup processes, between groups, the emphasis is placed on the study of the role of groups in the construction of people's identity.

Social psychology takes social phenomena into account but does not focus their study on them. Instead, analyze how these social phenomena have an effect on the individual. Social psychology tries to understand how most individuals are affected by social factors, regardless of their individual personality differences.

· **The sociology**

Sociology, in its research, studies how organizations and institutions that make up the social structure are created, maintained, or changed (Tezanos, 2006). In turn, it also studies the effect that different social structures have on the behavior of groups and individuals; and the changes that occur in these structures as a cause of social interactions (Lucas Marín, 2006).

In other words of Richard Osborne (2005), "sociology is to explain something that seems obvious (how our society works) to people who believe it is simple and who do not understand how complicated it really is." The acts we perform on a day-to-day basis sometimes have explanations that we would never think about.

Great representatives of both fields

Although, both in social psychology and in sociology, the representatives of these fields are counted by millions, some have excelled. Unable to honor all the great researchers who have left their mark, here are some of the theories and methods left by two of the best-known representatives of both fields and that will help to understand the differences between the two sciences:

- Pierre Bourdieu (1998) is known, among other things, for introducing the concept of habitus. He will tell us that the habitus is a set of schemes through which we perceive the world and act in it. The habitus has a great influence on our thoughts, perceptions, and actions. The habitus becomes the fundamental dimension that explains the social class. The social class is integrated from the characteristic habits of it. The performance of actions is what places us in a certain social class.

- Henri Tajfel, together with John Turner (2005), developed the theory of social identity. According to this theory, through categorization processes, we end up identifying with groups whose norms are going to modulate our behaviors. The greater the identification with a group, the more willing we will be to follow the rules of that group and even make sacrifices so that they continue to be maintained.

While Bourdieu proposes that the schemes from which we perceive the world are going to determine our behaviors, Tajfel interprets that group membership is going to be what determines their behavior according to the group's norms. As mentioned, they study the same thing but from different perspectives.

Why is psychology important?

Due to the breadth of the field of psychology, its importance depends largely on the specific application to which we refer. However, in this section, we will reflect on the relevance of psychology at a general level, emphasizing some of its key contributions.

1. To understand living beings

Psychological theories are fundamental to explain the behavior of animals, especially people: any activity produced in human society is likely to be analyzed from psychology since it will always involve the participation of basic mental processes. Concerning the study of human groups, social psychology is particularly important.

Behavior analysis is not only interesting in itself for a large number of people, but also allows the knowledge acquired to be applied to many different fields. Especially within the social and natural sciences such as medicine, sociology, economics, history, political science, demography, linguistics, veterinary medicine, or zoology.

2. To increase the quality of life

Many people believe that the ultimate goal of psychology is to increase the well-being and quality of life of others. Although other professionals have different conceptions, the truth is that service to other people has been a central aspect of the development of psychology and continues to be so today.

Psychology is useful for enhancing mental health and personal growth, but the benefits of this science are not limited to the psyche. Health psychology, for example, seeks physical well-being and disease prevention through the acquisition of healthy behavioral habits, a key aspect that medicine tends to set aside.

3. To improve relationships

The knowledge derived from psychological science is very important for the improvement of human relationships. Thus, it is the psychologists who are most qualified to improve the social skills of shy people, to mediate in cases of divorce, or to intervene in mobbing and bullying, among other functions.

4. To enhance professional performance

In today's societies, performance and productivity are extremely valuable on a professional level, and more and more people realize that having psychologists in their work team clearly enhances the results. Human resources, organizational psychology, and sports psychology are good examples of this role.

COGNITIVE BEHAVIORAL THERAPY MADE SIMPLE

By

Gary Scott

INTRODUCTION

In the way we live and think, everything is dedicated to material pleasure. We consider objects to be of utmost importance and materialistically devote ourselves to whatever makes us happy, famous and popular. Even though all this comes from our mind, we are so totally preoccupied with the external objects themselves that we never look within, we never question what makes them so appealing.

However, this mind is an integral part of us; as long as we exist, our mind is there within us. Thus we are always up and down; it is not our body that goes up and down; it is our mind, whose way of functioning we do not understand. Therefore, sometimes you have to examine yourself; not just your body but your mind, which is the thing that is telling you what to do. You have to know your psychology, or, in religious terminology, perhaps, your inner nature. But no matter what you call it, you have to know it.

Don't think that examining and knowing the nature of your mind is only an Eastern trip. That's a wrong conception; it's not an Eastern trip, it's your trip. How can you separate your body or the picture you have of yourself, from your mind? You can't say, "I have the power to separate my body from my mind." That's impossible. You think you are a free person in the world, enjoying everything. That's what you think, but you are not free. I'm not saying that you are under the control of someone else; it's your attachment, your uncontrolled mind that you are oppressed by. If you can discover how it oppresses you, the uncontrolled mind will disappear automatically. Thus knowing your own mind is the solution for your mental problems.

One day the world is so beautiful; the next day it is so bad. How can you say that! Scientifically the world can't change radically like that. It's merely your mind that makes this happen. Don't think that this is religious dogma; our going up and down is not religious dogma. I'm not talking about religion; I'm talking about the way you lead your life, which is what sends you up-down. The people and the environment don't change radically; the changes are in your own mind. Surely you can understand that—it's so simple.

Similarly, one person thinks that the world is beautiful and people are lovely and kind, but another thinks that everything and everyone is horrible. Who is right? How do you explain that scientifically? It's just the individual mind's projection of the sense world. Hence you feel, "Today is like this, tomorrow is like that; this man is like this; that woman is like that. Even seeing somebody beautiful is somehow a creation of your mind.

Also, you should not expect material objects to satisfy you and make your life perfect. How can you be satisfied with even vast amounts of material objects? How can you be happy with sleeping with hundreds of different people? Satisfaction comes from the mind. Your dissatisfied mind wanting to keep changing from one person to another, from one thing to another, can never satisfy you. All of this is in your mind only.

So you see, if you don't know your own psychology, you might ignore what's going on in your mind until it breaks down and you go completely crazy. People go mad through a lack of inner wisdom, the ability to examine their own minds. They cannot explain themselves to themselves; they don't know how to talk to themselves. They are not aware of their inner "world." Self-analysis, therefore, it is necessary as well as the ability to examine your mental attitudes. However, you don't need to embark on some emotional or religious journey to explore yourself. Some people, however, think that this kind of self-analysis is something spiritual or religious, although if you want to be happy, you do have to check the way you lead your life. Your mind can become "your religion."

You should be able to relax and face problems with positivity. Just be conscious of them and their origin, knowing their root. Introduce them to yourself. Then the problem will automatically ease. It's not too hard if you want it, be conscious that you have a mind. You cannot deny your mind. Therefore, treat yourself wisely and try to discover the real source of satisfaction.

When you were a child, you may have loved and craved things like sweets or toys or things that you couldn't afford, thinking "When I'm old like my parents, I'll have all the things I want, and then I'll be happy." Now you may have the things you were craving for, but you are still not satisfied and perhaps want more or different things you may or may not be able to afford. Therefore, you will search for other sources of happiness, but in the end, you would still be dissatisfied with something. Then, what is satisfaction? Examine your life from childhood to the present—meditate. You have changed your mind several times and not truly understood what makes you happy and you may feel somehow lost if you can not find your goals in life. Therefore, Lord Buddha is saying that you only have to know who you are, how you exist; that's all. You don't have to do anything. Just understand your mind: how it works; how attachment and desire arise; how lack of knowledge results; where the emotions come from. It is sufficient to know the nature of all that; just that gives so much happiness and peace. Your life changes completely; everything gets turned upside down; what you interpreted as horrible becomes beautiful. It's truly possible.

I'm sure that if I told you that all you were living for was chocolate and ice cream, you'd think I was crazy. No, no, no, your arrogant mind would say. But look deeper into your life's purpose. What are you here for? To gain a good reputation or to collect material things? Or maybe to try to look good to others? I'm not exaggerating—check for yourselves, then you'll see. Through examination, you can realize that if your entire life is dedicated to seeking happiness through superficial things there is no significance in your being a human. Birds and dogs have the same kind of attitude to life. If you think you're intelligent you should dedicate your life to goals higher than those of chickens!

I'm not dictating your life for you, but It's much better to have an integrated experience than to live in a mental disorder. Otherwise, your life is not worthwhile, not beneficial to yourself or others. Ask yourself what you are living for—for chocolate? For steak? Perhaps for education. But that also comes from the mind. Without the soul, what is knowledge, what is philosophy? A philosophy is somebody's way of thinking, thoughts put together in a certain way. Without the mind there's no philosophy no doctrine, no university subjects. These things are mind-made.

How to check the mind? Just watch how it perceives or interprets any object that it makes contacts with. What feeling—comfortable or uncomfortable is. Then you ask yourself, "When I recognize this feeling or emotion, I react in a certain way. This is how to check the mind; that's all; it's straightforward.

When you have checked your own mind correctly, you may stop blaming others, recognizing that actions come from yourself. When you are preoccupied with the material, external objects, you always blame them and others for your problems. Then you become miserable because you project that view onto external phenomena instead of seeing their reality. So you can realize your fade-conception view—the attitude, or nature, of your own mind.

You might think that this is all very new for you, but it's not. Whenever you are going to do anything, first you check whether to do it or not and then make your decision. Since you do this already, I'm not giving you something new; the difference is that you are not doing it enough. You have to do more checking. To do this you don't have to sit in some corner on your own—you can be checking your mind all the time, even while talking or working with other people. Also, you shouldn't think that examining the mind is something only for those who are abroad. Don't think that way.

You should also realize that the nature of the mind is different from that of the mesh and bone of this physical body. The mind is like a mirror, reflecting everything without discrimination. If you have understanding-wisdom, you will control the sort of reflections you allow in your mind-mirror. If you ignore what is happening in your mind, it will reflect all negative things that would make you psychologically ill.

Your checking-wisdom should distinguish between beneficial reflections and those that bring psychological problems. Eventually, when you realize the nature of subject and object, all your questions will dissolve.

Some people think they are religious, but what is spiritual? If you are not examining your own nature, not gaining knowledge-wisdom, in what way are you religious? Just the idea that you are religious—I am Buddhist, Jewish—does not help at all. It does not help you; it does not help others. If you have knowledge-wisdom, you can help others.

The most significant problems of humanity are psychological, not material. From birth to death, people are continuously under the control of their mental sufferings. Some people never check themselves when things are going well, but when something goes wrong—an accident or some other terrible experience—they immediately say, God, please help me. They call themselves religious, but they're aren't. In happiness or sorrow, a severe practitioner maintains constant awareness of God and his nature. You're not realistic or even remotely religious if you forget yourself when you are having a good time, surrounded by materialistic things and preoccupied with worldly sense pleasures, and turn to God only when something awful happens. That doesn't help.

No matter which of the many world religions we consider, their interpretation of God or Buddha or whatever is simply words and mind; only these two. Therefore words don't matter so much. What you have to realize is that everything—good and evil; all kinds of philosophies and doctrines—comes from mind. The mind is mighty; therefore it requires strong direction. A powerful jet plane needs a good pilot; your mind-pilot should be wisdom understanding the nature of it. Then powerful energy can directed to benefit your life instead of being allowed to run uncontrollably like a mad elephant, destroying yourself and others.

It's widely recognized that a few sessions of cognitive-behavioral therapy (or CBT) can be beneficial in treating the anxiety and depression that so many people experience. However, many people don't have access to a CBT therapist—maybe none are close by, or they're not in the person's insurance network, or they're prohibitively expensive. It can also be challenging to take time off from paid work or childcare every week to see a therapist.

If you're interested in CBT for anxiety or depression and you aren't able to see a CBT therapist, take heart—you may not need to. There are multiple options for doing CBT without a therapist, including self-help books and Internet-based treatment. Many studies have shown that self-directed CBT can be handy.

For example, a review of 33 studies found that self-help treatment led to significant reductions in anxiety; another review of 34 studies on depression found similar benefits of self-directed therapy, mainly when the treatments used CBT techniques. Both reports found that, on average, the self-help treatments were moderately helpful. In other words, people who did the therapy felt substantially better— maybe not like "a new person," but a noticeably less anxious or depressed version of themselves.

Data from these studies also suggest that people who do self-help CBT for anxiety and depression tend to hold on to their progress over time, which is very encouraging. One of the primary goals of CBT is for you to "become your own therapist" by learning skills that you can continue to practice after you've ended treatment. These studies show that people who learn CBT skills on their own can use these skills to keep feeling well.

Does this mean the end for therapists? Certainly not. One of the other findings from the studies above is that CBT with a therapist tends to be more effective than self-help CBT, so there can be an additional advantage to working with someone directly. Self-help treatment can also be done with a limited amount of input from a professional—for example, a brief phone call each week—which can provide an extra boost compared to self-help alone. I suspect that the added benefit from working with a therapist comes not only from having the input of an expert but also from having a caring person's consistent encouragement.

CBT is part of a movement toward stepped care, in which the goal is to match the intensity of treatment to a person's needs. Someone who is severely depressed and barely able to get out of bed is probably not a good match for self-directed CBT, and likely will need one-on-one treatment with a professional. On the other end of the spectrum, a person with mild to moderate anxiety or depression which is generally able to function well may be the right candidate for a less intense option like a book on CBT.

SELF-THERAPY

Because there are so many different ways of going about self-therapy – from CBT to Rational Emotive Behavior Therapy (REBT), IFS, and more, there are many different tips out there on how best to go about doing self-therapy.

Start by thinking about what you'd like to achieve. Are you hoping to learn techniques for managing anxiety? Are you looking to nip negative thoughts in the bud? Do you want to work on developing some positive current behaviors? There's no 'right' answer. Clarifying your overarching goal will simply make your different objectives easier to understand.

Study your feelings and behaviors more closely. Take a closer look at how your problem is presenting. Are you hoping to deal with a behavioral problem, like avoidance or coping behaviors? Or are you wanting to target unwanted feelings, like social anxiety or stress?

Studying your behaviors or emotions at a more in-depth level can involve describing your feeling or action, recalling times that you thought or acted a certain way and keeping a record of when and where these feelings or behaviours tend to show up.

Ask yourself: what were you thinking at that precise moment? How intense was the atmosphere? Where were you and who was there? Are there certain situations that lead to the problem?

Identify and explore any associated self-talk and thoughts.

Very often, irrational or unhelpful cognitive mental processes are behind unwanted feelings and behaviors. Stress, anxiety, depression, and even relationship difficulties can often be addressed by identifying the negative self-talk or distortions that go on in our heads.

Challenge your irrational thoughts and internal dialogue

Regardless of which direction you choose to take your self-therapy, the goal is to feel more positive. We can do this much more effectively by addressing the root cause of the problem, which a lot of medications don't do.

As an example, Sarah is given feedback on a work task by her boss. Instead of allowing herself to think negatively (e.g. "I'm not good enough"), she replaces this with a more objective, rational thought. Instead, she thinks: "My boss sees my full potential, and I'm excited to grow and realize that potential."

Practice

Every day, we face triggers and external events that we have no control over. As we practice, develop, and strengthen our rational and positive thought processes, we get better at managing our responses to them. Reward yourself with something you enjoy doing for keeping up the good work.

Self-Therapy questions

Self-therapy questions aim to probe a little deeper into the nature of whatever anxiety, depression, or emotional problems you might be experiencing.

These can take many different forms and may entail part of a much longer-term process.

Self-therapy questions require nothing more than something to write with, but keeping your answers on hand can be very helpful over the long term. You or your patients may find that being as honest as possible while answering makes for more powerful reflection at later points in time.

The Cycle of Anxiety Worksheet and questions

This worksheet and set of questions are best used together. The Cycle of Anxiety worksheet is designed to help those of us with anxiety understand how the symptoms often lead us to engage in avoidance behaviors. Because many therapeutic interventions (such as CBT) attempt to deal with anxiety by 'breaking the cycle,' the illustration can be helpful to visualize, understand, and target the source of our concern.

As part of self-therapy, you can use the Cycle illustration to introduce yourself or your client to the concept of how feedback and reinforcement contribute to the recurrence of avoidance behaviors.

This activity can help facilitate an understanding of why it's often essential to tackle the source of these negative emotions head-on when they occur. As a therapist, it is often not possible to be around when your client experiences external anxiety-inducing triggers, and this worksheet is very handy for them to have on hand.

The questions accompanying the worksheet help you or your client make the Cycle more meaningful, and include the following:

• What are three things that trigger your anxiety?

• What are three physical symptoms that you experience when you feel anxious?

• What are three thoughts you tend to have when you feel anxious?

• What are three things you do to cope when you are anxious?

By asking yourself these questions, you can develop a better sense of what triggers your anxiety, how it manifests physically and mentally, and the avoidance behaviors you commonly exhibit.

Questions for Challenging Negative Thoughts

Anxiety and depression often come together, being brought about by negative thought processes. These questions are designed to help you or someone you know to challenge these maladaptive thoughts and help you reassess them. Ideally, they should provide an alternative perspective and help you cope with or reframe the situation.

• Is there substantial evidence for my thought?

• Is there evidence contrary to my thought?

• Am I attempting to interpret this situation without all the evidence?

• What would a friend think about this situation?

• If I look at the situation positively, how is it different?

• Will this matter a year from now? How about five years from now?

Challenging our subjective or potentially distorted thinking patterns is a logical next step to being able to identify and recognize them, which the Cycle of Anxiety exercise above helps with. The questions can be very helpful if a client or you yourself realize that you might be catastrophizing, overgeneralizing, or magnifying/minimizing the importance of certain situations.

Questions for Cognitive Distortion

These questions are especially useful because they can be easily adapted to meet a whole range of different levels and stages of emotion. They are aimed at helping you or your client understand that the worst possible solution is not always right.

When you feel that you are at risk of catastrophizing when you feel the onset of either anxiety or an unnaturally low mood, ask yourself:

• What are you worried about?

• How likely is it that your worry will come true? Give examples of past experiences, or other evidence, to support your answer.

• If your worry does come true, what's the worst that could happen?

• If your worry does come true, what is most likely to happen?

• If your worry comes true, what are the chances you'll be okay…

- In one week? ____%
- In one month? ____%
- In one year? ____%

Discovering your Inner Critic

These questions are designed to be self-administered. The test itself shouldn't take longer than 8 minutes, and the results will be most helpful to you if you answer them using your first reaction.

Based on the answers you give, you will ideally be able to get some understanding of the internal parts of yourself that give you unnecessary negative messages.

Each question is answered on a five-point scale ranging from Never to Always.

• I set extremely high standards for myself.

Never / Seldom / Sometimes / Frequently / Always

• I push myself to work very hard so I can achieve my goals.

Never / Seldom / Sometimes / Frequently / Always

• When I think of trying something new and challenging, I give up before I begin.

Never / Seldom / Sometimes / Frequently / Always

• I have a hard time feeling OK about myself when I'm not acting in accordance with my childhood programming.

Never / Seldom / Sometimes / Frequently / Always

• It is hard for me to start on new projects because it is unacceptable to make mistakes even when I am just learning.

Never / Seldom / Sometimes / Frequently / Always

• I am troubled by something I have done that I cannot forgive myself for.

Never / Seldom / Sometimes / Frequently / Always

Using Self-Therapy for Anxiety

Unpredictability is part of the very nature of anxiety. Triggers can be internal or external, and it's easy to feel overwhelmed fairly quickly. As mentioned, not everyone can access a therapist instantly, so guided self-therapy can be incredibly helpful for dealing with daily occurrences that might lead to moderate or mild anxiety.

How does self-therapy work for anxiety?

Often, self-therapy is used as part of a stepped-care model. This means it is considered a low-intensity treatment which individuals with anxiety can do without therapeutic intervention. At the same time, carrying out self-therapy for anxiety can help us understand if a more high-intensity approach is required, while also being a useful tool to use alongside one-on-one therapy.

There are many different forms of self-therapy for anxiety and work-related stress including, but not limited to:

• Psychoeducation – resources to help you understand the nature of anxiety and the vicious Cycle of Anxiety are frequently found with self-therapy worksheets, questions, and exercises. We've given some examples above, and these sheets also provide valuable information about what treatments you or your client may be interested in pursuing;

• Relaxation – of course, relaxation is a huge part of treating anxiety. Meditations, guided breathing, music, exercise, and more can be part of self-therapy, and you can find more activities for targeting anxiety;

• Cognitive Restructuring – the 'Challenging Negative Thoughts' exercise above is a brilliant example of how cognitive distortions can contribute to anxiety and stress as well as depression. Cognitive restructuring involves identifying and changing the maladaptive thought processes underpinning negative emotions and symptoms;

• Anxiety Management Techniques – typically used alongside cognitive restructuring and relaxation, these can include 'grab-and-go' self-therapy techniques that work well in everyday life. These can include positive self-talk, grounding techniques, and related exercises, some of which we've included below in our worksheets section.

Self-Therapy for Depression

In a nutshell, self-therapy for depression uses a lot of the same techniques and approaches. Most self-therapy approaches to handling depression use CBT techniques to identify, combat, and change negative thoughts.

Individuals can easily learn to develop Cognitive Behavioural Therapy skills, and when self-directed, these can help to somewhat reduce feelings of anxiety as well – the two are often found together.

Neuroimaging research also provides evidence to suggest that CBT helps to reduce activity in our self-referential medial prefrontal cortex, which is typically 'on' when we're having negative self-thoughts.

OCD, Social Anxiety and Self-Therapy

Because both social anxiety and obsessive-compulsive disorder (OCD) are related to feelings of anxiety, self-therapy is frequently used as a means of addressing both. In fact, just under a quarter of those found to have OCD are also diagnosed with social anxiety.

Self-therapy, in this case, will often involve identifying the anxious 'parts' of our psyche that are driving obsessive thoughts, compulsive behavior, or feelings of fear relating to social situations.

Social anxiety can often drive behaviors, particularly avoidance-related behaviors, and self-therapy directed at treating it often starts with psychoeducation.

Research points towards the effectiveness, in particular, of cognitive-behavioral bibliotherapy and internet-based programs for individuals with social anxiety. Even more encouragingly, these improvements showed signs of having endured in follow-up trials a year later.

Gratitude Exercises Worksheet

You can easily use this worksheet yourself, or to help your clients learn how to practice gratitude by getting involved in several activities:

Journaling: By taking time each day to record a few nice things that happened, you can reflect on these if and when you feel anxious or depressed.

Letter Writing: Composing letters to those who you're thankful for and getting it down on paper can really trigger some strong positive emotions. The worksheet guides you through this.

Expanding on this theme, other exercises in the worksheet include:

- Visiting those you appreciate, or those who have had a big positive impact on your life;
- Saying 'Thank You' and looking for reasons to thank people;

- Gratitude Walks, during which we can focus externally rather than internally, looking around us at things that make us feel appreciative.

The Internal Family Systems Model (IFS) and Self-Therapy

The Internal Family Systems (IFS) Model is a type of psychotherapy based on the concept that our psyches comprise multiple subpersonalities. These multiple separate parts, which can be thought of as painful emotions, exist within our mental systems and can be at conflict with one another, and with our spiritual center, the Self.

Our Inner Parts

Each subpersonality has a distinct set of motivations, goals, feelings, and emotions, such as 'the angry part', 'the loving caretaker', 'the inner critic' and more.

Developed by Dr. Richard Schwartz, IFS therapy allows us to recognize, target, and transform these different parts into inner strengths. In other words, resources of strength, love, and freedom that we can draw on to deal with depression, anxiety, and other manifestations of imbalance between our 'inner parts'.

The ultimate goal of IFS in self-therapy is to engage directly with these facets of our psyche and heal them in order to access the Self, a source of creativity, compassion, clarity, and courage.

According to the IFS Model, we experience our inner parts through our feelings, thoughts, as well as through physical symptoms such as anxiety and depression. Some are proactive, while others can be 'exiled' – meaning they can't carry out their intended roles of acting to help you.

Protective inner 'parts'

The Managers – these proactive 'organizer' parts of our psyche strive to keep balance in our systems by keeping feelings associated with 'exiled' parts in check. 'Manager' parts help us control our behavior in different situations by avoiding risks and worry, by evaluating ourselves and others, and related protective behaviors.

The Firefighters – more reactive than 'Managers', these inner parts aim to distract you or dissociate from the exiled parts of your psyche when these come into play. Physically, they can be felt as anxiety, hypervigilance, or related symptoms such as panic and digestive problems.

Exiles

A detailed descriptions suggest, 'Exiles' are young parts or the psyche that have become separated from the rest of our systems for their own, or our, protection.

Traumatic, difficult, or painful experiences may have lead to this isolation, and these parts carry the feelings and sensations of these past experiences. When situational factors, or the IFS psychotherapy process are used to access these 'exiled' parts, they can lead us to feel extreme emotions in an attempt to be heard and attended to.

MOST EFFECTIVE TOOLS OF CBT THERAPY

The basic idea of cognitive behavioral therapy is that your thinking determines your quality of life. If you change your thinking, you will improve your life. External factors influence your life to some degree, but it is mostly how you interpret external factors that has the greatest impact.

If you feel the need to be perfect, small disappointments will feel like major failures. If you dwell on your worries or fears, you will eventually feel overwhelmed. If you hold on to disappointments or resentments, you will sap the joy out of life. How you choose to interpret events, and your ability to reframe them, is the power of mind over mood.

Ask your therapist or doctor if cognitive therapy is right for you. These techniques can complement the work you do with your therapist or doctor, but they are best done in combination with professional guidance.

What is Cognitive Behavioral Therapy?

It is a step-by-step method for identifying your negative thinking and replacing it with healthier thinking. It changes your inner dialogue. Numerous studies have shown that cognitive behavioral therapy is effective for treating anxiety, depression and addiction.

Negative Thinking

Negative thinking leads to negative consequences. It is based on false beliefs or on a few selective facts, and it ignores important facts that would lead to better consequences. Negative thinking is usually rigid, absolute, and not supported by most of the facts.

When your thinking is rigid and absolute, you tend to take an all-or-nothing approach and you are resistant to change. For example, you may think that you are a failure at everything, and you may be resistant to hearing encouraging advice from your friends.

Sometimes it's hard to recognize negative thinking. Cognitive therapy is designed to help you recognize your negative thinking and discover healthier thinking patterns.

Common Negative Thinking Patterns

1. *All-or-Nothing Thinking:* "I have to do things perfectly, and anything less is a failure."

2. *Focusing on the Negatives:* "Nothing goes my way. It feels like one disappointment after another."

3. *Negative Self-Labeling:* "I'm a failure. If people knew the real me, they wouldn't like me. I am flawed."

4. *Catastrophizing:* "If something is going to happen, it'll probably be the worst-case scenario."

5. *Excessive Need for Approval:* "I can only be happy if people like me. If someone is upset, it's probably my fault."

6. *Mind Reading:* "I can tell people don't like me because of the way they behave."

7. *Should Statements:* "People should be fair, and when they are not fair they should be punished."

8. *Disqualifying the Present:* "I'll relax later. But first I have to rush to finish this."

9. *Dwelling on the Past:* "If I dwell on why I'm unhappy and what went wrong, maybe I'll feel better."

10. *Pessimism:* "Life is a struggle. I don't think we are meant to be happy. I don't trust people who are happy. If something good happens in my life, I usually have to pay for it with something bad."

Causes of Negative Thinking

Negative thinking is learned thinking. If you see important people in your life using negative thinking, it will start to seem normal, you won't question if it is healthy or not or where it came from.

Negative thinking turns into automatic thinking through repetition. By the time you are independent enough to do your own thinking, you may have been exposed to numerous examples of negative thinking. Without even questioning it, you will automatically assume that you are wrong, or a failure, or disliked.

Automatic thinking is helpful in everyday life, because you have so many minor decisions to make that you can't take time to ponder every choice. It allows you to navigate life efficiently. Automatic thinking can also be unhelpful if your assumptions are false. If you have absorbed a negative way of thinking, then you will often come to the wrong conclusions.

With cognitive behavioral therapy, you can unlearn what you knew and learn new skills and new ways of thinking that can lead you to a better life.

Consequences of Negative Thinking

The consequences of negative thinking are cumulative. One negative thought piled on top of another starts to take a toll on how you view yourself and your future.

If you think that any mistake is a failure, this all-or-nothing thinking can lead to anxiety. You worry that any mistake may expose you to criticism or judgment. Therefore you don't give yourself permission to relax and let down your guard.

If you think that you are broken, unfixable, or unlikeable, this negative self-labelling can lead to depression. You are trapped by your own unrealistic view of yourself. Feeling trapped is one of the common causes of depression.

Negative thinking that can lead to anxiety or depression can also lead to addiction, because anxiety and depression feel so uncomfortable that you may turn to drugs or alcohol to escape.

Negative thinking not only leads to unhappiness, it is also an obstacle to self-change. When you think in an all-or-nothing way, then the idea of change feels like an overwhelming challenge. You can't see the small steps, and you don't have the energy to take big steps, therefore you feel stuck.

CBT Worksheets (Thought Record)

A CBT Worksheet (also called a Thought Record) helps you reflect on your way of thinking. A basic tool of cognitive therapy, it is a series of questions that lead you step-by-step through the process of identifying your negative thinking and changing it.

This worksheet gives you a chance to analyse your thinking and actions after the fact has happened, so that strong emotions won't affect you during the process and you can easily identify your negative thinking.

A Thought Record helps you see what your negative thought are based on, what might have triggered it and finding ways to deal with the problem and find healthier ways of interpreting the facts.

CBT Worksheet/Thought Record Template

1. *The trigger:* Briefly describe the situation that led to your unpleasant feelings. This will help you remember the situation later if you review your notes.

2. *Initial thought:* What thought first crossed your mind? This was probably a subconscious or automatic thought that you have had before.

3. *Consequences:* Why do you want to change this thinking? What will be the consequences if you don't change? Look at the psychological, physical, professional, and relationship consequences.

4. *Challenge your initial thought:* How successful has this thinking been for you in the past? What facts do you have that support or challenge your initial thought? What strengths do you have that you may be overlooking? What advice would you give someone else in the same situation?

5. [Optional] *Negative thinking:* Summarize the kind of negative thinking behind your initial thought. Identify one or more of the basic types of negative thinking, for example all-or-nothing, focusing on the negatives, catastrophizing, or negative self-labelling.

6. [Optional] *Origin:* When did you first have initial thoughts like this? How deep do the roots go? Do you know anyone else who thinks like this? How successful has this thinking been for them?

7. *Alternative thinking:* Now that you understand your negative thinking, how could you have handled the situation differently?

8. *Positive thinking and affirmation:* Write down an affirmation, in a positive form, that reflects your healthier approach. Choose something that you can use as a reminder.

9. *Action plan:* What can you do if this situation arises again? How can you prepare for the situation? Write a list of strengths you bring to the situation. Knowing your tendencies, what can you do if you fall back on old habits?

10. *Improvement:* Do you feel slightly better or more optimistic? This step reinforces the idea that if you change your thinking, you will change your life.

How Effective is Cognitive Behavioral Therapy?

Cognitive behavioral therapy has been proven to be more effective than other forms of psychotherapy for anxiety and depression, as it helps to change the wiring of your brain. When you challenge your negative thinking, you create new neural pathways. The more you practice your new way of thinking, the more you strengthen those pathways.

MRI studies have confirmed that cognitive therapy changes the wiring of your brain and this is why the benefits of cognitive behavioral therapy are not just temporary.

The principles of cognitive behavioral therapy are so sound that it can be used effectively in a number of settings. Cognitive behavioral therapy has been shown to be effective when delivered in primary care, via computer, and through internet-based self-help programs.

Behavioral Therapy

CBT is a combination of two forms of therapy: cognitive and behavioral therapy. Behavioral therapy is sometimes used initially with individuals who are too anxious or too depressed to even acknowledge that their thinking is part of the problem.

Behavioral therapy encourages you to try simple tasks and as you succeed, you gradually improve your belief in yourself. Once you see that you can change your behavior, you may be more willing to change your thinking. In most cases, individuals who are ready to change are encouraged to start directly with cognitive therapy rather than begin with behavioral therapy.

History of Cognitive Behavioral Therapy

In the 1950s, American psychologist Albert Ellis introduced Rational Therapy in which people were taught the A-B-C-D approach for dealing with uncomfortable situations. When a person is confronted with an adversity (A) their beliefs (B) will influence the way they respond to that adversity and lead to emotional and behavioral consequences (C).

If the beliefs (B) are rigid, absolute, and unrealistic, the consequences (C) will likely be self-defeating and destructive. If the beliefs (B) are flexible and constructive, the consequences (C) will likely be positive. People can change their thinking and their lives by disputing (D) and challenging their beliefs.

Rational therapy was partly developed as a reaction to psychoanalysis, which was considered inefficient because individuals went through years of therapy, but were not explicitly directed to change their thinking. Psychoanalysis was based on the approach that understanding your subconscious thoughts would eventually lead to self-change. Rational therapy takes a more directive approach. You are encouraged to challenge your beliefs in order to achieve faster and more efficient change.

In the 1960s, American psychiatrist Aaron T. Beck introduced Cognitive Behavioral Therapy partly based on the ideas of Albert Ellis and used it as a treatment for depression. Beck developed the idea of the thought record, in which individuals could challenge their thinking through writing their thoughts down and looking for healthier ways of thinking. He also developed self-reporting measures for anxiety and depression including the Beck Anxiety Inventory (BAI) and the Beck Depression Inventory (BDI).

Ineffective ways people try to stop negative thinking

People often try many different ways to get rid of their negative thoughts, including distractions or diversions, only to later mentally beat themselves up for being still stuck in their negativity. It can feel like a real internal battle.

Key one – recognise & step back from negative thought patterns

Negative thought patterns are repetitive, unhelpful thoughts. They directly cause what we could describe as 'negative' (unwanted or unpleasant) emotions like anxiety, depression, stress, fear, unworthiness, shame etc.

Once we learn to recognise and identify negative thought patterns as they occur, we can start to step back from them. This process of stepping back from thoughts is called 'cognitive defusion.' In cognitive defusion we learn to see the thoughts in our head as simply thoughts and not reality.

When we can step back into cognitive defusion, we do not take our thoughts too seriously. We hold them lightly and only listen to them if we find them valuable or helpful.

As an example, imagine this: you wake up one day and look out the window and see that it's raining. A common thought some people might have is that the day is going to be bad because of the weather. Now, is it true that it's a bad day? No, it is simply raining. However, if you believe that thought (called 'cognitive fusion') you might actually end up thinking yourself into having a bad day. In other words, if you believe a negative thought, it can and will generate what we might call negativity.

It's completely normal to have negative thoughts. We all have minds that have evolved to be constantly on the lookout for problems and dangers, so most of us have minds prone to have many negative thoughts.

The problem arises when we believe our thoughts are true. When you are no longer entangled in thoughts they lose their grip on you and lose their power to generate unpleasant emotions.

It's important to be able to recognise the kinds of unhelpful thinking styles that can arise, so here are some other negative thinking patterns that are most common.

Anxious thoughts and worry: worry is when the mind projects into an imagined future and conjures up scenes and thoughts about what could go wrong. Here it often creates 'what if' scenarios.

Sometimes it takes the form of imagining or expecting that bad things will happen or that nothing good will ever happen for you. You might fret about your health deteriorating, your relationship going downhill, your car breaking down or your career being ruined—even though nothing has actually happened yet.

Criticism and self-beating: do you have a harsh inner critic? Are you always trying to whip yourself into shape, mentally beating yourself up for not being good enough yet? Are you on a perfection mission? Another pattern of negative thought is to constantly criticise and 'self improve' because you're not good enough yet. You may be very harsh on yourself, focusing in on all of your weaknesses and perceived flaws.

You may even extend this habit of criticism to others in your life. This can be the cause of tremendous strain on relationships. Negative self-talk and self-criticism often results in low self-esteem and a lack of confidence.

When the mind continuously hones in on what is wrong with yourself (and your life) and disassociates from what is going well and is good, we can become stuck in negativity.

Regret and guilt: ruminating on mistakes made in the past often creates feelings of shame, guilt and negativity. Feelings of worthlessness may arise when you play over and over in your mind, 'bad' choices or 'wrong' actions you feel you have made.

There is nothing negative about simply reflecting on past experiences. This is how we can learn, grow and mature as people. Negativity arises when you dwell on a situation repeatedly with no real intention to learn and grow, but instead you are self-beating or wishing things were different instead of being accepting of things as they are.

Problems: negative thoughts often revolve around what's wrong with your life. Your attention becomes fixated on, and exaggerates the so called negative aspects of your life. Here your mind will often downplay what is going well.

For example, you may have a wonderful family, food to eat and shelter, but your car breaks down and it's all you can think about and focus on all week long. You allow the situation with the car to dominate your thinking and negative emotions arise as a result.

Constantly focusing on that single problem is not constructive at all and is another way we can get trapped in negativity.

Key Two: Coming To Your Senses

Notice that many negative thoughts mostly flow from two directions. The first is dwelling on the past, the second is worrying about the future.

This may take the form of stress over whether or not you will achieve certain goals or anxiety about the security of your finances or relationships. Whatever your particular negative thoughts are, notice that in order to engage in negative thought patterns the mind needs to cast its focus mostly into past or future.

When lost in negative thinking, we tend to be so engrossed in thoughts that we completely lose touch with what is actually happening in the present moments of our lives. To become more present, and able to step out of negative thinking, one powerful method is to 'come to your senses'. To do this simply redirect your attention out of the thoughts in your head and bring your focus to your sense perceptions.

Whether you're in your home, at the office, in the park or on a subway, notice everything around you. Use your senses to their fullest. Don't get into a mental dialogue about the things you see, just be aware of what you're experiencing in this moment.

Research from Prof. Mark Williams from Oxford University showed that when difficulties arise in life, many of us tend to get caught up in excessive unhelpful thinking. Sometimes people try to stop constant unhelpful thinking, but we don't have to try to stop our thoughts. A more effective way to ease all that internal noise is to pay attention to our direct sensory experience. This way, there is little to no room left in our attention for all that excessive thinking. Coming to our senses calms the mind and grounds us in the present moment.

Key Three: Regular Mindfulness Practice

Mindfulness is the practice of waking up to that wellspring of wholeness and peace. It's waking up out of mind wandering (where we are lost in our heads, our old beliefs, habits, reactions and thinking patterns) so that we are able to live deliberately. Through mindfulness, we build our capacity to live from that deeper awareness and tame the mind.

Regular mindfulness meditation has been shown to decrease stress, depression and anxiety as well as improving immune function. People who practice meditation report overall levels of satisfaction with life higher than others. In fact, researcher and psychologist Matt Killingsworth found that what makes people most happy is being fully present in the moment and that the more our minds wander the more unhappy we become.

Four Ways You're Strengthening Your Mind When You Practice Meditation: each time your mind wanders in meditation, your task is to notice it and then detach from your thought stream and come back to your senses. This is a practice of untangling from thoughts over and over again, a habit which translates in the rest of your life too. It becomes a habit to notice and let go with ease.

Each time you let go of the thought stream and come back into the present moment, you tap into the stillness and wholeness at the heart of who you are. A sense of peace, lightness and joy arises more and more with each time you practice.

Key Four: Helpful questions For Unhelpful Thoughts

Some kinds of negative thinking patterns can be quite 'sticky'. You may find that you try to 'name it to tame it' and come back to your senses, but the thoughts continue to have a grip on you. If you find yourself in this position, there are some further tools you can use to untangle from your thoughts and change your focus. These are called the 'Helpful questions for Unhelpful Thoughts'. These are drawn from ACT (Acceptance and Commitment Therapy).

Here are some questions you can ask yourself to help you untangle from negative thoughts.

• Is this thought in any way useful or helpful?

• Is it true? (Can I absolutely know that it's true?)

• Is this just an old story that my mind is playing out of habit?

• Does this thought help me take effective action?

• Is this though helpful or is my mind just babbling on?

• What do I really want to feel or create in the situation? How can I move towards that?

• How can I make the best of this situation?

• Who would I be without this negative thought?

• What new story or thought can I focus on now?

• How can I see this in a different or new way?

• What can I be grateful for in this moment?

Constructive thinking allows you to be happy when things are going good, and puts problems in perspective when times get tough so you can stay calm and clear headed and deal with them in a practical and efficient way.

Practicing The Four Keys

The four keys are not a quick fix method for creating permanent change of long standing patterns. You will find that in any given moment of negativity, these tools will be of great help in assisting you and change your way of thinking and your mindset. The more you practice these tools, the more they will become like second nature to you. It is essentially like building a muscle.

How to Improve Your Mental Health

Mental health is much more than a diagnosis. It's your overall psychological well-being—the way you feel about yourself and others as well as your ability to manage your feelings and deal with everyday difficulties. And while taking care of your mental health can mean seeking professional support and treatment, it also means taking steps to improve your emotional health on your own. Making these changes will pay off in all aspects of your life. It can boost your mood, build resilience, and add to your overall enjoyment of life.

Tell yourself something positive: research shows that how you think about yourself can have a powerful effect on how you feel. When we perceive our selves and our life negatively, we can end up viewing experiences in a way that confirms that notion. Instead, practice using words that promote feelings of self-worth and personal power. For example, instead of saying, "I'm such a loser. I won't get the job because I tanked in the interview," try, "I didn't do as well in the interview as I would have liked, but that doesn't mean I'm not going to get the job."

Write down something you are grateful for: gratitude has been clearly linked with improved well-being and mental health, as well as happiness. The best-researched method to increase feelings of gratitude is to keep a gratitude journal or write a daily gratitude list. Generally contemplating gratitude is also effective, but you need to get regular practice to experience long-term benefit. Find something to be grateful for, let it fill your heart, and bask in that feeling.

Focus on one thing (in the moment): being mindful of the present moment allows us to let go of negative or difficult emotions from past experiences that weigh us down. Start by bringing awareness to routine activities, such as taking a shower, eating lunch, or walking home. Paying attention to the physical sensations, sounds, smells, or tastes of these experiences helps you focus. When your mind wanders, just bring it back to what you are doing.

Exercise: your body releases stress-relieving and mood-boosting endorphins before and after you work out, which is why exercise is a powerful antidote to stress, anxiety, and depression. Look for small ways to add activity to your day, like taking the stairs instead of the elevator or going on a short walk. To get the most benefit, aim for at least 30 minutes of exercise daily, and try to do it outdoors. Exposure to sunlight helps your body produce vitamin D, which increases your level of serotonin in the brain.

Eat a good meal: what you eat nourishes your whole body, including your brain. Carbohydrates (in moderate amounts) increase serotonin, a chemical that has been shown to have a calming effect on your mood. Protein-rich foods increase norepinephrine, dopamine, and tyrosine, which help keep you alert. Vegetables and fruits are loaded with nutrients that feed every cell of your body, including those that affect mood-regulating brain chemicals. Include foods with Omega-3 polyunsaturated fatty acids (found in fish, nuts, and flaxseed.) Research shows that these nutrients can improve mood and restore structural integrity to the brain cells necessary for cognitive function.

Open up to someone: knowing you are valued by others is important for helping you think more positively. Plus, being more trusting can increase your emotional well-being because, as you get better at finding the positive aspects in other people, you become better at recognizing your own.

Do something for someone else: being helpful to others has a beneficial effect on how you feel about yourself. Being helpful and kind, and valued for what you do, is a great way to build self-esteem. The meaning you find in helping others will enrich and expand your life.

Take a break: in those moments when it all seems like too much, step away until you feel a little better. Sometimes, the best thing to do is a simple breathing exercise: close your eyes and take 10 deep breaths. For each one, count to four as you inhale, hold it for a count of four, and then exhale for another four.

Go to bed on time: sleep deprivation has a significant negative effect on your mood. Try to go to bed at a regular time each day, and practice good habits to get better sleep. These include shutting down screens for at least an hour before bed, using your bed only for sleep or relaxing activities, and restricting caffeinated drinks for the morning.

You have the power to take positive steps right now to improve your resilience and emotional health. Don't wait until you're in a crisis to make your mental health a priority. Pick something from this section that resonates with you and try it. Then, try something else. Slowly putting in place routines, habits, and regular patterns will help you feel better through gradual change.

APPLYING BEHAVIORAL TECHNIQUES

You and your therapist can mix and match techniques depending on what you're most interested in trying and what works for you. You can also try the following Cognitive Behavioral Therapy techniques as self-help.

Pleasant Activity Scheduling

Pleasant activity scheduling is a surprisingly effective Cognitive Behavioral Therapy technique. It's particularly helpful for depression.

Try this: write the next seven days down on a piece of paper, starting with today. For each day, schedule one pleasant activity (anything you enjoy that is not unhealthy) that you wouldn't normally do. It could be as simple as reading a chapter of a novel or eating your lunch away from your desk without rushing.

An alternative version of this technique is to also schedule an activity a day that gives you a sense of mastery, competence, or accomplishment. Again, choose something small that you wouldn't usually do. Aim for something that will take you less than ten minutes.

An advanced version of this technique would be to schedule three pleasant activities per day - one for sometime during your morning, one for the afternoon, and one for evening.

Doing activities that produce higher levels of positive emotions in your daily life will help make your thinking less negative, narrow, rigid, and self-focused.

Situation Exposure Hierarchies

Situation exposure hierarchies involve putting things you would normally avoid on a list. For example, a client with an eating disorder might make a list of forbidden foods, with ice cream at the top of the list and full fat yogurt near the bottom. A client with social anxiety might put asking someone on a date at the top of her list and asking a woman for directions near the bottom of her list. For each item on your list, rate how distressed you think you'd be if you did it. Use a scale from 0-10. For example, ice-cream = 10, full fat yogurt = 2. Order your list from highest to lowest. The theme of the list should reflect your problem.

Try to have several items at each distress number so there are no big jumps. The idea is to work your way through the list from lowest to highest. You would likely experiment with each item several times over a period of a few days until the distress you feel about being in that situation is about half of what it was the first time you tried it (e.g., you can eat full fat yogurt with only 1/10 distress instead of 2/10). Then move to the next item up the list.

Imagery Based Exposure

One version of imagery exposure involves bringing to mind a recent memory that provoked strong negative emotions. Imagery based exposure can help counteract rumination because it helps make intrusive painful memories less likely to trigger overthinking mechanisms. Because of this, it also tends to help reduce avoidance coping. When a person is less distressed by intrusive memories, they're able to choose healthier coping actions.

Cognitive Rehearsal

In this technique, the patient is asked to recall a problematic situation from his/her past. The therapist and patient work on the problem to find a solution for it. The therapist asks the patient to rehearse positive thoughts in his/her mind; rehearsing positive thoughts helps in making appropriate changes to the patient's thought processes. The power of imagination proves to be of great help when you are doing such type of exercises.

Validity Testing

Validity of thoughts of the patient are tested by the therapist; the patient is allowed to defend his/her viewpoint with the help of an objective evidence. The faulty nature or invalidity of beliefs held by the patient is exposed if he/she is unable to produce any kind of objective evidence.

Guided Discovery

The purpose behind using this technique is to help patients understand their cognitive distortions. Patients are offered the necessary assistance and guidance by therapists to understand how they process information. It allows patients to alter the way they process of information. Upon completion of this treatment, the patient's perception of the world undergoes a profound change and he/she starts seeing things with a new outlook. A change in perception enables the patient to modify his/her behavioral patterns.

Modeling

This is one of the important cognitive behavioral therapy techniques wherein therapists perform role-playing exercises. These cognitive behavioral therapy exercises teach patients how to respond in difficult situations. The patient sees the behavior of the therapist as a model to overcome his/her own behavioral problems.

Homework

'Homework' is actually a set of assignments to be completed by patients. During their sessions with therapists, the patients are asked to take down notes, review audiotapes of these sessions and read books related to this therapy.

Aversive Conditioning

In this technique, the appeal of maladaptive behavior is lessened with the help of 'dissuasion'. The patient is exposed to an unpleasant stimulus while he/she is engaged in a particular behavior for which treatment is needed. The end result of this exercise is that the patient learns to associates the unpleasant stimulus with the maladaptive behavior in question; he/she becomes averse to behaving in such a manner.

Systematic Positive Reinforcement

A technique in which a certain kind of behavior (positive) is rewarded with positive reinforcement. A reward system is used to reinforce the importance of positive behavior in the minds of patients.

Cognitive Behavioral Therapy for Depression

CBT is one of the effective therapies used for treating mild depression. This therapy is considered to be as effective as treatment with antidepressant medication. CBT is known to deliver good results in adults as well as adolescents. This kind of treatment can be most effective when the patient is motivated enough to overcome his/her behavioral problems.

CBT for Children

Cognitive behavioral therapy for children requires the therapist to play an active role in the treatment. This is because children are not capable of labeling or describing their thoughts and feelings as accurately as adults do. Therefore, the therapist has to perform the crucial job of extracting necessary information about the child's thoughts and behavioral patterns. It is also important that CBT sessions for children are completed in a short span of time.

Structured Format of CBT

The structured model of CBT makes this therapy more effective than most other psychotherapy techniques. CBT is basically a time-bound therapy during which the client (patient) has to attend sessions with a therapist. The patient has to do some homework before attending the next; which means, he/she is required to actively participating in the whole process.

The cognitive behavioral therapy techniques help in solving many problems that occur from maladaptive thoughts and behavioral patterns. Therapists and patients (clients) make use of the above-mentioned techniques to cure most of the psychological problems in a time-bound and effective manner.

LEARNING TO ANCHOR
THE POSITIVE CHANGES

For most people procrastination, irrespective of what they say, is NOT about being lazy. In fact, when we procrastinate we often work intensely for long stretches of time just before our deadlines. Working long and hard is the opposite of lazy, so that can't be the reason we do it. So, why do we procrastinate? And, more importantly, what can we do about it?

As suggested above, some say they procrastinate because they are lazy. Others claim they "do better" when they procrastinate and "work best" under pressure.

Virtually everyone who says this habitually procrastinates and has not completed an important academic task in which they made a plan, implemented it, had time to review, etc. before their deadline. So, in reality, they can't make a comparison about the circumstances they work best under. If you always procrastinate and never really approach your tasks systematically, then you can't accurately say that you know you "do better" under pressure. Still, other people say they like the "rush" of leaving things to the end and meeting a deadline

Procrastination is not a matter of solely having poor time management skills, but rather can be traced to underlying and more complex psychological reasons. These dynamics are often made worse by schools where students are constantly being evaluated, and especially in college where the pressure for grades is high and a lot can be riding on students' performance. In reality, procrastination is often a self-protection strategy for students. For example, if you procrastinate, then you always have the excuse of "not having enough" time in the event that you fail, so your sense of your ability is never threatened. When there is so much pressure on getting a good grade, it's no wonder that students want to avoid it and put off their work. For the most part, our reasons for delaying and avoiding are rooted in fear and anxiety-about doing poorly. We avoid doing work to avoid our abilities being judged. And, if we happen to succeed, we feel that much "smarter." So, what can we do to overcome our tendencies to procrastinate?

Awareness: The First Step

To overcome procrastination you need to have an understanding of the reasons why you procrastinate and the function procrastination serves in your life. You can't come up with an effective solution if you don't really understand the root of the problem. As with most problems, awareness and self-knowledge are the keys to figuring out how to stop procrastinating.

Time Management Techniques: One Piece of the Puzzle

To overcome procrastination, time management techniques and tools are indispensable, but they are not enough by themselves. Not all methods of managing time are equally helpful in dealing with procrastination. For instance, making a huge list of things to do or scheduling every minute of your day may increase your stress and thus procrastination. Instead, set reasonable goals (e.g. a manageable list of things to do), break big tasks down, and give yourself flexibility and allot time to do things you enjoy as rewards for the work you have completed.

Motivation: Finding Productive Reasons for Engaging in Tasks

To overcome procrastination, it's critical that you stay motivated in order to be productive. A good way to put positive motives in motion is to set and focus on your goals. Identify and write down your own personal reasons for enrolling in a course and monitor your progress toward your goals using a goal-setting chart. Remember to focus on your reasons and your goals.

Staying Motivated: Be Active to be Engaged

Another key to overcoming procrastination is to stay actively engaged in your classes. If you are passive in class you're probably not understanding the course and its topics, and that weakens your motivation. If you are passive, you are probably not making as much sense out of the course and course materials as you could. Nonsense and confusion are not engaging; in fact, they are boring and frustrating. Prevent that by aiming to really understand course material. Try seeking out what is interesting and relevant to you in the course materials, setting your own purpose for every reading and class session, and asking yourself (and others) questions about what you are learning.

Summary of Tips for Overcoming Procrastination

Awareness: Reflect on the reasons why you procrastinate, your habits and thoughts that lead to procrastinating.

Assess: What feelings lead to procrastinating, and how does it make you feel? Are these positive, productive feelings? Do you want to change them?

Outlook: Alter your perspective. Looking at a big task in terms of smaller pieces makes it less intimidating. Look for what's appealing about, or what you want to get out of, an assignment (beyond just the grade).

Commit: If you feel stuck, start simply by committing to complete a small task, any task, and write it down. Finish it and reward yourself. Write down on your schedule or to do list only what you can completely commit to, and if you write it down, follow through no matter what. By doing so, you will slowly rebuild trust in yourself that you will really do what you say you will, which so many procrastinators have lost.

Surroundings: When doing school work, choose wisely where and with whom you are working. Repeatedly placing yourself in situations where you don't get much done, such as studying in your bed, at a cafe or with friends, can actually be a method of avoiding work.

Goals: Focus on what you want to do, not what you want to avoid. Think about the productive reasons for doing a task by setting positive, concrete, meaningful learning and achievement goals for yourself.

Be realistic: Achieving goals and changing habits takes time and effort; don't sabotage yourself by having unrealistic expectations that you cannot meet.

Self-talk: Notice how you are thinking, and talking to yourself. Talk to yourself in ways that remind you of your goals and replace old, counter-productive habits of self-talk. Instead of saying, "I wish I hadn't... " say, "I will ..."

Un-schedule: If you feel stuck, you probably won't use a schedule that is a constant reminder of all that you have to do and is all work and no play. So, make a largely unstructured, flexible schedule in which you slot in only what is necessary. Keep track of any time you spend working toward your goals and reward yourself for it. This can reduce feelings of being overwhelmed and increase satisfaction in what you get done.

Swiss Cheese It: Breaking down big tasks into little ones is a good approach. A variation on this is devoting short chunks of time to a big task and doing as much as you can in that time with few expectations about what you will get done. For example, try spending about ten minutes just jotting down ideas that come to mind on the topic of a paper, or skimming over a long reading to get just the main ideas. After doing this several times on a big task, you will have made some progress on it, you'll have some momentum, you'll have less work to do to complete the task, and it won't seem so huge because you've punched holes in it (like Swiss cheese). In short, it'll be easier to complete the task because you've gotten started and removed some of the obstacles to finishing.

HOW TO OVERCOME NEGATIVE BELIEFS

People's emotional reactions and behaviour are strongly influenced by core beliefs. Core beliefs are essential part of the individual's cognition. Cognition comprises thoughts, beliefs and interpretations about the self or the situations. In other words, one's cognition is the meaning one gives to the events of his/her life.

Different cognitions generate different emotions

If we ask people what has made them sad (or happy, or angry) they often give us accounts of events or situations. If an event automatically gave rise to an emotion in such a straightforward way, then it would follow that the same event would have to result in the same emotion for anyone who experienced that event. What we see actually is that to a greater or lesser degree, people react differently to similar events. Even events such as suffering bereavement, or being diagnosed with an inoperable stage of cancer, which are obviously terrible, do not produce the same emotional state in everyone. Some may completely be crushed by such events, while others cope reasonably well. When two people react differently to an event it is because they are seeing it differently.

Different levels of cognitive processes

Cognition has different levels. Some cognitive processes are in the consciousness and we are aware of them. Negative thinking and negative thoughts automatically generated when an incident occurs are in the uppermost level.

Core beliefs

Core beliefs represent the bottom line of a person's mind. These are the fundamental beliefs about oneself, other people and the world in general. Characteristics of core beliefs are:

1. They are not immediately accessible to consciousness. They may have to be inferred by observation of one's characteristic thoughts and behaviours in many different situations.

2. They manifest as general and absolute statements. (E. g. I am bad. Others are not to be trusted.)

3. Unlike negative automatic thoughts, core belief do not vary much across times or situations, but are seen by the person as fundamental truths that apply in all situations.

4. They are usually learned early in life as a result of childhood experiences, but they may sometimes develop or change later in life, e.g., as a result of severe traumatic experience.

Change your core beliefs to avoid stress and prevent psychological disorders

Psychological disorders like generalized anxiety disorder, panic disorder, depression, phobias, and obsessive compulsive disorder spring from the negative core beliefs. Changing negative core beliefs helps the individual to deal with their psychological disorders. The first step in changing a core belief is to identify it. When you do a thorough job of identifying the core beliefs, you are more than halfway to changing them. This task can be a little challenging in the beginning, but gets easier with practice.

How to identify the core belief?

Identifying a core belief is like solving a mystery of the illusions in your mind. You have to follow some clues to get down to the hidden beliefs in the unconscious. Let's use the example of fear of public speaking. Fear of public speaking is an emotional reaction to a belief. The underlying thought a person has is that, "They will think I'm stupid." This is the fear, but not the belief. Fears associated with what other people think of us are very common. This same thought can occur in the mind when asking for what we want.

However the thought is not a core belief. One has to be careful here because they are often misleading. When finding core beliefs you follow the emotion. We have to keep asking how the emotion of fear is created by the act of what someone else thinks.

If someone pointed at your hair, claimed it was green, and then started to laugh out loud at how silly you looked would you feel hurt? Probably not. You know the issue is with their perception and not with you. Having someone make fun of you and laugh at you when you know it is their perception is not a problem for you. What people think of you doesn't hurt you at all.

When you don't believe you look foolish you are not affected by what others think. Being aware that their mental image of you is not actual you, gives you immunity to their opinion. With this understanding, it is obvious that one cannot be hurt emotionally by what others think and say about him/her.

Steps to Changing Core Beliefs

When you fully identify a set of beliefs, you instinctively divest your belief in them. This shift happens just through your expanded awareness. Just by identifying your beliefs, you facilitate change in your emotions and behavior without a lot of work.

Changing a core belief is surprisingly easy. You simply stop believing in them. It doesn't take much effort to not believe something. However, it does take some effort to develop the awareness to identify them.

It sounds simple, but does require some work. There is also one very important step in the process that is often missed. You have to change your point of view in order to change a core belief. Where you shift your point of view in your mind is critically important. Certain points of view will make it easy to dissolve a core belief and others will stop the process.

Changing Core Beliefs by Shifting Point of View

An easier way to change a belief is through shifting point of view. A new perspective allows you to have awareness that changes the way you see things.

Without this shift in perspective, it is very difficult to change a belief. When you are within the paradigm of a false belief, it appears completely true thus you continue to believe in it.

A belief paradigm acts very much like a dream when you are asleep. When you are in a dream, it seems completely real. You believe what is happening in the dream is really happening to you. You might feel like your life is in danger and feel the corresponding emotions of fear, but when you wake up from the dream, you begin looking at it from the perspective of sitting up in your bed in an awakened state. With that shift in point of view, you immediately drop your fear and the notion that you are in danger. Changing your point of view in this way allows you to quickly change beliefs. This kind of paradigm shift is very powerful. Numerous people have had near death experiences that completely dissolved their fears of death and dying. Real life change involves changing core beliefs. One of the fastest ways to change core beliefs is by shifting your point of view.

Keeping a thought diary helps to identify negative core beliefs

Following this guideline for writing a thought diary:

1. *The situation:* Briefly describe the situation you would like to have handled better. This will help you remember it later if you want to review your notes.

2. *Initial thought:* What thought first popped into your mind? This was probably a subconscious or automatic thought that you have had before.

3. *Negative thinking:* Identify the negative thinking behind your initial thought. Choose one or more from the list of common types of negative thinking.

4. *Source of negative belief:* Can you trace your thinking back to a situation or person? Is there a deep belief or fear driving your thinking?

5. *Challenge your thinking:* Look at the evidence both for and against your thinking. Have you been in a similar situation before? What did you learn from it? What strengths do you bring to this situation? Make sure you see the whole picture.

6. *Consider the consequences:* What are the short-term and long-term consequences if you continue to think like this? Look at the physical, psychological, professional, and emotional consequences.

7. *Alternative thinking:* The previous steps of the thought record helped you understand your thinking and lower your defenses. Now that you've considered the facts, write down a healthier way of thinking.

8. *Positive belief and affirmation:* Write down a statement that reflects your healthier beliefs. Find something that you can repeat to yourself.

9. *Action plan:* What action can you take to support your new thinking?

10. *Improvement:* Do you feel slightly better or more optimistic? This step reinforces the idea that if you change your thinking, you will change your mood. Gradually, your thinking and life will begin to improve.

If you write a thought record every day for a few weeks, you will begin to change your thinking. You'll spot your negative thinking quickly and let it go. You will come up with better alternatives. You will practice your healthier way of thinking and incorporate it into your life.

A Negative Thought as a Flame

Visualize a negative thought as a flame. A flame burning in an empty concrete parking lot cannot do much damage. These fires are left to burn out on its own or easily extinguished.

Put that flame in a closed room filled with combustible material, and you have a potential disaster on your hands.

Unless quickly extinguished, the fire will use every piece of flammable material in that room to burn hotter, longer and faster. Left uninterrupted, that single flame will become an inextinguishable inferno that will burn until it has nothing left to fuel its flames.

People experience a similar situation when they are a host for so much negativity. By the time it finally runs its course, all the anger, frustration, and blame has destroyed a person from mental, physical and spiritual exhaustion.

Recognizing the triggers

In order to avoid a negative spin, you need to recognize the triggers that set off the cycle and the environments that make you more susceptible to these triggers.

Being in a positive state of mind or in a secure and nurturing environment allows for a measure of protection from a negative cycle.

Add another layer of defence by being mindful of your work environment, the type of career you choose and the interactions you have with people.

Weakening Triggers

Create an inventory of positive truths about yourself and your life. It takes a little bit of effort to remember the positive aspects of your life, but it is well worth the work.

Disarming triggers requires that you counter any negative thought with a relevant and equally powerful positive truth.

For example, if you think "Everyone hates me, I'm unlovable", you can counteract this thought by thinking, "My wife and children love me and they are always happy to see me when I come home." Extinguish the negative thought as quickly as it arises.

Be truthful and celebrate the good in your life. Take five minutes every night to write down all your successes, positive qualities and the things that make you happy. This creates a natural defence against negativity.

Disrupting the cycle by disrupting the pattern

There are going to be times when you are unable to recognize a trigger because you are in a weak mental state.

For example, you go to sleep in a positive state of mind and then unexpectedly wake up angry and grumpy. In these scenarios, breaking a negative cycle with positive thoughts is hard, if not impossible, to do.

In cases like this, starve yourself of any additional negative energy that might strengthen your state of mind. This requires you to break any established patterns.

If the usual routine includes having a coffee and reading a newspaper, then you have to catch your mind off guard and go straight to the shower.

FEAR IN THE BRAIN

Fear may be as old as life on Earth. It is a fundamental, deeply wired reaction, evolved over the history of biology, to protect organisms against perceived threat to their integrity or existence. Fear may be as simple as a cringe of an antenna in a snail that is touched, or as complex as existential anxiety in a human.

Whether we love or hate to experience fear, it's hard to deny that we certainly revere it – devoting an entire holiday to the celebration of fear.

Thinking about the circuitry of the brain and human psychology, some of the main chemicals that contribute to the "fight or flight" response are also involved in other positive emotional states, such as happiness and excitement. So, it makes sense that the high arousal state we experience during a scare may also be experienced in a more positive light. But what makes the difference between getting a "rush" and feeling completely terrorized?

We are psychiatrists who treat fear and study its neurobiology. Our studies and clinical interactions, as well as those of others, suggest that a major factor in how we experience fear has to do with the context. When our "thinking" brain gives feedback to our "emotional" brain and we perceive ourselves as being in a safe space, we can then quickly shift the way we experience that high arousal state, going from one of fear to one of enjoyment or excitement.

When you enter a haunted house during Halloween season, for example, anticipating a ghoul jumping out at you and knowing it isn't really a threat, you are able to quickly relabel the experience. In contrast, if you were walking in a dark alley at night and a stranger began chasing you, both your emotional and thinking areas of the brain would be in agreement that the situation is dangerous, and it's time to flee!

But how does your brain do this?

Fear reaction starts in the brain and spreads through the body to make adjustments for the best defense, or flight reaction. The fear response starts in a region of the brain called the amygdala. This almond-shaped set of nuclei in the temporal lobe of the brain is dedicated to detecting the emotional salience of the stimuli – how much something stands out to us.

For example, the amygdala activates whenever we see a human face with an emotion. This reaction is more pronounced with anger and fear. A threat stimulus, such as the sight of a predator, triggers a fear response in the amygdala, which activates areas involved in preparation for motor functions involved in fight or flight. It also triggers release of stress hormones and sympathetic nervous system.

This leads to bodily changes that prepare us to be more efficient in a danger: The brain becomes hyperalert, pupils dilate, the bronchi dilate and breathing accelerates. Heart rate and blood pressure rise. Blood flow and stream of glucose to the skeletal muscles increase. Organs not vital in survival such as the gastrointestinal system slow down.

A part of the brain called the hippocampus is closely connected with the amygdala. The hippocampus and prefrontal cortex help the brain interpret the perceived threat. They are involved in a higher-level processing of context, which helps a person know whether a perceived threat is real.

For instance, seeing a lion in the wild can trigger a strong fear reaction, but the response to a view of the same lion at a zoo is more of curiosity and thinking that the lion is cute. This is because the hippocampus and the frontal cortex process contextual information, and inhibitory pathways dampen the amygdala fear response and its downstream results. Basically, our "thinking" circuitry of brain reassures our "emotional" areas that we are, in fact, OK.

Similar to other animals, we very often learn fear through personal experiences, such as being attacked by an aggressive dog, or observing other humans being attacked by an aggressive dog.

However, an evolutionarily unique and fascinating way of learning in humans is through instruction – we learn from the spoken words or written notes! If a sign says the dog is dangerous, proximity to the dog will trigger a fear response.

We learn safety in a similar fashion: experiencing a domesticated dog, observing other people safely interact with that dog or reading a sign that the dog is friendly.

Fear creates distraction, which can be a positive experience. When something scary happens, in that moment, we are on high alert and not preoccupied with other things that might be on our mind (getting in trouble at work, worrying about a big test the next day), which brings us to the here and now.

Furthermore, when we experience these frightening things with the people in our lives, we often find that emotions can be contagious in a positive way. We are social creatures, able to learn from one another. So, when you look over to your friend at the haunted house and she's quickly gone from screaming to laughing, socially you're able to pick up on her emotional state, which can positively influence your own.

While each of these factors - context, distraction, social learning - have potential to influence the way we experience fear, a common theme that connects all of them is our sense of control. When we are able to recognize what is and isn't a real threat, relabel an experience and enjoy the thrill of that moment, we are ultimately at a place where we feel in control. That perception of control is vital to how we experience and respond to fear. When we overcome the initial "fight or flight" rush, we are often left feeling satisfied, reassured of our safety and more confident in our ability to confront the things that initially scared us.

It is important to keep in mind that everyone is different, with a unique sense of what we find scary or enjoyable. This raises yet another question: While many can enjoy a good fright, why might others downright hate it?

Any imbalance between excitement caused by fear in the animal brain and the sense of control in the contextual human brain may cause too much, or not enough, excitement. If the individual perceives the experience as "too real," an extreme fear response can overcome the sense of control over the situation.

This may happen even in those who do love scary experiences: They may enjoy Freddy Krueger movies but be too terrified by "The Exorcist," as it feels too real, and fear response is not modulated by the cortical brain.

On the other hand, if the experience is not triggering enough to the emotional brain, or if is too unreal to the thinking cognitive brain, the experience can end up feeling boring. A biologist who cannot tune down her cognitive brain from analyzing all the bodily things that are realistically impossible in a zombie movie may not be able to enjoy "The Walking Dead" as much as another person.

So if the emotional brain is too terrified and the cognitive brain helpless, or if the emotional brain is bored and the cognitive brain is too suppressing, scary movies and experiences may not be as fun.

All fun aside, abnormal levels of fear and anxiety can lead to significant distress and dysfunction and limit a person's ability for success and joy of life. Nearly one in four people experiences a form of anxiety disorder during their lives, and nearly 8 percent experience post-traumatic stress disorder (PTSD).

Disorders of anxiety and fear include phobias, social phobia, generalized anxiety disorder, separation anxiety, PTSD and obsessive compulsive disorder. These conditions usually begin at a young age, and without appropriate treatment can become chronic and debilitating and affect a person's life trajectory. The good news is that we have effective treatments that work in a relatively short time period, in the form of psychotherapy and medications.

Surefire ways to get rid of bad habits

Success, happiness and good health often elude us not because we lack good habits but because we have bad habits. Sometimes they are habits like procrastination or mindless spending. But at other times they can be addictions like smoking and gambling.

Knowing how our bad habits negatively influence our lives is rarely enough to break them. For example, all smokers are aware of the health consequences of smoking. Diseased lungs are displayed prominently in every cigarette pack. There would be no smokers in the world today if that worked.

This fails to work because we don't do our bad habits for the reasons we should not do them. No smoker has ever smoked a cigarette to get cancer. Students don't procrastinate to fail. So in order to break our bad habits, we must first remove the reason why we do them. In other words, we need to eliminate the desire to do the habit.

Once the desire is gone, it takes no willpower to break bad habits, just as it doesn't take willpower to not do things we have no desire to do. It doesn't take much effort to stop yourself from eating live frogs because you have no desire to do it. Breaking your bad habits can be just as effortless. You just need the right belief and the right system.

Our Habits Controls Us

From the outside, it would seem that our bad habits is a matter of choice. Smokers, for example, do make the choice of trying their first cigarette. But no smoker has ever made a decision that they will keep smoking for the rest of their lives. We often fall into the trap thinking we can stop whenever we want, only to realize that we no longer have any control. When we watch the first episode of a TV show, we end up binge watching multiple seasons at a stretch because we cannot stop ourselves. Every addict wishes inside that he had never started because life was fine before their addiction but now they are hooked and cannot enjoy life without satisfying their craving.

Researchers from National Institute on Alcohol Abuse and Alcoholism trained rats to press a lever to get a piece food. The researchers later electrified the floor so that when the rat walked to get the food, it received a shock. In a different experimental setting, the rat recognized the danger in the electric floor and would avoid it. But when the rat saw the lever, the habits took over and the rat would press the lever and go for the food and get electrocuted every time. The rat could not stop itself in spite of being aware of the danger because the habits were so strong.

Similarly, dieters find it hard to resist junk, smokers struggle to quit and students procrastinate on their assignments in spite of being aware of the consequences it has on their lives. Strong habits create an obsessive craving which makes our brain behave on autopilot even if there are strong disincentives like loss of job, health, reputation, family or home.

When We Use Willpower to quit, We Fail

We usually try to break bad habits using willpower, which makes us feel we are making a sacrifice. A Harvard study showed the 12 month success rates of people who used the willpower method to quit smoking with no education or support was 6%.

When using willpower to quit, we find life extremely unpleasant and difficult and have to be cautious all the time to prevent relapse. This is because the desire to do the habit always remains inside us.

10% of former smokers who abstained from smoking for ten years showed ongoing cravings even years later. Mere abstinence does not mean we have broken our habit. It just means we don't allow ourselves to do our habit. A person who does not drink alcohol but who is constantly thinking about alcohol is not a non-alcoholic but is an alcoholic who does not let himself drink.

We see the benefits of breaking our habits but also believe it provides us with something which we are now depriving ourselves of. This makes us miserable, vulnerable and increases desire that begins to obsess us. We try to overcome this by not thinking about our craving but that only makes us more obsessed.

Believing our problems can be easily solved by doing our bad habits we begin to question our decision to break our bad habits. Finally, we accept defeat and cave in. This minor relapse makes us feel bad and we indulge in the very same habit that made us feel bad, to feel better.

We fail to break our bad habits not because we lack willpower but because we don't eliminate desire. Without desire, willpower is not required to stop, just as it doesn't take willpower to not do the things we have no desire to do.

Why Does Our Brain Form Habits If They Are Bad?

Habits is a way for the brain to save effort by making rewarding behaviour automatic. Without habits, you will have to relearn how to brush your teeth every morning. Habits are useful but the problem is our brain cannot tell the difference between good and bad habits. Behavior that gives us short-term rewards often becomes habits, even if they cause long-term harm. Overeating, procrastinating and smoking becomes habit easily because the rewards are instant and the pain comes later. Developing the habit of exercising is harder because the reward comes later.

Schultz from the University of Cambridge, trained a monkey named Julio to pull a lever when a shape appeared on computer screen. Pulling the lever gave Julio a drop of blackberry juice which made the pleasure centres of his brain light up. When his brain started craving for the juice, Julio was glued to the monitor like a gambler in a slot machine. If the juice arrived late or diluted, this craving would turn into anger & depression.

Charles Duhigg's book, "The Power of Habit" focuses on the 3 components of a habit. The first component is the trigger, which tells the brain to start doing a particular behaviour (shapes in Julio's monitor). The second component is the behaviour that is done (Julio pulling the lever). The third part is the reward for doing the behaviour (Julio's blackberry juice). The habit is formed when the brain starts to crave for the reward as soon as the brain sees the trigger. There is nothing programmed in our brains that makes us want to overeat or smoke. But over time we slowly develop a neurological craving for these things.

Break The Habit By Seeing The Reward As An Illusion

The first step to breaking your bad habit is identifying the reward.

What do you really get doing your habit?

If the rewards you think your habits provided were actually real, then you can break your bad habits, simply by switching your existing habit with a healthier behavior that provided the same reward. For example, if you eat junk at work for distraction, then you can break your habit simply by replacing eating junk with a healthier distraction that does not add to your waistline. This is the premise of the book "The Power of Habit" and this works well for weaker habits. But try telling a smoker to resist his urge for smoking when he is bored by entertaining himself on YouTube. He won't be a successful non-smoker for very long. This is because most rewards of our habits are illusions.

We often rationalize why we do our bad habits but all the reasons we use to justify our behaviour are an illusion, excuses, fallacies or based on myth. For example, smokers believe they need cigarettes to relax, relieve stress, to concentrate or to relieve boredom. But cigarettes do not give them any of this. If it did, they should be a lot more relaxed, focused and less bored than non-smokers.

Most of us brainwash ourselves in a certain way that keeps us doing our bad habits. Only by identifying what we think is the reward can we address and remove the myths we have about the reward. When we begin to see through the illusory rewards, we eliminate desire by realizing that there is nothing to give up.

What We Give Up When We Break Bad Habits?

What are we giving up when we break our bad habits? Well, most of the time you are giving up absolutely nothing.

We don't do our bad habits for pleasure. We do it to feel normal. This feels like pleasure. A drug addict feels miserable, anxious, stressed and angry when he is deprived of his drug. When he shoots up his drug, he gets relief from all the negative symptoms. The subsequent dose partially relieves the symptoms but also ensures that the addict goes through withdrawal again. This keeps the addict stuck in the vicious habit loop. Normal people do not experience the symptoms of the drug addict. When we look at this it is obvious to us that the symptoms the drug addict experiences are caused by the drug, not removed by it. But we fail to have the same understanding when it comes to our bad habits.

Our bad habits cause symptoms of craving that normal people don't experience. We do our bad habits to partially relieve the symptoms but it only keeps us stuck in the vicious habit loop ensuring we experience the symptoms of craving again.

Unlike drug addiction which might require a visit to rehab, the craving caused by most bad habits including alcohol and smoking can be killed immediately when the belief system is changed. If you are not entirely convinced that there is nothing to give up, you need to examine the rewards of your bad habits and see them for what they really are. Otherwise, you will feel craving and will have to use willpower to prevent relapse.

The 4 Illusory Rewards

If you think your habit provides any of the following 4 rewards, you probably have an illusory reward:

1. Relieves stress

2. Relieves boredom

3. Improves concentration

4. Relieves anxiety and gives confidence

We will address the common myths people have about each of these rewards which will help dispel the illusion.

Reward 1 - Relief From Stress & Relaxation

For many, habits provide relaxation and relief from stress. We all have several things stressing us out. Not just big tragedies but relatively minor things like work deadlines. We do our bad habits to relieve this stress and the stress does seem to go away. But what has really happened?

Apart from the environmental stress, we experience additional stress because of the aggravation caused by craving. Bad habits relieve this portion of stress it created through craving. But our real-world stress like work deadlines continues to exist. When we do our habits we feel better able to cope with this stress because we temporarily don't have the additional stress caused by the craving to deal with.

A study has shown that we fall back into our habits when we are stressed because we feel less anxiety and more in control when we do our habits. People who have been sober for years relapse when a major life catastrophe happens like a death of a loved one or divorce. This is because of a failure to understand that alcohol does not relieve stress but only adds to the problem.

The habits that we fall back on during times of stress need not be bad. In a study, students who habitually ate a healthy breakfast continued to eat healthy during the stressful period of their exams. Whereas students who gained extra weight during their exams had a habit of eating unhealthy. Consciously engineering your habits is important so that your habits make you better and not worse during times of stress.

Reward 2 - Relief From Boredom

Some people do their habit because they are bored. Boredom is a frame of mind and not a physical condition that can be cured. Initially, we are bored. Now we are bored and engaged in self-destructive behaviour. Our bad habits do not cure boredom. It just creates a temporary distraction that allows us to forget that we are bored.

If our bad habits did relieve boredom, then why do we have to engage in it multiple times or do it for longer periods at a stretch?

Most bad habits rob us of our energy and make us more lethargic, putting us in a state of mind where we cannot do anything else. Instead of doing something when bored like how a normal person would, we lounge around, do our bad habit and feel more bored.

If you know someone who plays excessive video games or who spends hours in front of the TV, you will see they are not any less bored. They will be extremely tired and will feel like shit for wasting so much time.

Reward 3 - Helps Concentration & Removes Mental Block

If you think your bad habits removes mental blocks and improves concentration, then you are not alone. Some of the greatest artists of the world including Van Gogh and Beethoven were addicts. But curing addiction does not lower creativity because your genes do not change. It is just your craving that goes away. So what really happens?

A study done on 96 undergraduates showed a reduction in the student's ability to do tasks that required visuospatial memory, when they experienced craving for chocolate. In other words, craving negatively affected the student's ability to remember.

Our bad habits cause craving which creates a distraction that makes it difficult to concentrate. When we need to concentrate we do our habits to eliminate the distraction caused by our craving. We give credit to our bad habits for helping us concentrate when it was responsible for the distraction to begin with. People without bad habits will not have problems with concentration because they don't experience the craving.

Over time people who believe that their bad habits help them concentrate begin to believe that it removes mental blocks. After you do your bad habits, your block will still exist, but only now you will get the job done just like how anybody would have done it. But your bad habits get the credit for helping you get the work done.

Your bad habits provide no mental performance advantage and believing it does is based on fallacy and myth.

Reward 4 - Confidence & Anxiety Relief

We acknowledge the relief provided by our bad habit as it removes the small amount of emptiness and insecurity. But we don't acknowledge that this emptiness and insecurity are the symptoms of our bad habits in the first placek.

People who have had their bad habits for many decades have been in a perpetual state of anxiety and emptiness so their bad habits seem to be the only way to get confidence and a relief from this feeling. Our bad habits do not relieve the anxiety in our lives, it causes it. People without bad habits never feel this insecurity or anxiety, to begin with.

Freedom from the self-loathing and dependency is one of the biggest positive changes people see in their lives when they break their habits. They are more relaxed and confident after breaking their bad habits and are better able to deal with their anxieties if it is not gone altogether.

Relief From Craving is The Only Reward

Craving and withdrawal can make you insecure, irritable, anxious or agitated. Though there is no physical pain, it causes mental agony giving us a feeling that something is not right. For example, smokers believe that withdrawal is a physical trauma caused by not satisfying their craving. But eight hours after putting out the last cigarette, a smoker is 97% nicotine-free. This happens every night during sleep. Only during the day does he feel the need to smoke every hour to fix his craving. After three days of not smoking, a smoker is 100% nicotine-free. Yet smokers relapse because of craving after months of abstinence. The truth is withdrawal and craving is almost always psychological even for smokers & alcoholics.

We associate our bad habits with pleasure because we see them satisfy our craving, but don't see them causing it. Our craving is not cured by our bad habits but is caused by it.

We might have started doing our bad habits for many reasons, but the only reason why we keeping doing them is to feed the craving. Every time we do our habit, the craving is satisfied temporarily. This provides a temporary relief, putting us in a normal state of mind. But by doing our habit, we have set ourselves up to experience craving again in the future. The more we feed our craving, the more it takes to satisfy it. Smokers go from one cigarette to chain smoking fairly quickly.

What we really enjoy is not our bad habits but the feeling we get when our craving is satisfied. It is like putting on tight shoes just for the pleasure of taking them off. This is why by breaking bad habits, you are giving up nothing.

Hidden Drivers of Bad Habits

Alcoholics Anonymous (AA) have a concept called dry drunk, where alcoholics stop drinking but still remain angry, selfish and narcissistic. Our bad habits are often symptoms of some inner conflict. Things like anger, shame, loneliness, fear and hopelessness that makes people start doing their bad habits, needs to be addressed first. Until the flawed beliefs are fixed, we will always remain vulnerable to relapse. The habit of procrastination, for example, can be fixed only temporarily, if the underlying fear of failure is left unaddressed.

Bad habits are a way for our sub-conscious mind to avoid the real inner conflict that exists inside us. The inner conflict is either a bitter truth ("I am ashamed of my past") or a distorted assumption ("I screw up everything" or "I am better than everybody"). This inner conflict is never a mystery but we make it a mystery because acknowledging the truth is uncomfortable. It is easier to think we have no choice or control over our lives than it is to take responsibility for fixing it.

The best way to fix inner conflicts is through therapy which works by bringing our inner conflict to light causing them to vaporize like a vampire. The next best way is service. Helping others has helped AA members reduce their desire to drink. A study of 195 addicted adolescents showed that treatment showed substantial improvement when it was accompanied by service. 10 This works because love neutralizes shame and service to others reduce obsession and craving by eliminating the inner conflict. Helpfulness may not help break bad habits by itself, but it addresses the internal conflicts that create craving.

The System To Break Bad Habits

Now that we have addressed the core beliefs and issues that make us do our bad habits, let us look at the step by step system to break bad habits. With this system, you will be able to break any habit easily and effortlessly without using willpower.

Helping Others Break Bad Habits

Do not patronize the person you are trying to help, by telling them why their habits are bad. They already know this and don't do their bad habits for the reasons they shouldn't do it. They do their bad habits to feel normal.

Do not tell them breaking bad habits is easy as it will only irritate them. Give them the support and praise to keep them moving forward.

Do not force them to break their bad habits. Even if they try, they will use willpower to quit and end up failing. Tell them that people who succeeded in breaking their habits did not use willpower but instead addressed their flawed beliefs. Tell them how their bad habits only remove their need to do the habit which is perceived as pleasure by the brain. But in reality, their bad habit do not give them anything.

When they start believing that they can break their bad habits, their mind will begin to open up and that is when they are ready to read this book. Mention that there is no pressure to break their bad habits. If they want to continue to do their bad habits after reading this book, they can.

Where To Go From Here

The key to making it easy to break bad habits is to make your decision final and certain. Don't worry whether or not you have broken your bad habit. Know that you have. Do not ever doubt your decision. Celebrate it. Withdrawal is entirely psychological and if you are sulking, it only means you have not addressed your belief systems yet. Revisit Steps 2 to 4 in the system.

Don't make the mistake of procrastinating and not applying what you have learnt. You can wait for as long as you want to break your bad habits but the right time will never come and your habits are not going to be any easier to break tomorrow.

Some people think their bad habits has not caused any problem yet, so it is not a big deal if they don't break their habits now. The best time to fix the roof is when it is not raining. Don't wait for things to go wrong before you fix your bad habits. Break your bad habits now.

OBSESSIVE-COMPULSIVE DISORDER

Obsessions are more than thoughts we keep coming back to. They are constant, overriding all other thoughts, they are often impulsive and are typically inappropriate, forbidden socially or simply disgusting. These obsessions create a high level of anxiety and are referred to as "ego-alien" and "ego-dystonic" because they are typically completely out of character for the person dealing with them. The person will not be able to control the thoughts and may leave with a high level of fear that the thoughts will translate into an actual loss of control with the thoughts or impulses being acted out. Many people who are suffering from OCD may have irrational fears of germs or body fluids, or they could suffer from constant doubts that they have forgotten or overlooked something. The obsession might also center on a desire for things to be placed in or done in a certain order. They can also involve a fear of losing control, or the constant battle against impulses that are violent or sexual in nature.

When people suffering with OCD are faced with these obsessions and thoughts, they engage in compulsions to help ease the anxiety. The compulsions are repetitive, comforting behaviors or mental processes. Compulsions can be obvious and clear behaviors; such as checking, repetitive hand washing, or some other behavior. They can also be mental acts that are less obvious such as praying, reciting or counting. Compulsive rituals can consume many hours a day for some people. The rituals can be complex, taking up several hours; or several hours can be consumed on the repetitive tasks.

Some people are more neat and tidier than others naturally but someone who suffers with obsessive compulsive disorder takes neatness to the next step, to an extreme degree. A sufferer will spend many hours tidying, cleaning, checking and re-checking that objects are in order etc. to the point of it interfering with their everyday lives.

An obsession is a recurring thought, idea or image that although not making a lot of sense will continue to intrude on your mind. An example may be the thought of leaving your door unlocked, you recognize this fear as irrational but you cannot get it out of your mind, hence you repeatedly check and re-check that the door is locked.

A compulsion is the ritual you perform to dismiss the anxiety which has been brought on by the obsession. An example would be washing your hands continuously to dismiss the fear of being unclean or contaminated. You fully realize this ritual to be unreasonable but feel compelled to carry it out to ward off the anxiety associated with the compulsion.

Obsessions can occur independently of compulsions, it is thought that around 25 percent of sufferers will only struggle with obsessions, so the fear is there but they do not feel compelled to carry out the ritual to free themselves of the anxiety.

The most common of compulsions would be the hand washing ritual. You would be continually concerned about avoiding any contamination so much so you avoid coming into contact with anything associated with dirt or germs, an example here would be shaking hands with someone or even touching a door handle. You could literally spend hours washing hands to reduce your anxiety about contamination. It is thought that women are more likely to be compulsive about cleanliness but men would outnumber women when it comes to checking and re-checking items, as in the example of repeatedly checking if a door is locked.

It is common for obsessive compulsive disorder to first set in with males when they are in their teens to early twenties, and for females when they are first entering adulthood. The course of the disease can vary; but people can expect that the symptoms will become worse during periods of great stress. Certain disorders are commonly co-morbid with OCD; including major depressive disorder and generalized anxiety disorders. Roughly twenty to thirty percent of those people undergoing clinical trial for obsessive compulsive disorders report that they have previously experienced tics and another one-third of people suffering from OCD also have Tourette's disorder. Among people with Tourette's disorder, up to fifty percent of them will develop some form of obsessive compulsive disorder.

Obsessive-compulsive disorder is more often than not accompanied by depression and in some cases can also develop into phobic avoidance, for example, a sufferer will completely avoid public restrooms.

Obsessive-compulsive behavior was at one time considered a rare disorder but recent studies have shown that four or five percent of the world's population may suffer to a degree with this disorder. It is important for anyone who has obsessive-compulsive disorder to realize it has nothing whatsoever to do with being crazy or having a form of madness. You recognize that what you are doing is irrational and you are very frustrated that you cannot control your thoughts and actions.

Studies have shown that about half of all obsessive-compulsive disorders actually begin in childhood with the majority of the remaining cases developing in early adult life, a fairly small number of cases will appear in later life.

Obsessive compulsive disorder is clearly a genetic disorder that shows a higher level of familial specificity than many other anxiety disorders. First-degree relatives who have Tourette's disorder have a greater chance of developing obsessive compulsive disorder. There are many mental disorders that can fall into the category of obsessive compulsive disorders such as trichotillomania (compulsive hair pulling), sexual behavior disorders, compulsive gambling and compulsive shoplifting. These other conditions are not as ritualistic as those commonly associated with obsessive compulsive disorder; however they do provide the same level of pleasure or gratification. Another disorder than can occur comorbidly with OCD is body dysmorphic disorder; with this disorder, the compulsive and obsessive behaviors will center very specifically around some feature of a person's appearance.

For some the thought of Obsessive Compulsive Disorder Symptoms may seem a little funny but for those suffering from the disease find the thoughts far from funny. It is reported that some 2.2 million people are diagnosed with this disorder every year. When you factor that some of these people have already suffered for a few years before seeking medical treatment their daily quality of life has suffered for some time with debilitating thoughts and crippling actions to their everyday routine. You may feel as though you are alone and that there is no one in the world that can help you, but I am here to tell you that there are thousands of people who have had OCD and beat it, including myself!

Obsessive Compulsive Disorder Symptoms - Elaboration On Various Symptoms Of OCD

Obsessive compulsive disorder (OCD) consists of two parts. If you want to understand the symptoms of obsessive compulsive disorder, you should have the full understanding of both parts. The first part of OCD contains obsession while, the second part consists of compulsions. Now, I will separately elaborate both of the parts.

1) Obsessions. Obsessions are ill thoughts of a person with particular characteristics. These thoughts are not normal thoughts rather they are unwanted, penetrating and appear again and again in one's mind. This is the part which relates to mind of a person and, no other person can see it. Only the sufferer knows about his obsessions while, others may know through his overt behavior or verbalizations. Whenever these thoughts strike one's mind, they produce anxiety such as, the thought that one's hands are dirty. Whenever, this thought will come into one's mind, person will start feeling that his hands are dirty, and should be washed.

2) Compulsions. Compulsions are the repetitive, fixed-pattern behaviors. A person feels drive to perform these behaviors. We have seen that when obsessions come into one's mind, they produce

anxiety. Thinking that one's hands are dirty, one gets anxious and feels compel to wash his hands in order to reduce that anxiety. Obsessions strike mind repeatedly, producing mental anxiety. As a consequence, person performs particular behaviors repeatedly to get rid of anxiety.

Sometimes, people are over conscious about certain things. For example, there may be a person who is over conscious about his hygiene. He may wash his hands several times during a day. Psychologists diagnose obsessive compulsive disorder when these symptoms take the form of ritualistic behavior and, start interfering in daily functioning of the person. A person with obsessive compulsive disorder may get one or two hours late from office because he was busy in washing his hands.

There are different types of obsession such as, concern with germs, dreadful happenings (death, fire), perfectionism, religious concerns, lucky or unlucky numbers, sexual and aggression impulses and counting things. Compulsions may include excessive handwashing and bathing, checking (doors, locks, emergency brakes), touching, ordering/arranging things again and again, counting, cleaning households and miscellaneous rituals (writing, speaking, moving) etc. people may suffer from one or more symptoms of obsessive compulsive disorder simultaneously. Sufferers know that their thoughts are ill, and their behaviors are inappropriate. In some of the cases, children leave their schools, because their obsession regarding cleanliness compels to leave the classroom and go for handwashing.

Generally, sufferers think that their ritualistic behavior (compulsions) will prevent them from obsessions. These compulsions reduce their mental anxiety for a brief period of time, but they keep on experiencing obsessions. Repetitive behaviors are observable in young normal children. Sometimes, it becomes difficult to distinguish between normal repetitive behavior and pure compulsive behavior. Usually it can be diagnosed when they grow older and, this is the time when their compulsions become firm.

There is some difference between onset of the disorder among males and females. Males develop this disorder at an average age of nine whereas; females develop at an average at of eleven years. Moreover, children are more affected by compulsion whether; adults experience obsessions and compulsions at an equal base. The reason behind this may be that children are less likely to verbalize their mental processes and thoughts. Whatever the case, one should be vigilant about symptoms of obsessive compulsive disorder because, once they become fixed, they are most difficult to eliminate.

Obsessive Compulsive Disorder Causes - Elaboration On Various Causes Of OCD

Understanding the precipitating factors or causes of obsessive compulsive disorder (OCD) is essential because this disorder is most difficult to manage once it strikes an individual. Sometimes, there are some causes of disorders that can be controlled before the onset of the disorder. It is equally important to understand the various causes of a disorder because; causes are not same for all the sufferers. Management may be different for the sufferer who has adopted disorder from his family whereas, different for the one who has developed the same disorder after facing stressful family circumstances.

Obsessive compulsive disorder occurs at an early age and sometimes it is not differentiated from normal ritualistic behavior of the children. The disorder becomes obdurate till the time it is diagnosed. For such kinds of disorders, it is preferable to locate the causes of disorder for the sake of prevention.

There are different precipitating factors of OCD, and I will discuss each of them, separately.

1) Biological/Physiological Causes. Firstly, in most of the cases of obsessive compulsive disorder, we can find biological basis of the disorder. Empirical data has shown that individuals with OCD have first degree relatives with the same disorder. The idea of the biological basis of the disorder is strengthened by the co-morbidity

of Tourette's syndrome and OCD which shows that the neurological factors which cause Tourette's syndrome, are involved in OCD, as well. Brain pictures of individuals suffering from OCD demonstrate abnormality in structure of basal ganglia. This is the brain structure which is located under cerebral cortex. Sometimes, antibodies react with strep cells and produce inflammation in cells of basal ganglia. This reaction can produce obsessive compulsive symptoms in an individual.

According to researchers, worry circuit in the brain seems to be involved in causing obsessive compulsive disorder. Worry circuit is a set of neurons that produce signals of danger and warns an individual in anticipation of a threatening situation. It is hypothesized that this circuit consistently sends messages regarding threat and demands for urgent attention. This condition leads to obsession and compulsive behavior eventually. Serotonin is the neurotransmitter which is involved in obsessive compulsive behavior. Lower levels of serotonin in brain can produce obsessions and compulsions in an individual. This is all about biological or physiological causes of obsessive compulsive disorder.

2) Reinforcement. Negative reinforcement makes compulsive patterns stable. Individuals indulge in compulsive activities because these activities reduce their mental anxieties. Once, the individual know that carrying out some behavior will reduce his anxiety; he makes a habit to perform those behaviors. Psychologists from learning perspective strictly follow their views about the role of reinforcement in development of different disorders.

3) Social Causes. Element of prevention becomes significant when we talk about social causes. Some social factors have the potential to induce obsessions and compulsions in an individual. For example, child sexual abuse is the factor that can produce obsessive compulsive behavior in an individual. Such children remain preoccupied with feelings of incest and try to clean their selves through repetitive bathing and handwashing. Parental neglect during

childhood can also cause OCD. Any traumatic event that has potential to induce higher levels of anxiety, can be rated among causes of obsessive compulsive disorder.

Obsessive Compulsive Disorder Treatments

Obsessive compulsive disorder (OCD) treatments include a wide variety. Sometimes, clinicians (psychologists or psychiatrists) are unable to treat obsessions fully. In such situations, clinician tries to manage disorder as much as possible. In most cases, obsessions exist but, the patient learns to manage his anxiety, and prevents himself from indulging in compulsive or ritualistic behaviors.

Treating OCD takes time because obsessions are embedded in the mind and one finds it difficult to distract his mind. These obsessions produce anxiety. To reduce this anxiety, an individual performs compulsive behavior. Difficulties exist at two levels during treatment. Firstly, difficulty appears when an individual becomes habitual to reduce anxiety through compulsions. Secondly, difficulty appears when a clinician stops an individual to perform compulsion after occurrence of obsession.

Treatments for obsessive compulsive disorder includes a variety of techniques and therapies.

1) Pharmacological Treatment. Empirical researches have shown that neurotransmitter serotonin is involved in obsessive compulsive disorder. Low levels of serotonin can produce obsessions and compulsions in an individual. If this is the case, psychiatrists recommend Serotonin Reuptake Inhibitors. These inhibitors include Prozac, Paxil and Zoloft etc.

2) Psychotherapies. Different types of psychotherapies can be used for treating OCD.

The first thing, which a clinician can do, is to psychoeducate the sufferer and his family about the disorder. Psychoeducation consists of developing the full understanding regarding any psychological issue. When a clinician will psychoeducate someone about OCD, he will develop the full understanding of causes, symptoms and various treatment modes of disorder.

Clinicians widely use relaxation therapy as a treatment for obsessive compulsive disorder. In this kind of therapy, clinician teaches an individual to calm down himself. Self-talk or self-instruction is the technique which can be most beneficial for an individual with obsessive compulsive disorder. During self-talk, an individual talks to himself in order to guide. This self-talk is also helpful in preventing an individual from performing compulsions.

Treatments for obsessive compulsive disorder include family therapy. There are certain reasons for giving family therapy. Sufferer of obsessive compulsive disorder is already victimized in social gatherings for his repetitive behavior, but sometimes, family does not support its member, as well. During family sessions, family members of the sufferer are instructed to provide him social support and to empathize with the sufferer.

Exposure Response Prevention (ERP) is one of the most popular psychotherapies. In this therapy, the sufferer is exposed to anxiety provoking condition such as, the sufferer is asked to touch the handle of the door but, after that he is not allowed to wash his hands. In this way, his anxiety diminishes automatically, and sufferer learns that compulsive behaviors are not essential to reduce anxiety.

Hypnotism can be used to reduce symptoms of obsessive compulsive disorder. Hypnotist tries to reduce particular ritualistic behaviors through instructions. Cognitive therapy can be used for altering the meaning or interpretations of obsessions and compulsions. Mostly sufferers consider their obsessions as threatening that can cause harm for them. The task of the clinician is to challenge these obsessions and replace them with accurate thoughts. So all these therapies are included in the treatments for obsessive compulsive disorder and, these therapies can benefit a sufferer a lot.

PANIC DISORDER

Anxiety is a normal reaction that we all have when we are confronted with a stressful situation in our lives, but a panic disorder is a much more serious condition that can strike suddenly without any warning or reason. People with this disorder will have a panic attack which is a response to fear, however the response is normally out of proportion for the given situation. A person with a disorder will develop a fear overtime that they will have another panic attack. This constant fear of having another attack can eventually affect the daily functions and the overall quality of one's life. If not treated, having a disorder can ultimately rule your life. Normally serious conditions that include alcoholism, drug abuse or depression can greatly increase the probability that a person will develop a panic disorder.

People that suffer from a panic disorder experience a panic attack that can last around 10 minutes and even longer for more severe cases of panic disorders. When a person has a panic disorder and they suffer a panic attack, they often feel an intense and overwhelming feeling of terror, with difficulty breathing. A panic attack can also cause a pounding feeling in the chest and a dizziness feeling accompanied by a feeling that they may faint. Other symptoms can include sweating, nausea, and trembling or uncontrollable shaking. A panic attack can cause hot flashes or chills and a feeling of numbness or tingling. A panic disorder can be very dangerous if the proper treatment isn't sought. Experiencing a panic attack while behind the wheel of an automobile is not only scary, but can be dangerous. During a panic attack, a person my feel that they are losing control and that can be dangerous if that happens while driving.

Having a panic disorder can rule your life and make you very fearful to step outside of your door. One of the worst problems for people that have this disorder is the constant fear of suffering future panic attacks. Having this fear is how a disorder can easily start to rule your life. The fear of future attacks can cause a person to change many things in his or her daily routine, including avoiding certain places, situations and even driving or the willingness to travel because of that fear of having another panic attack.

An individual experiencing a panic attack feels an undeniable wave of fear for no particular reason at all. The individual heart begins to beat rapidly, his chest hurt and it became increasingly more difficult to breathe; at which time the individual believes he is having a heart attack and will die if he does not receive proper intervention.

One patient defined his symptoms in this way: I am so afraid; every time I start to go out I get that awful feeling in the pit of my stomach, and I am terrified that another panic attack is coming or that some other unknown terrible thing is going to happen to me or someone in my family."

Panic attack generally last no more than a few minutes, but it can be the most distressing condition that a human being can experience. Individuals who experienced one attack will have others. Those who experience repeated attacks, or feels heightened anxiety about having another attack are considered to have developed panic disorder.

Panic disorders are a serious health problem in the United States. Recent studies concluded that about three million people will experience panic attacks at some time during their lives. The symptom is strikingly different from other types of anxiety. Panic attacks are very sudden and often unexpected, seemingly unprovoked, and are often disabling.

When a person has sudden overwhelming fear and anxiety they are having what we call a panic attack (PA). The heart will pound and they find it hard to breath. They can feel dizzy and feel like they are going to vomit. Sometimes they feel like they will dye. If (PA) are not treated they can escalate into other problems and panic disorder.

Severe cases can cause a person to withdraw from everyday activity. With treatment you can take control of your life once again and eliminate or reduce the symptoms.

Mary's story

Mary first had a (PA) about six months ago. When she had this attack she was in her office getting ready for an important meeting. Without any advanced notice she felt a very intense feeling of fear. After this she was feeling sick and felt as if she would vomit. Mary's heart was pounding and she was finding it hard to breath, her body was also shaking uncontrollably. After several moments the the attack had passed and she was feeling better. Mary became deeply worried about this as nothing like this had ever happened to her before.

About two weeks later Mary had her second (PA). From then on her attacks started happening more and more often. Mary is never sure when her next (PA) will come or where she will be. Out of a deep fear of having an attack while in public, Mary has been going home after work and staying there. Mary has also developed places she avoids such as elevators. She is not afraid of elevators just of having a (PA) while on one.

A (PA) can come on at any time without warning. Most of the time there is not a reason for the (PA). Panic attacks can even occur when you're relaxing or sleeping. (PA) can happen just one time or they can be something that happens repeatedly. Most people who suffer from (PA) have them repeatedly. Many times (PA) that are recurring, are triggered by a specific situation. These triggers can be things like high places, public speaking or riding in a car. This can be especially true if the situation has caused a (PA) in the past. Most of the time the (PA) comes on when you feel like you are in danger or cannot escape. You can have one or two panic attacks in your life and besides that you live a normal life. Sometimes (PA) can happen in association with panic disorder and depression. Whatever you may think, this is treatable. Many techniques have been developed to help deal with the symptoms.

Some of the symptoms of the onset of a panic attack

Most (PA) occur when you are not at home. You can have (PA) virtually anyplace - driving, at a party, taking a shower, at the grocery store.

The symptoms of a (PA) come on quickly and with very little warning. Most (PA) will be at their worst about ten minutes into them and be over in about twenty or thirty minutes. It is very rare for a (PA) to last more than one hour. A complete full panic attack can combine some or all the symptoms listed below.

- Hyperventilation or being short of breath
- Pounding or racing heart
- Pain or discomfort in the chest
- Shaking and trembling
- Feeling like you are choking
- Feeling like you are not connected or detached from your surroundings
- Perspiration
- Feeling like you are going to vomit
- Feeling lightheaded or faint
- Tingling sensations in your limbs
- Hot and / or cold flashes
- Afraid you could dye or losing control

A panic attack can feel like a heart attack.

Symptoms of a (PA) tend to be physical and sometimes these can be so bad, that people think they are having a heart attack. It is not uncommon for people who have panic attacks to make trips to the doctor, because they think they are having a heart attack. It is very important to have any possible problems checked out, but do not overlook the possibility of a panic attack.

Lots of people will experience a panic attack without ever having another one or any complications. Do not worry if you have had only one or two (PA). Be aware that if panic attacks persist you are most likely developing panic disorder. Panic disorder is having several, repeated panic attacks. Panic attacks combined with constant anxiety and changes in your behavior are most likely panic disorder.

Some Symptoms Of Panic Disorder

You have frequent, sudden and unexpected panic attacks that are not related to a specific situation.

You worry a lot about having more panic attacks.

You are changing your routine because of the panic attacks, such as avoiding place you had a panic attack in the past.

One panic attack can last only a couple minutes, but this one panic attack can leave a lasting negative impression on a person. Panic attacks that happen over and over can take a huge emotional toll on a person. Just the memory of the fear and overwhelming terror can hurt your self-esteem and create harmful disturbances in your life. This can lead to the panic disorder symptoms listed below.

Anticipatory anxiety - You feel anxious and tense between panic attacks. This is caused by the fear that you will have another attack.

Phobic avoidance - You avoid certain places and situations. You do this because you fear the place or situation will cause another panic attack. If you start avoiding places most the time, phobic can turn into agoraphobia.

Panic Disorder Causes

One approach to understanding the cause of panic disorder is that the body's normal alarm system the mental and physical mechanisms that allows a person to react to a threat, tends to be triggered unnecessarily, when there is no real danger in the immediate environment. Most medical studies are unable to explain exactly why this happens.

However, several psychological studies have showed, the root cause of panic disorder may begin on the emotional level or the physical side, or it could be both. The feeling of heightened-anxiety always begins with a trigger that initiates the fight or flight response from the limbic system. For example, the first hint of apparent danger your brain chemistry, blood hormones, and cellular metabolism all goes into action.

When you have a chronic anxiety disorder over time your anxiety symptoms may be triggered by less and less serious events because the limbic system has been sensitized to react in a highly panicky manner.

For example, if as a child you were constantly yelled at; as an adult you may feel anxious whenever there is potential for confrontation with an authority figure; and you may go to extreme measures to avoid such confrontation, even in a situation as benign as refusing a simple request by a family member or anyone of authority figure. At this point your conscious mind has lost track of the connection between your current feeling and your past emotional experience. You now have no idea why you are feeling panicky about something of so little significant.

No one knows exactly what the panic disorder causes are although there is evidence to suggest that it is the result of a combination of the following influences.

Genetics:

The chances are 8 times greater to develop this disorder if a family member, such as a parent or grandparent, also had it. Also, if one identical twin has it there is a 40% chance that the other twin will also get it.

Environmental/Social Factors:

Some panic disorder causes center around major stresses in life or in a person's upbringing. These include overprotective parents, parents who were always anxious, child abuse or some childhood trauma or high stress levels in the home, to name a few.

Other panic disorder causes may be attributed to the use of illegal drugs (cocaine, marijuana), drinking a lot of alcohol or caffeinated beverages, using certain medications that treat heart problems or asthma or ending the treatment of certain ailments like anxiety and sleeping disorders.

Medical Conditions:

Panic attacks can also be caused by other existing medical problems such as hyperthyroidism, certain heart problems, epilepsy and other seizure disorders as well as asthma.

Biological Factors:

There are a few theories here, one of which is that your fight or run reaction is triggered for no reason although researchers don't know why. Another theory is that when an imbalance of oxygen and carbon dioxide occurs in your system, a signal is sent out that you are going to suffocate which results in a state of panic. A third theory suggests the symptoms of a panic attack are caused by an imbalance of serotonin which is a chemical messenger in the brain that helps regulate anxiety.

Mode Of Treatments

There are a wide variety of treatments available for panic disorders, including several effective psycho pharmacology interventions, and specific forms of psychotherapy. Psychotherapy for panic disorder is equally important as drug intervention. Several studies shows that the combination of medication and psychotherapy treatment for panic disorder is more effective than either intervention alone.

Cognitive Behavioral Therapy (CBT) is widely accepted as the superior form of psychotherapy. CBT is designed to help those with panic disorder identify and decrease the irrational thoughts and behaviors that reinforce panic symptoms.

Psycho dynamic psychotherapy is another form of intervention that is seldom mentioned as an appropriate treatment for panic disorder. In fact, many therapist strongly reject the idea of using psycho dynamic techniques as an intervention to reduce the symptoms associated with panic disorder.

What set psycho dynamic therapists apart from the rest is their ability to recognize one indisputable fact: Panic states may, symptomatically, appear to be identical weather they are produce from a neurotic condition or from a manic-depressive state.

Clinical research indicated that neurotic type of panic states should be treated solely with psychotherapy; and manic-depressive states are to be treated with one of the many effective anti-depressive drugs. Proper differential diagnosis is the super-highway to symptom reduction for all psychological disorders, including panic disorder.

Treating Panic Disorder With Psycho Dynamic Techniques

Although studies have shown the effectiveness of cognitive-behavioral and psycho pharmacological treatments; many patients fail to respond positively to these interventions or have had persistence or recurrence of symptoms. Given the high costs and reappearance of panic disorder; there is a need to explore treatment options.

Psychoanalytic techniques are commonly used to treat panic disorder but have rarely been exposed to the rigor of scientific research procedures. Such a study would highlight and describe the psychoanalytic concepts involved in understanding panic disorder. While at the same time proposes a more "client-friendly" psycho dynamic psychotherapy for panic disorder called panic-focused psycho dynamic psychotherapy.

The potential benefit of this form of therapy is based on the belief that panic patients have a psychological vulnerability to panic disorder associated with personality disturbances, relationship problems, difficulties tolerating and defining inner emotional experiences, and unconscious conflicts about separation, anger and sexuality. Psycho dynamic psychotherapy focuses more, but not exclusively, on these impairments than other therapies, including psycho pharmacology, potentially reducing vulnerability to symptoms recurrence.

Unconscious emotions

According to psychoanalytic theory, panic symptoms are based at least in part on unconscious fantasies and affect In fact, both clinical and research observation suggests that panic patients have special difficulties with anger feelings and fantasies, such as wishes for revenge. These wishes often represent a threat to important love ones, especially those we have a close attachment to; therefore triggering a panic attack.

Patients are often unaware of the power of these affects and the revengeful fantasies that accompany them. Becoming aware, by bring them to consciousness, of this negative aspect of mental life and render them less threatening are important components of psycho dynamic psychotherapy.

Panic Disorder With Agoraphobia!

Panic disorder is at its most severe when it becomes panic disorder with agoraphobia. Panic disorder with agoraphobia creates such anxiety that a person will do anything to avoid being in what he or she considers 'unprotected space'. Public places are feared as 'unprotected' merely because a panic attack could happen there.

When a panic attack sufferer begins to avoid public places, agoraphobia has set in. The agoraphobic tries to stop attacks by making his or her world very small.

Agoraphobics have difficult networks of fears that totally control their lives. Major symptoms of agoraphobia are:
- Frequent intense panic attacks and severe anxiety.
- Avoiding attacks by staying home all the time.
- Depending too heavily on others.
- Never wanting to be alone.

- Avoiding any place where you can't escape.
- Fear you'll lose control in a public place.
- Feelings of detachment plus isolation.
- Helpless feelings.
- A persistent feeling of unreality.
- A feeling that your body is not quite real.
- Twitching, trembling, or emotional outbursts.

Agoraphobics have symptoms which are periodically disrupted by panic attacks. Agoraphobics have very intense panic attacks. Heart attacks and agoraphobic panic attacks look and feel very similar. The following symptoms are typical during a panic attack:

- Trouble breathing.
- Extreme disorientation or dizziness.
- Feeling like you may faint.
- Numbness plus tingling sensations.
- Blushing uncontrollably.
- Chest pain.
- Worry that you are dying.
- Thinking you are going crazy.
- Rapid pulse.
- A spike in blood pressure.

A disorder with agoraphobia is serious and will not got away on its own. Agoraphobia usually develops after years of panic issues.

The negative effects of panic disorder with agoraphobia come with social isolation, unemployment, and broken private relations. Panic disorder with agoraphobia can be successfully treated even though the symptoms are severe.

Early diagnosis is critical. Early treatment creates the fastest cure. Cognitive Behavioral Therapy (CBT) combined with systematic desensitization is the standard treatment for agoraphobia. Medication may also be prescribed.

CBT is a method for changing the way an agoraphobic thinks about fear and the world. Systematic desensitization actually desensitizes agoraphobics to fear so they never become afraid of specific stimuli.

Agoraphobics could start out by being asked to simply imagine leaving the house. When that can be done without panic, the next step might be to imagine opening the door. Stepping outside might be the final step. Agoraphobics are all different, but generally the prognosis for a full recovery is excellent.

Antidepressant medications may be prescribed to relieve the most intense symptoms. Drugs can improve the effectiveness of therapy. Agoraphobics may be weaned off medication when therapy is complete. Patients occasionally continue to take medications in order to maintain a full recovery.

Treating the panic problem early can prevent agoraphobia. The cause of panic disorder with agoraphobia is unknown. No other mental disorder is more common than anxiety and panic. Anxiety disorders are responsible for thirty percent of all the cash spent on mental illnesses.

Since panic disorder remains a major health problem in the United States it is important to continue to develop effective approach to its treatment. Panic-focused psycho dynamic psychotherapy will be a useful alternative or adjunct to cognitive-behavioral approach and medication. Psycho dynamic therapy addresses intra-psychic conflicts, defense mechanisms, and developmental issues not likely to be focused on in other therapeutic methods.

Psycho dynamic approach also affect psychological factors that lead to vulnerability to recurrence panic state, or other difficulties connected with a panic disorder. A complete and randomized controlled trial should shed further light on the effectiveness of panic-focused psycho dynamic psychotherapy.

CONQUERING DEPRESSION

You know exercise, eating right, and engaging your mind are vital steps for a healthy, well-functioning brain. But how can you hit the gym when just getting out of bed seems like a monumental effort? Even cooking a healthy meal or tackling a simple crossword puzzle might seem overly ambitious for someone struggling with depression.

Depression, after all, alters the brain's chemistry in a way that reduces a person's energy level, lowers motivation, reduces the ability to sustain attention, and heightens the perception of pain. It may increase irritability or anxiety, making it hard for people to engage in social activities. Depression has even been shown to shrink the hippocampus, a key part of the brain that plays a vital role in memory and learning. As a result of these brain changes, depressed patients may experience memory lapses, sluggish thinking, or an inability to "connect the dots."

The exciting news is that for most people depression is highly treatable. And not just with medication. In addition to medication and therapy, there are a host of simple lifestyle changes that can help reduce the symptoms of depression and put you on the path to recovery. As a bonus, many of these changes have also been shown to improve brain fitness, leading to a brain that functions better now and well into old age.

The key for those suffering from depression is to start small and to recognize that every tiny step they take makes a real, measurable difference in their brain health. A five-minute walk, for example, might not seem like a boast-worthy accomplishment to a healthy person, but to someone who spends most of his day on the couch, it may be the first critical step on the path to better health. Of course, any lifestyle changes should be made under the watchful eye of a medical professional, so if you are depressed, or suspect you may be, be sure to talk to your doctor.

Nine things that can help you conquer depression

Get a checkup: This may seem like a no-brainer, especially if you've already been to your doctor for your diagnosis and treatment of depression, but many long-standing health conditions can contribute to reduced brain fitness, while not being the primary cause of your depression. Being overweight, for example, has been shown to reduce brain function and can contribute to depression. It may also lower your ability to exercise, robbing you of a key brain and mood-booster. High blood pressure, high cholesterol, diabetes, anemia, thyroid problems, concussions or other brain injuries, stroke and other health problems can all take a toll on brain fitness, as can low levels of Vitamins B12 and D, and testosterone (in men). Getting these conditions under control can help boost your brain, which in turn will put you in the best condition to bounce back from depression.

Check your medications: I often see patients who have no idea their medications are causing side effects. In particular, medications given for anxiety, insomnia, pain and even depression can cause mood changes, brain fog, or other cognitive and health problems, so it's a good idea to review your total medication list with your doctor to ensure they're not interfering unnecessarily with your brain function or health.

Sleep: Insomnia and sleep apnea, in particular, have been shown to reduce brain function, which can contribute to depression. Many people put up with sleep disorders and incorrectly assume they're untreatable. Not only are both conditions often treatable, but treatment can help reverse the damage done to the brain and lead to dramatic improvements in brain function. Diagnosis is easier than ever before – with a small device provided by your doctor you can do a sleep study in your own home.

Get moving: you no doubt know that exercise is good for the brain. Recent research has shown us that exercise can actually grow the hippocampus and improve brain function. Exercise is a also a tremendous mood booster and an invaluable tool in the treatment of depression. Depressed people may find the thought of exercise physically and mentally daunting, so always start small. Walk five minutes a day for four days, then add two minutes every other day until you're walking 30 minutes a day, five days a week.

Get connected: Depression can be socially isolating, but making a strong effort to socially engage is brain and mood-boosting on many levels. Taking a dance class, attending a spiritual gathering, or volunteering helps to engage parts of the brain that are vital for brain fitness. Even Skyping with a far-away grandchild can help kick the brain into gear and offer long-lasting cheer.

De-stress: Stress is a major brain drainer and can be both a contributor to depression and a byproduct of depression, so stress reduction is a worthwhile cause. Cognitive behavioral therapy and other therapies can help change unhealthy thinking patterns, while simple stress reducers can help you take some of the pressure out of your life. Set aside time to think about the stressors in your life and brainstorm ways to reduce them.

Be mindful: Meditation has been shown to help in the treatment of depression and has also been shown to boost brain function, even in healthy people. If you can't take a class, look online for tutorials on how to go it alone, or borrow a DVD from your library. If even that is too much, enlist the help of a friend or loved one to take the basic steps to get you started. Begin with just a few minutes of meditation or calm breathing a day and then work your way up to 20 minutes, several times a week. Yoga, and tai chi are other pursuits that may have mood and brain benefits and drumming therapy – which involves rhythmically banging on a drum – shows similar promise in helping people calm their mind and body.

Get thinking: Fascinating research in recent years has shown that the adult brain is malleable in ways we once didn't even imagine. Using your brain – by performing complex mental tasks – has been shown to boost brain health, which in turn can help you reduce the symptoms of depression. It's hard for a depressed person to muster the energy mental gymnastics require, so start by simply making an attempt each day to do something slightly mentally challenging – read the newspaper for 10 minutes, try to memorize five items on your grocery list, learn the names of three flowers that grow in your garden. Then aim to increase your daily "thinking time" each week.

Simple Ways To Overcome Depression And Sadness

Depression can be debilitating and is very different from just feeling unhappy. Depression is a pervasive feeling. It's almost as if you are in a black tunnel with no light. Hope disappears and the things you used to find enjoyable become a chore. Even winning the lottery would not snap someone out of depression and it is never a good idea to tell someone who is depressed to sort themselves out and pull themselves together. Unfortunately, it isn't that simple, but there are ways to alleviate the symptoms of depression.

1. *Practice Mindfulness:* A depressed mind tends to mull over all that is wrong and worries unnecessarily about all the negative possibilities that may emerge in the future. This negative thought cycle reinforces misery and is not helpful in managing to overcome depression. Mindfulness involves focusing on the present moment and is a skill that needs to be practiced. More often than not, our brains are full of thoughts and focusing on the present moment seems unnatural for our minds. Practice on engaging your senses in the moment. Focus on touch, taste, sight, sound and smell. Engaging the senses leaves less time for worry.

2. *Listen to Upbeat Music:* I have always thought of music as food for the soul. An upbeat tune can change an atmosphere instantly and create a more positive vibe. Listening to upbeat, happy music alters brain chemistry and can improve your mood.

3. *Use Touch:* Science shows that touch therapies can help some people overcome depression, lower the stress hormone cortisol and increase the feel-good hormone oxytocin. Therapies to consider include acupuncture, acupressure, massage, reiki and reflexology.

4. *Include Omega 3 Fatty Acids in Your Diet:* Research has shown that depressed people often lack a fatty acid known as EPA. Participants in a 2002 study featured in the Archives of General Psychiatry took just a gram of fish oil each day and noticed a 50-percent decrease in symptoms such as anxiety, sleep disorders, unexplained feelings of sadness, suicidal thoughts, and decreased sex drive. Omega-3 fatty acids can also lower cholesterol and improve cardiovascular health..

5. *Stop the Negative Self Talk:* Depressed people tend to see the world in a negative way. When things go wrong they blame themselves and when they go right, they put it down to luck. Depression reinforces self doubt and feelings of worthlessness. Monitor your inner negative talk and make allowances for this type of thinking by reminding yourself that your thinking is that of a depressed person, not a healthy functioning person. Don't take your thoughts seriously when you are feeling low. Acknowledge the thoughts but this doesn't mean you have to believe them. Keep perspective.

6. *Bide Your Time:* Accept that your mental state is not entirely balanced. During depression, we tend to see the negatives in everything and find it harder to be balanced about what is going on. Gently remind yourself that you are tuned into the 'negativity channel' and don't listen to your thinking. It is definitely distorted when you are depressed. This idea alone can provide some comfort when the world appears bleak. It won't last forever. Remind yourself that change is constant and that you won't always feel this way. Be patient and do your best to look after yourself in the meantime. Eat well and get a decent amount of sleep.

7. *Distract Yourself:* If possible, do your best to distract yourself from overthinking. Your thoughts are your enemy when depression sets in. Play with a pet or go for a walk. Read a book if you are able to concentrate, or finish a puzzle. Do anything that takes your mind

off your fears and worries. Keeping busy is an effective way to overcome depression.

8. *Use More Light:* Seasonal Affective Disorder (SAD) is known for causing low mood over the winter months when there is less sunlight. Investing in a sunlamp – a 300 watt bulb within three feet for 20 minutes three times a day can help. SAD symptoms can include problems sleeping, anxiety, depression, irritability, fatigue, apathy and loss of libido. Using light can help to overcome depression and these other symptoms.

9. *Try Cognitive Therapy*: Cognitive therapy can be extremely useful in counteracting depression and is based on the principle that certain ways of thinking can trigger certain health problems, such as depression. The counselor helps you to understand your current thought patterns and identify any harmful or false ideas and thoughts that you have that can trigger depression or make it worse. The aim is to change your ways of thinking to avoid these ideas as well as help your thought patterns to be more realistic and helpful.

10. *Write in a Journal*: A journal can work in two ways. Use it to write down fears and worries. Sometimes, having an outlet in this way can be soothing and ease your mind. Another good way to use a journal is to write at least five things down every day that you are grateful for. This forces us to think more positively and can help to remind us that things are never that bad. In a gratitude journal, you can write about anything that happened in the day that made you feel appreciative. A stranger smiling at you, the sun shining..anything positive will do!

11. *Connect with Friends*: This can be one of the hardest things to do when feeling depressed, but it is one of the most rewarding activities. Force yourself to go out. Isolating oneself from others may seem a good idea, but put a limit on it and then get out there again. This can have a huge positive effect on your mood.

12. *Get Enough Sleep:* Sleep and mood are closely connected. Inadequate sleep can cause irritability and stress, while healthy sleep

can enhance well-being. Studies have shown that even partial sleep deprivation has a significant effect on mood.Taking steps to ensure adequate sleep will lead to improved mood and well-being. The quality of your sleep directly affects the quality of your waking life, including your mental sharpness, productivity, emotional balance, creativity, physical vitality, and even your weight. No other activity delivers so many benefits with so little effort so aim for between 7.5 and 9 hours sleep per night.

13. *Forgive Others:* When we hold a grudge, we are the ones that feel the anger. The person whom we are angry with is probably merrily going about their business completely oblivious to your feelings. Don't allow others to have this power over you. They may have caused you grief in the past, try not to allow that grief to continue – it only affects you, not them. Lighten the emotional load and you will improve your mood and help you to overcome depression.

14. *Exercise:* Regular exercise has benefits for helping to overcome depression. Exercise releases endorphins which improve natural immunity and improve mood. Besides lifting your mood, regular exercise offers other health benefits, such as lowering blood pressure, protecting against heart disease, cancer and boosting self-esteem. Experts advise getting half an hour to an hour of moderate exercise, such as brisk walking at least three to four times per week.

15. *Don't give up:* Depression can make you want to hide away from the world and disappear. It's okay to take some time out, but give yourself a time limit and then do something productive to improve your mood. Depression can be well managed and there can be a wonderful life beyond depression. Hang in there and keep the faith.

How to Define a Specific Goal to work toward over the course of 6 weeks

Because of CBT's success, some of its tenants have become well-known. You might already have heard, for example, that thoughts affect feelings, or that behavioural change can affect negative thoughts.

But what other Cognitive Behavioral Therapy techniques and tools are there, and how do they help you? How are these CBT techniques used in a session?

AGENDA SETTING IN CBT

This is a collaborative process between your therapist and you to determine how to best make use of each session. At the start of each appointment both you and your therapist suggest items you'd like to discuss. A decision is then made on the order the points will be discussed, and how much time each one needs.

The point of agenda setting is to make sure that the session is well spent, and that the hour isn't lost to something that isn't of itself productive, like simply rehashing the events of the week. It is always a good idea to be thinking before your session about what you want to put on the agenda, so you don't walk away feeling something important was missed.

In the first few sessions your therapist will model for you how to set agendas. So you don't have to instantly feel comfortable enough to add items to the agenda yourself, but can learn over time. This is itself a valuable process, helping you take charge of your problems and their solutions.

GOAL-SETTING IN CBT

Again, this is a collaborative process designed to maintain structure and focus. The point is to make the goals for your therapy those that are relevant to you, with input from your therapist to make sure they are clear and are what you actually want as opposed to what you think you should want. Goal-setting makes CBT productive by highlighting the possibility of change, making insurmountable problems appear more manageable, and increasing your hope of overcoming them.

While there are many different approaches to goal setting, one of the more common techniques used by CBT therapists is the SMART way.

SMART goal setting creates a clear and vivid picture of your goal and helps you maintain your motivation for achieving it.

This is what the acronym stands for:

Specific: Avoid generalisation. Be clear and focused on exactly what you want. A specific goal has a much greater chance of being accomplished than a general goal.

Measurable: Establish concrete criteria for measuring progress toward the attainment of each goal you set. Ask yourself questions such as, "How much?" and "How many?" "How will I know when I have met my goal?"

Achievable: Make your goals attainable and feasible! How are you going to make this goal a reality? What can you do to make it more achievable?

Realistic: Is your goal realistic given your skills, time frame, etc? While setting high goals can be a great way of increasing motivation, it can also be disheartening when they are so high that you cannot reach them. This can leave you feeling like a failure.

Timely: Set realistic time-frames to avoid procrastination or giving up on your goal.

In pursuing your goals, if you find that that you are not able to complete a particular step along the path to your goal, take a closer look at it. It is possible that the step was too big, so do not be afraid to break it down further and go from there. It could also be that the step was not SMART from the start. See if you can rework it to make it one you can tackle.

Learning goal setting skills takes practice, but can be invaluable in helping you do those things you have been avoiding or "just don't seem to get to" and feel a sense of accomplishment. Consider consulting with a CBT therapist if you think therapy may be helpful for you in reaching your goals.

Understanding the importance of Goad setting

A lot a people who come for therapy it is usually because their relationships are suffering, and so they are suffering. It could be a teenaged boy whose severe social anxiety prevents him from spending time with his friends, a woman with depression that makes it hard to be the partner she wants to be, a father whose expressions of anger have put distance between him and his kids, or the college student whose alcohol-fueled behavior has alienated her friends. It's hard for our relationships to thrive when we're hurting.

Effective therapy can improve our relationships, whether or not those relationships are the specific target of the treatment. A relatively brief course of cognitive behavioral therapy (CBT)—which has been tested more than any other treatment—can lead to marked benefits not only for the person in therapy but for those close to that person. Some of the major relationship benefits of CBT include:

1. Greater presence. It's hard to overstate the importance of our presence in a relationship, since we can't truly "relate" to someone who's not there. One of the biggest complaints about partners that I hear in my practice is that "s/he isn't there for me." Sometimes the person means quite literally that their partner is absent—always traveling for work, for example. Just as often the problem is that even when the person is there in body, his or her mind is elsewhere.

Mindfulness-based CBT can address both these issues; for example, training in mindfulness has been shown in multiple studies to increase one's ability to attend to the person we're with (as described in this previous post). A CBT framework can help translate one's intention to be present into a plan of action to make it happen.

Try it: The next time your partner talks with you about something, bring your full attention to what they're saying. Practice seeing the person as though for the first time, really focusing on them and what they're saying.

2. Less anxiety. When we're overwhelmed by anxiety, we're not our best selves. It's no surprise that untreated anxiety disorders take a toll on our closest relationships. For example, the need for a "safety companion" in panic disorder and agoraphobia can lead to strain as the supporting partner has to adjust his or her schedule to accommodate the other person's travels. Similarly the chronic worry in generalized anxiety disorder frequently leads to tension and irritability, causing conflict between partners.

For any anxiety diagnosis, the treatments with the most evidence for their effectiveness come from CBT. The relief a person feels from a marked reduction in anxiety extends to greater harmony in the relationship.

Try it: If you've struggled with uncontrollable anxiety, consider looking into the best treatments for your condition on the website for Division 12 of the American Psychological Association. You can also search the therapist directory of PsychologyToday.com for a therapist who provides the treatment you're looking for. If a suitable therapist is not available, you might pursue self-guided CBT (such as with this book or my own workbook), which has been shown to be effective.

3. Improved mood. As with anxiety, untreated depression wears on couples. It's a struggle to be the partner we're capable of being when we have no energy, little enthusiasm even for activities we would normally enjoy, and no sex drive, among other symptoms. After a typical course of CBT for depression—12 to 16 weeks—the average person will not only feel substantially better but will be able to function much more effectively. And happier individuals make happier couples.

Try it: As with anxiety, you can search for a CBT therapist through the PsychologyToday.com therapist directory. There is also evidence that self-guided CBT can be effective for treating depression (e.g., CBT in 7 Weeks or Cognitive Behavioural Therapy), so CBT is available even when a therapist is not. You can even do Internet-based CBT, such as this program.

4. Better sleep. As many as 23% of adults in the US suffered from bad sleep in the past month. When we're not sleeping well we tend to be cranky and impatient—not a recipe for the best interactions with the people who love us. Furthermore, insomnia can turn the bed into a place of worry and stress, which interferes with a cozy night's sleep beside our partner. CBT for insomnia (CBT-I) is typically 4 to 6 sessions and is the treatment of choice for insomnia. It helps a person fall asleep faster and sleep more soundly, and restores a strong association between the bed and sleep. And better sleep helps with pretty much everything.

Try it: If you've struggled with sleep, consult these guidelines for healthy sleep habits. The National Sleep Foundation has suggestions for finding a CBT-I therapist. CBT-I is also available through self-guided books (e.g., End the Insomnia Struggle) and apps.

5. Healthier relationship with alcohol. Problematic drinking can kill a relationship. Alcohol use disorder is tied to higher divorce rates, greater intimate partner violence, lower relationship satisfaction, and a host of other problems. CBT can effectively target the thoughts and behaviors that maintain problems with alcohol, and replace drinking with healthier ways of coping. Interestingly, the treatment with the strongest research evidence is Behavioral Couples Therapy, with both the patient and his or her partner actively involved in the treatment.

For many individuals with an alcohol use disorder, lifelong abstinence is necessary. However, there is modest support for a treatment program that includes the possibility of moderate alcohol consumption for some people.

Try it: If you're interested in learning more about the Moderate Drinking program, information is available here. You can also consult the PsychologyToday.com directory to find a therapist who provides Behavioral Couples Therapy for alcohol use disorders.

6. Happier kids. When a child is struggling with intense fears (e.g., phobias, obsessive-compulsive disorder), it can lead to tremendous stress for the family. Parents inevitably feel the strain when a child is refusing to go to school, struggling socially, or having problems at bedtime. As the saying goes, "You're only as happy as your least happy child."

Furthermore, most couples have somewhat different parenting styles, with one partner more lenient and the other more of the disciplinarian. A child's intense struggles will tend to amplify these differences, leading to conflict between the parents. At the end of the night when the kids are finally in bed and both parents just want to unwind, they may instead find themselves arguing about how best to help their child. Thus they may feel like their reserves are exhausted, with little left to give their child or each other.

The American Academy of Child and Adolescent Psychiatry recommends CBT as a first-line approach for treating many childhood conditions, including anxiety and OCD. Similarly, the American Academy of Sleep Medicine recommends behavioral treatments for sleep problems in infants and children, which can help both the child and the parents sleep through the night.

Try it: There are books available that detail how to apply the techniques of CBT to help your child with anxiety (e.g., Helping Your Anxious Child) or OCD (e.g., What to Do When Your Brain Gets Stuck). There are also many CBT-focused web resources available, such as from the International OCD Foundation and the Society of Clinical Child and Adolescent Psychology.

7. Healthier Thought Patterns. Even if we're not dealing with a diagnosable condition like anxiety, depression, insomnia, or a substance use disorder, the tools of CBT can have powerful effects on our relationships. CBT is based on an understanding of the connections among thoughts, feelings, and behaviors (see figure). When our thought patterns are aligned with reality, they generally lead to positive feelings and behaviors. However, when our thoughts become distorted in some way, they start to work against us, including in our relationships.

For example, we might notice that our partner left his clothes on the floor and think, "He expects me to pick up after him. He thinks I'm his maid." The result might include a fight driven by resentment and defensiveness. Or we could think that our partner seems distant and tell ourselves, "She's unhappy with me and our relationship," leading us to withdraw in turn.

The cognitive part of CBT encourages us first of all to notice the thoughts we're telling ourselves; oftentimes they happen so quickly and automatically that we don't even recognize the story our mind is creating. Once we've identified the thoughts we can test them out to see if they're accurate. Maybe our partner's clothes on the floor say nothing about his view of us, or expectations that we clean up his mess. And perhaps our partner's preoccupation has nothing to do with our relationship and everything to do with her worries about her ailing mother. With practice we can replace distorted and destructive thoughts with more accurate and constructive ones.

(Importantly, cognitive techniques are not about fooling ourselves or pretending things are better than they are. It would be important to know if our thoughts are actually valid so we can deal with the situation directly.)

Try it: The next time you're upset with your partner, write down the thoughts you notice and the emotions you feel. Then ask yourself the following questions (adapted from Retrain Your Brain: Cognitive Behavioral Therapy in 7 Weeks):

What is the evidence for my thought?

Is there evidence that contradicts my thought?

Based on the evidence, how accurate is the thought?

How could I modify this thought to make it fit better with reality?

8. Greater enactment of our intentions. All of us want to be the best significant other we can be. We want to be attentive, supportive, generous, patient. And like anything else, the road to impoverished relationships is paved with the best of intentions. If we're not deliberate about living out our values, we risk leaving them in the abstract—vague platitudes without substance.

For example, we might tell ourselves, "My family matters to me more than anything," and then live as though family is our last priority. We might idealize presence in our relationship yet attend more to our phone than to those around us.

The tools of CBT can help even when there is no "disorder"—when we simply want to commit to sustained action that supports our deepest values. It starts with taking an inventory of our relationship, and setting clearly defined goals based on what we find—for example, To listen when my spouse talks to me.

It includes identifying specific behaviors we want to practice that will move us toward our goals.

We might plan, for instance, to turn off our phone during dinner and focus on our conversation. The goals and activities can be anything that's important to us in our relationship—we get to decide. It can be very beneficial to collaborate with our partner in the process by asking what they need more of from us.

A CBT approach also includes planning activities as specifically as possible so they stay on our radar, like putting "Come home early to make dinner" in our calendar, and protecting the time. Through daily practice of our intentions, we give our relationship the nourishment it needs not only to last but to be extraordinary.